Angels with Dirty Faces

THE *SUNDAY TIMES* BESTSELLING AUTHOR

CASEY WATSON

Angels with Dirty Faces

HARPER
element

*These books are works of non-fiction based on the author's experiences.
In order to protect privacy, names, identifying characteristics,
dialogue and details have been changed or reconstructed.*

HarperElement
An imprint of HarperCollins*Publishers*
1 London Bridge Street
London SE1 9GF

www.harpercollins.co.uk

The Little Princess first published by HarperElement 2016
No Place for Nathan first published by HarperElement 2014
Daddy's Boy first published by HarperElement 2016
The Wild Child first published by HarperElement 2015
Scarlett's Secret first published by HarperElement 2014

This collection first published by HarperElement 2017

17 18 19 20 LSCC 10 9 8 7 6 5 4 3 2 1

© Casey Watson 2016, 2014, 2016, 2015, 2014, 2017

Casey Watson asserts the moral right to be
identified as the author of this work

A catalogue record of this book is
available from the British Library

ISBN 978-0-00-826211-2

Printed and bound in the United States of America

Find out more about HarperCollins and the environment at
www.harpercollins.co.uk/green

Contents

Introduction

Dear readers,

I'm excited to share with you a collection of short stories about some of the children who have briefly passed through our lives yet left a lasting impression. Although Mike and I are specialist carers, and ideally are meant to look after children for much longer periods of resettling, we are often asked to take in emergency or short-term children in between placements. We love doing this, of course, and through it we have met some delightful new people, both of the little variety (the children) and the larger kind (social workers and new teams of staff), whom we otherwise wouldn't have met.

These shorter placements can bring a feeling of achievement, when we've been able to play some part in helping a particular young person in need, but they can often leave us feeling sad and discontented that we've only been a stopgap, a stepping stone on a much longer journey that we won't be part of. That, unfortunately, is the nature of the beast, and we are well aware that fostering doesn't always guarantee a happy ending. But it doesn't stop us from hoping and trying.

When I was a small child I remember watching a James Cagney film with my grandmother called *Angels with Dirty Faces*. That film – and the morals behind it – have always stayed with me; the idea that circumstances determine what will become of us and our ability to change lives. I often think of our foster children as angels with dirty faces, and although I am neither a racketeer nor a priest, I like to think that I can play a small role in helping these kids move on to lead stable, happy lives.

The Little Princess

Chapter 1

It was the Sunday before Christmas. Almost my favourite time of year. Actually, in some ways my most favourite time of year, because it was the date of our annual family pre-Christmas dinner – or my practice run, as my son Kieron had always called it. Which was just like the main one, only in lots of ways nicer, as it involved all the fun without any of the stress, plus the anticipation of Christmas proper still to come.

Well, to my mind, at any rate. I should have known better than to mention it to my ever-loving husband Mike. 'More like a prelude to a nightmare,' he quipped, 'with this gaggle of little monsters around. Look at them. If this level of mania is anything to go by, heaven help us when we get to the actual day!'

I knew, what with the house full of grandkids and mayhem, that he was probably only half-joking. He had a point, too. I winced as I watched Marley Mae, who was deep in the realm of the terrible twos now, almost collide with the Christmas tree. And for the umpteenth time today, while the film I'd put on (in the vain hope of keeping Riley's three occupied) blared to itself in the corner. Much as I loved Arnie Schwarzenegger – the film was *Jingle All the Way* – I could barely hear myself think.

'Shut up, you old Grinch,' I told Mike. 'You know you love it really. And how can you say such a thing? Bless them,' I added, scooping Marley Mae into my arms. 'You're not a monster. You're our little princess, aren't you?'

It was a phrase that would very soon come to haunt me.

We'd had the luxury (in a manner of speaking, since it had been a pretty hectic time) of taking a few months off from fostering. After seeing our last foster child, Flip, off to her forever home the previous spring, we'd decided to take a bit of a break. With our Kieron and his partner Lauren having given us our fourth grandchild, Dee Dee, we'd taken the decision to devote some time to just being there for them. With Kieron's Asperger's (which is a mild form of autism), we'd been all too aware that they could really use the extra support. So, apart from Tyler, our permanent foster child, and very much now part of the family, we'd only accepted a couple of short-term emergency placements. We'd had a singular lad called Connor, veteran of the care system, for a brief but intense period, and a misunderstood five-year-old called Paulie, who'd been rejected by his mother and stepfather, and who was now settled with a long-term foster family.

Both had proved to us – if proof were needed – that you couldn't fix everything for every child; sometimes you could only help smooth the transition from one kind of life to the next. Life was different for us too now – keeping Tyler had changed everything. With the fostering we did at present, we had to keep his needs always in mind.

It had been a happy time. And at the centre of it was the joy of being grandparents. That and the gratitude – Mike and I counted our blessings daily. And not least because Dee Dee had proved to be an amazingly easy baby – and Kieron and Lauren, despite the usual wobbles, very natural parents. I could still find myself welling up whenever I thought about it; just how lucky we'd all been that our anxious, fretful son had met, in Lauren, such a perfect and loving soulmate.

Today, then, was all about the simple joys of family, and as I beavered away in the kitchen, putting pans on and keeping an eye on my roast potatoes, that was what was very much on my mind. So when I saw a car pull up and soon after disgorge our fostering link worker, John Fulshaw, I found myself smiling. Trust him to be working on a Sunday. And how nice it would be to welcome him in – perhaps I'd even be able to persuade him to have a festive glass of sherry.

John always appeared at some point in the run-up to Christmas. It was one of his traditions to 'do the rounds' at this time of year, bestowing all his foster families with a poinsettia. 'All the way from sunny San Diego!' he'd always remind us as he handed it over, San Diego apparently being the poinsettia capital of the world.

There was sun for us too that particular Sunday. Sun, and the sort of frosty air that promised ice tonight, if not snow. But as I watched John walk up the path, there was no pot plant in his hand, just his usual battered briefcase. And, worryingly, no seasonal smile on his face, either. Just a deeply etched frown. I could see it clearly, even in the gathering December dusk.

I dried my hands and went out into the hallway. No poinsettia for me today, I thought, glancing down at the place I usually reserved for it – at the back of the hall table where it was generally safe from little hands.

'Can you keep an eye on the veg for me? We've got a visitor,' I called to Riley. She was still playing lion tamer in the living room with Mike, Kieron and Lauren, till Tyler returned from an outing with his half-brother, Grant, when he would assume his role as chief entertainer of the little ones till we ate.

I opened the door just as John was reaching for the knocker. Nope, it was a definite. There was no pretty red plant behind his back. 'Come in, come in,' I said, gesturing with my hand. 'You look half-frozen.'

He put his case down just inside the door and rubbed his hands together. 'Brrr,' he said. 'Too right. It's really cold out there today.'

I agreed, and hurried to help him off with his coat. But I could already see he was somewhat distracted. 'What's up, John?' I asked him as I threw it on top of the pile over the newel post.

He sighed. 'I'm so sorry,' he said, glancing towards the

living room. 'This is not the best time is it? I did call, but ...' He gestured towards the cacophony. 'But thought I'd try popping over, since I was out and about anyway. I was hoping you and Mike could help us out.'

By 'us', I immediately knew he meant the fostering team. Christmas was always a stressful time of year for them, for all the usual, depressing reasons. Family flare-ups, often compounded by the stresses of the festive season. And compounded too by the fact that – for the same festive reasons – foster carers were temporarily thin on the ground. Sad though it was, it was part and parcel of the job. He must need us to take a child in. That much was immediately evident. Not a poinsettia, but a child – most likely one in distress. And it must be urgent for him to turn up after only trying to call once. He knew what I was like, and how often I mislaid my mobile.

'If we can, you know we will,' I immediately reassured him. 'But hang on – let me grab Mike and get the little ones out of the way, so we can have somewhere quiet to talk.'

Which was easier said than done, obviously, given the size of the house and the number of people currently in it. But in the end I set Riley and Lauren to work in the kitchen, minding the dinner, while Mike, Kieron and David minded the children in the living room, leaving us the conservatory – the only room in the house not yet festooned with fairy lights, which, given John's grim expression, seemed the most appropriate.

'I'm so sorry,' he said again as we went in.

* * *

I have seen and heard an awful lot in my fostering career, some of it the sort of thing I wished I hadn't had to. The sort of thing that, once seen and heard, you couldn't un-see or un-hear; testament to the reality that the world could be a cruel, ugly place. And you get a sixth sense, when you've worked with someone as long as Mike and I had with John. Seeing his expression as he sat down in one of the two wicker armchairs, I realised this might just be one such occasion.

'We are desperate,' John began, 'or I wouldn't have come to you. I know how much Christmas means to you, and particularly this Christmas. But the truth is that I don't have anywhere else to turn.'

Nowhere else to turn. The kind of statement that's almost a cliché. Not to mention one I'd heard before, as it's a bit of a theme in fostering. And sadly, when a link worker or social worker says it, it's usually the literal truth.

Riley popped her head round the door. 'I've made some coffees. You both want one?'

We both nodded and she smiled John a hello. She knew the potential score. She and David fostered too these days, though, sensibly, with three little ones on their hands, they only did it intermittently, to provide respite for full-time foster carers.

I pulled the table across in readiness, while she went to get our drinks for us. I could still hear Arnie and co jingling their merry way in the living room.

John was anything but merry, and I wondered quite what he was about to tell me.

'So,' I said, 'you want us to take a child in.' He nodded. 'Just for over Christmas? Or are we looking at a more permanent thing?'

John rubbed his hands together again. They were pinkish, and mottled from the cold. 'I don't know yet. It's a big mess. Police involved. Shocking. All very sudden, so there's no care plan in place yet, obviously. Shocking,' he said again. John wasn't easily shocked. 'It's a little girl,' he went on, grimacing. 'Literally just been brought in to us. And you'll need to prepare yourselves. Ah, Mike,' he said, looking up. 'Good.'

Mike came in with the coffees, having presumably left Riley and the others to deal with what needed dealing with – which, it occurred to me, could usefully involve turning the TV off.

'Go on, then,' I urged John, once Mike had pulled up another chair. 'Exactly how shocking? How bad is it?'

Pretty bad, as it turned out, even to our experienced ears.

'Her name is Darby,' John began. 'Six years old. Lives with both parents.'

I knew this could mean everything and nothing. Many foster kids – most of the type we tended to foster – came to us having already been involved with social services, from dysfunctional families, fractured ones, the kids of addicts of various kinds – and a fair few who'd already been in the care system for a while. That this girl came from a home with a mother and father could mean lots of things, good or bad, so I couldn't pre-judge. What I knew it wouldn't be was some sort of tragedy, such as both parents having been killed in a road accident. Police, he'd said. A big mess. That was telling.

'She's come to our attention,' John continued, 'via a known paedophile. And, as I said, you'll want to brace yourselves ...'

The word was galvanising. We did. In fact, I don't think I'd sat so stiffly to attention since I'd last been to a lecture on fostering protocols. Though this time it wasn't so I didn't drift off to sleep. On the contrary, I'd rarely been so riveted.

The little girl, Darby Sykes, had indeed come to them via a known paedophile – one who'd been browsing through his usual diet of hardcore child pornography when he thought he recognised a child that he knew. That the images would have been disturbing wasn't in question – physical abuse of small children was the kind of material he mostly went for, but in this case, realising he knew the child lit some flame of disquiet in him. Identifying the actual victim meant he couldn't switch off the part of his brain that was required to pipe down in order for him to enjoy what he was doing.

And what he'd been doing, John explained, in a quiet, measured voice, was watching little six-year-old Darby, on film, on his laptop, initially dressed up, and made up, but soon almost fully naked, and acting out various scenarios with a variety of sex toys. Above each moving picture was apparently a banner. It read 'Our Little Princess'.

Chapter 2

The known paedophile, John continued, had been sickened. He smiled grimly, once he'd told us that, as if to say *I know* – even paedophiles as depraved as this one had their limits. 'He was apparently really sickened,' John went on. 'Which he must have been, mustn't he? Because he reported it to the police even knowing the probable consequences – that, when they seized his computer, which they obviously would do, he'd be in big trouble himself. They live on the same estate,' he continued. Then spread his palms wide. 'Doesn't bear thinking about, really, does it?'

'I feel sick too,' Mike said, echoing my own sentiments. 'Six? You say she's *six*?' He shook his head. 'And her parents are *filming* her for paedophiles? I honestly just can't imagine anything more terrible.'

John sipped his coffee. 'Yes, six, and an only child, thank God. Which is not to say the couple haven't …'

'*Jesus*,' said Mike. 'It's so *sick*.'

'But she's safe now. The police acted swiftly, thank goodness. She's safe with us now.'

'Since when?' I asked.

'Since two hours ago.'

'At the office?'

He nodded. 'But look – listen, both – don't say yes if you don't think …'

'How could we possibly say no, John? God!' I said. 'What kind of a state must she be in?' I tried to imagine what kind of mental turmoil the child was in. Had she been held prisoner in her own home? Forced to 'perform' under threat? Would she be glad to have escaped? Desperate? Hysterical? Or, on the other hand – and the thought crept unavoidably into my brain – was she more distressed at being taken away from all she knew? Was what she'd been forced to do her version of normal?

Mike and I exchanged glances. I knew his thought processes would be similar. A few years previously we'd fostered siblings who'd been born into a family that were at the centre of a terrifyingly huge paedophile ring. The older one, Ashton, was his grandfather's son – one of several children he'd sired with his own daughters. Most chillingly, however, was that, groomed virtually from birth, these two terrified innocents had been distressed, no doubt about it, but not about the sexual abuse, which for them was just another way of showing love – no, they were distressed at being taken from their ever-loving granddad.

Hearing the shouts and whoops of my own grandchildren coming from the other room, my heart felt suddenly leaden. 'Then go and fetch her,' I told John, returning Mike's affirmative nod. 'Bring her here. Of course we'll have her. That's settled.'

John's frown lines smoothed out slightly. A box had been ticked. A problem shared and halved. 'Thank you,' he said, and I knew he really meant it. 'I knew I could depend on you two. And, of course, I'll go back and organise for her to be brought to you right away. But you need to be aware of what you are taking on. *Seriously*. I know you've a lot of experience of this sort of thing –' He spread his palms. 'Would that it were otherwise, eh? But this appears to be a severely damaged little girl. And in all kinds of ways. It's in a different league, honestly –'

Mike laughed grimly. 'You said it, mate. Sheesh. You're telling me.'

'Horrific,' John agreed.

'And the parents,' I said, thinking suddenly about the monsters who'd done this evil. 'What's happened to them now?'

'Arrested,' John said. 'Not sure what's happening next there. But if you're absolutely sure you're happy to take little Darby, even if just in the short term, I'll go back and sort things. She's already been allocated a social worker – though I've not met her myself yet – and she's the one who'll bring Darby over to you. Say an hour or so?' He glanced back towards the kitchen, sniffing the air. 'Give you time to have your dinner at least.'

* * *

13

Dinner, understandably, was the last thing on my mind. And, unsurprisingly, I had entirely lost my appetite. We ate anyway, because, aside from everything else, the rest of the family were all starving – all bar Tyler, who pitched up not long after John had left us, and in doing so reminding me why we did what we did. I hugged him extra hard, as if he were a living, breathing talisman against the evil that was going to come and visit, in the shape of the reality it forced into our minds.

We told Riley the bare minimum, and a white lie to Kieron – he found any kind of child abuse extremely distressing, so we simply said her parents had been arrested for unrelated offences, which, having no other family, had left her with nowhere to go over Christmas.

We also took the decision to end the family gathering early. Again, the kids were used to such things, and, with Christmas still to come, the little ones weren't bothered either. We just explained to Levi and Jackson that we were taking in a little girl over Christmas and, so she wouldn't be too traumatised, we needed a slightly quieter household when she arrived. Which was probably true anyway. John had told us that she'd been inconsolable. There'd been much clinging and screaming and sobbing apparently. It would be a pretty intense job for the poor social worker.

Levi, who'd just turned nine, was excited. A sociable little chap and a typical eldest, he was always in his element when there was a new young friend to take charge of, and wouldn't leave without a promise that he'd be meeting her soon, which I was only too happy to make for him. Once she'd settled, I told him, what she'd need would be the same as all kids need. Comfort and routine and to be enveloped in love. 'I'll give her *lots* of hugs, Nana,' he solemnly promised me.

First of all, however, she'd need a bedroom. So, as soon as we'd waved everyone off (in my case, with a pang of regret, as I watched the cars disappear down the road, Mike and Tyler in one of them, taking Kieron, Lauren and a rudely awoken Dee Dee) I hotfooted it upstairs to the bedroom.

Which wasn't so much bedroom as junk room just lately. Since little Paulie had left it had slowly reassigned itself, almost without me realising it was happening. Knowing we'd not be needing it for a good while, we'd both found it all too easy to say 'I'll just pop this here' and 'It can stay there for the moment,' and to such an extent that there was very little floor space – particularly since Mike had one of his major garage clear-outs and earmarked a ridiculous amount of stuff to go on eBay. 'Yeah, *right*, Dad,' Tyler had said. I remembered that well now. 'Yeah, right, bet you a tenner it'll still be here this time next year.' Though to his credit, he'd downloaded some 'app' (apps were still something of a mystery to me) and managed to sell a good deal more than a tenner's worth, at a hard-won but decent commission.

Still, there was a fair bit that still needed shifting, not to mention the fact that our Christmas presents were all stored there, safely away from several pairs of prying eyes, till such time as I poured myself an eggnog, popped on a favourite Christmas movie and settled down to wrap them in peace.

John had laughed about that, the tension broken as he'd left, having correctly identified the look of sudden stress on my face. 'Look at her, Mike,' he said. 'Full-on panic mode now. Thinking about how she won't have time to go out buying new curtains and duvets.'

Mike had laughed too. 'You know her too well, John. But under the circumstances, Casey,' he'd placed a hand on my shoulder, 'I don't think you need to be worrying about *that*.'

It had set the tone again, that, after our brief moment of levity. He'd been right. What this poor kid needed was a safe place. A sanctuary. Not a frilly duvet and a pair of matching bloody curtains.

Still, she needed a clean space, and this definitely wasn't that, so once I'd cleared the floor somewhat and piled the presents in our bedroom wardrobe, I ran back downstairs for a bin liner, disinfectant spray and cloth. And then, as an afterthought, ragged the small set of fairy lights from around the hall mirror. After all, they weren't going to be needed to illuminate any poinsettia, by the looks of things. And, for all that little Darby wouldn't need a new *Frozen* quilt cover, she would need a light in her current darkness, however small.

Chapter 3

Mike and Tyler were back within half an hour and, to at least stem the tide of typical Tyler-questions (which was totally reasonable, as he'd come to us as a traumatised child himself) we told him just a little – just enough to satisfy his curiosity. We told him Darby had been abused by her parents, that it was physical rather than just mental, but we left it at that. We were of one mind, Mike and I – and it had never been any different. No child should have to know about such things – that such things went on in apparently normal families. Not until they had to, at any rate. Of course, the hardest thing when Darby came to us would be to ensure that remained the case, but as Tyler, now off school for Christmas, had a packed programme of football and various teenage gatherings, I hoped we'd be able to achieve that much at least.

'So what do you think?' I asked Mike as we all trooped up to the bedroom, their presence required to relocate some of the junk from landing to loft.

'It's fine,' Mike reassured me, while Tyler pulled down the loft ladder. Then, 'Love, stop fretting about the décor. More important is how we're going to play this. You know, I *hate* this. And it seems to be the way more often than not now. Going in blind. Nothing to go on … not knowing how to *deal* with her.'

I could see what we'd been told was still weighing heavily on him, and I got that. How could it not? He was a father. And, more specifically, of a daughter – not to mention two granddaughters. Though you'd have to be naïve not to be well aware that it could equally have been a little boy.

'I think there's a car pulling up,' Tyler shouted down from the loft, being blessed with superhuman hearing.

And indeed there was. A swift glance out between the spare bedroom curtains confirmed it. The headlights snapped off and I could see the car door opening. 'Well, here goes nothing,' I said, as Mike followed me down the stairs, Tyler clattering down the ladder and close behind.

The social worker, whom I'd not come across before, was as grim-faced and stressed-looking as John had been. She introduced herself as Katy Morris, and gently touched the shoulder of the little girl by her side. 'And this,' she said, smiling down at the tiny child, 'is Darby.' She leaned down slightly. 'Are you going to say hello, Darby?' she said gently. 'This is Casey, and that's Mike. Remember, I told you all about them in the car?'

'And this is our son Tyler,' I added, conscious of how the little girl kept her head down, unwilling to look at us, but sufficiently interested to briefly look up at the sound of my voice. Her gaze flickered past us and I imagined Tyler beaming his mega-wattage smile. He could be a handful – he was a teenager – but I don't think he'd ever forget what it felt like to be dumped on a stranger's doorstep.

'Oh, I'm sorry,' Katy Morris said. 'I literally had about ten minutes to read your file.'

She looked so apologetic that I felt like patting her reassuringly on the shoulder too. She must have been on call. What festive delights had she been dragged away from? She was also quite young. No more than late twenties, I reckoned. Though with a reassuring air of quiet confidence.

Even so, this would have been a grim day for her too. 'No apologies necessary,' I reassured her, liking her immediately. 'Come on. Come on in. Follow me,' I chirped, leading the small procession into the living room, where it still looked as if a small typhoon had recently passed through. 'Grab a seat anywhere you like,' I added, willing myself not to start straightening cushions. 'How about a hot drink? It's so cold out, isn't it?'

She nodded. 'Can I?' she answered. 'I'd love a quick one. It's been manic, as you can imagine.' She put her bag down on the floor and started unbuttoning Darby's coat, talking to her all the time in soothing tones. It was an old coat and cheap-looking, and I belatedly realised it was the only thing she had with her. Had they not even had the chance to gather up some familiar clothes and toys? Evidently not.

Mike, ever practical, put the TV back on, flicking from DVD player to the channels as he did so. 'How about some cartoons?' he suggested to the girl, as he navigated the remote for something child-friendly. 'Would you like that, Darby? While the grown-ups have a quick chat? And a biscuit, perhaps? And a drink of juice or milk?'

At the mention of food and drink, Darby finally properly looked at us, and I was immediately struck by the arresting nature of her looks. She had the sort of dirty-blonde hair that young actresses paid a fortune for, shoulder length, fine, with a messy, choppy fringe that looked like it had been done with kitchen scissors. Behind it, I could now see a hauntingly beautiful little face. She had clearly been crying a lot – her cheeks were streaked with tear stains and very grubby, but those eyes! They were an amazing, almost luminous electric blue. Wide set and almond shaped, they were framed by thick lashes. Of the kind young actresses probably paid good money to have stuck on, too. It was a face that could stop you in your tracks, and, along with an appreciation of her gorgeous elfin looks, came the same sense of revulsion as had come earlier. People *had* paid good money. Bad people.

Sick people, I mentally corrected myself, trying to banish the image. Sick people watched her – I intuitively knew that – but it was bad people, evil people, who put her on show.

She smiled shyly at Mike. 'Yes, please,' she said politely. 'I'd like milk.' She glanced at her social worker. 'And I'm hungry.'

'I saved you a chicken dinner, Darby, if you'd like that?' I asked her. 'D'you think you could eat a dinner?' I gestured towards the coffee table. 'You can eat it in here if you want to watch some cartoons.'

Again she nodded and, again, gave that ghost of a smile. 'Yes, please,' she said simply. 'And then I'll go home to Mummy and Daddy.'

It was a statement rather than a question, which spared us the necessity of having to answer, so I went straight to the kitchen, Tyler following along behind, while Mike showed Katy Morris to the dining-room table, where Darby could still see them. And while Tyler microwaved the plate of food for her and poured her a tumbler of milk, I made us strong coffees. It could well be a long night, after all.

'I'm sorry about that,' Katy said, once we were assembled around the table, and Tyler had plonked himself down in front of the telly while Darby set about her food. 'It must be her age. She's very young to make any sense out of what's happened this afternoon. Although I explained it all to her as simply as I could during the ride over, she just isn't taking it in. I think she assumes that we've collected her for an outing and that she'll be going back home after she's eaten.'

'She's not going to understand,' I said, grateful for the volume coming from the box now, and mindful that we were all of us reeling at the moment. 'She's probably in shock ... This must be extremely confusing for her after all. But she'll be fine,' I added. 'Honestly. Don't worry. Once you leave, she'll get that she's staying with us for a bit.' I smiled reassuringly. 'We'll take it from here.'

Katy sipped her coffee, and I noticed the way her hands gripped the mug, whitening her knuckles. 'It was *horrible*,' she said, lowering her voice. 'I was there. The police just burst in. And I followed.' She looked like she was reliving it as she spoke. 'And there was a whole filming setup in the back bedroom – camera on a tripod, arc lights. The lot. And manacles attached to the bedhead – seriously, it was *horrible*. The mother was screaming. The father was trying to drag Darby from me. It was just *awful*. The poor kid didn't know what was going on and just kept crying for her mummy. Honestly, just when you think you've seen it all …'

She left the rest of her sentence hanging. I could see she'd been badly affected by the afternoon's events. I smiled gently at her. She was so young herself.

'I know what you mean,' I said. 'And it doesn't get any easier, does it?'

'It shouldn't,' Mike said. 'The day we are no longer shocked by this kind of thing is the day we become desensitised. And that can't happen – not in this job.' He glanced across at Darby. 'God help us.'

The handover paperwork was minimal, so, given that Darby had begun stealing glances across at us as she ate, I left it to Mike and went to join her in the living room.

'Blow on it, sweetie,' I prompted as she was about to load a forkful of hot potato into her mouth. 'Do you normally have a fork, or would you like a spoon?'

Darby blew hard as directed, and bristled a little.

'I'm six,' she said, before putting it to her mouth. 'I'm allowed a fork. *And* a knife,' she added accusingly. Tyler grinned.

'Wow! You're a big girl, then,' I said, dropping down to my knees on the other side of the coffee table. 'A fork *and* a knife! It's almost like you're seven – not six!'

That earned me a smile, once she'd finished chewing, followed by a belch. 'Pardon me,' she said, smiling sheepishly. There was no faulting her manners. What kind of humans made a child say please and thank you, and, at the same time, abused her so foully?

Darby speared a piece of broccoli. 'Is the lady taking me back to Mummy when I'm finished? 'Cos I have to go back for bedtime.'

'Sweetie,' I said, leaning in towards her. 'We have a lovely big girl's room here for you to sleep in tonight. It's got fairy lights and a pink rug. And teddy bears.' I tried to gauge her reaction, but her blue eyes betrayed nothing. Just stared. And a horrible thought flew into my head. Did they drug her with something when they had her perform? I'd heard of such things more than once.

But no. She was just trying to take things in, clearly. 'There was some trouble earlier, wasn't there?' I persisted gently. 'At home. You remember? And Mummy and Daddy have had to go and speak to some policemen. Which means, well –' I glanced over at Katy, who was just closing her folder. 'Well, Katy, there, who brought you, well, she has to leave you with us for a bit. So you're going to spend some time with us – us and Tyler here. That's right, isn't it,

Tyler?' He nodded and smiled encouragingly. 'Just till things are a bit better. Sorted out. Do you understand?'

The broccoli sat untouched on the end of Darby's fork. Then began to wobble, then was thrown down, fork and all, on the plate. The wailing began almost immediately. 'I want to go *home*!' Darby cried, making fists and rubbing her eyes hard with them. 'I want my mummy and daddy! I'm sorry if I was a bad girl! Tell the lady! I'm *sorry*! I'll be good! I *promise* I'll be a good girl. Oh, please, lady, *please* let me go home!'

I came around the table and sat beside her on the arm of the sofa, trying to pull her towards me for a hug, but was repeatedly pushed away. She was surprisingly strong.

'Oh, darling, you haven't been bad,' I said, trying to get a grip on her, to help calm her. 'That's not it at *all*. The grown-ups just have to sort some things out so that you don't get hurt. and then, once that's happened, we can talk about what comes next.'

'*Please*!' Darby cried. 'No one will hurt me! They won't. I want to go home!' She seemed to have a revelation. 'If you take me home, Daddy will give you some of his pennies. I promise. And I've got some in my piggy. You can have those as well. Please, lady, *please* ...'

She was shaking as she sobbed now, and I finally got a hold of her, even though she was still trying to drum angry fists against my chest. Ransom money. Was that it? That she thought she'd been kidnapped?

Behind Darby's back, Katy took in the jerks of my head and, with a thumbs up, she mouthed her goodbyes. And in responding I obviously loosened my grip on Darby too much, because she sprang from me, almost knocking over both tea tray and coffee table, and sprinted to where her little coat was over a chair.

Katy looked at us helplessly, and took a step to gently part child and coat, but Mike, who's so good in such situations, beat her to it. Sweeping Darby up, with a bright 'Come on, let's see your bedroom, shall we?' he took her off up the stairs, one decisive step at a time, weathering her kicking and bucking and screaming.

Chapter 4

Darby had cried her eyes out for almost two hours after Katy had left. Having seen the bedroom and having allowed Mike to bring her back down again, she'd sat briefly on the sofa, seemingly drained of all emotion – or, more likely, realising resistance was useless – then was off again, in some sort of panic attack, stamping her feet, pulling her hair and railing at us all to go away, then dissolving into paroxysms of gulping, racking sobs, which went on well into the evening.

Unable to comfort her, I let her cry. She probably needed to cry it out a bit in any case. At least if she did so she'd have a chance of falling into an exhausted sleep. Because, in truth, there was almost nothing anyone could do for her – not in the short term, anyway. We couldn't grant her wish to go home, and we couldn't make any promises about the future. From the few details we already did know – particularly about the collusion of the mother – there seemed little possibility she'd be allowed to return home ever again.

And she did eventually tire, and she did eventually stop, and though I had to accept that there was no way we'd be able to bath her or get her into pyjamas, I was happy enough for her to sleep in her clothes.

And now it was morning. Tyler, being naturally curious about why she'd come to us, was bombarding me with questions I couldn't answer.

'But what did they *do*?' he wanted to know. 'Why did the police have to bang the door down?'

'Tyler, they didn't exactly bang the door down.'

'But the social worker said they burst in.'

'*Knocked* on the door –'

'And wasted no time in taking Darby out, Mum.'

'You, young man,' I said sternly, 'do a great deal of earwigging.'

'So did they beat her up? She looks okay. And she obviously loves them. And they obviously didn't want her taken away, did they?'

I didn't miss the look of wistfulness that visited his face briefly. No matter how much love he was showered with by his new forever family, the memory of his rejection by his father would never wholly go away.

I pointed towards the kitchen clock. 'Don't you have to be showered and dressed in ten minutes, my lad?' I asked him pointedly. Mike, who was thankfully now off till New Year, the factory he worked at being closed, was taking Tyler and Kieron, and Tyler's mate Denver, on some tour of their beloved football club's ground. Santa was said to be putting in an appearance but, of course, everyone was much too old to care about *that*. It was a gift for me, however. A big one. It meant the day I'd earmarked for a long list of wrapping and prepping was at least free for me to focus on our tiny visitor.

'Okay, okay,' Tyler said, picking up his last half-slice of toast. 'But you know, Mum, I *am* old enough to *know* this stuff, you know.'

'So you are,' I said. 'And ugly enough, too,' I teased. 'Seriously, I *know* that. Not just right now, though, eh, Ty? We barely know anything ourselves.'

Which seemed to satisfy him. And would give me time to decide on the edited version. You were never old enough – or ugly enough – to need to know this particular kind of ugliness.

Once Mike and Tyler had left, I kept popping upstairs and listening stealthily at the bedroom door. I could see only the shape of Darby's lower half from my vantage point, and didn't want to disturb her because I was keen that she wake up naturally. Which she did eventually, having slept a solid thirteen hours.

While I was waiting I used the time productively, going through the piles of children's clothes I kept in the wardrobe in the other spare bedroom – the one I didn't use for foster kids on account of the wardrobe being the kind that, in a happy kid, would conjure dreams of trips through a forest of coats to Narnia and, in an unhappy one, just your bog standard nightmares. It was a family heirloom, however, so there was no question of getting rid of it, and it did sterling service as a repository for all my fostering essentials – clothing and bedding, plus all kinds of toys and games that I'd picked up from various charity shops down the years.

I pulled out a selection of items to which clung familiar memories – of Olivia, one of the siblings who'd been in such similar straits. I wondered how she was now and tried to calculate her precise age. Tried to picture the beautiful young woman she'd soon become. Physically perfect, yes, but how badly scarred? Would she ever be able to form normal relationships? I tried to console myself that her youth when she'd been abused was always on her side. More so, I remembered grimly, than her elder brother, Ashton. What scars – and proclivities – would he carry through his adult life? The saying *the abused often becomes the abuser* came to mind, and I shook it away as I shook out the little outfits.

I didn't want to think such things. There was no benefit in doing so. What I had to do with Darby was live entirely in the moment. Take care of her needs to the best of my ability, and leave the professionals to chew over The Bigger Picture.

I picked up my selection and made my way back across the landing, and seeing the shape in the bed had moved, pushed the door gently open with the pile of clothes in my arms.

Darby was sitting up in bed, knees to chest, the butterfly duvet cover pulled up to her chin, and she visibly flinched when she saw me.

She'd been crying again, and continued to as I put the clothing down on the chest of drawers and went to her.

'I want my mummy,' she sobbed. 'I want to go home to my mummy and daddy.'

I sat on the edge of the bed and stretched out a hand to comfort her. She pulled her hand away. 'Darby, I'm sorry, baby, but, like I said last night, you need to stay with me and Mike for a little while. Do you remember?'

'But I want to go home!' she sobbed. 'Why can't I go *home*?'

'Because you can't, sweetie, not right now. And I'm very, very sorry. I know how scared you must be. And how strange this will all seem. But nothing bad is going to happen here, I promise you. Come on, sweetie,' I said, taking hold of her hand more firmly. 'Let's go downstairs to watch some cartoons and have some breakfast. How about that? I have banana or chocolate milk. Do you like either of those?'

She didn't answer the question, but at least she didn't try to fight me as I gently pulled the duvet back so she could get out of bed.

Her T-shirt had ridden up and I noticed that her tiny, elasticated-waist jeans had left a deep red weal around her waist. I really needed to get her into the bath as soon as I could and into some fresh clothes. But not until I'd fed her. She'd eaten hardly anything the previous evening, and I knew a full belly would be at least a little of the battle won.

And she clearly *was* hungry, especially when I told her she could have anything she wanted. 'Well, as long as it's not toenails of toast,' I had quipped, 'because I'm all out of those,' which at least elicited a wan smile.

So, chocolate milk and jam sandwiches it was – apparently her favourite – and while she got stuck in I chattered on about the family – about my own children and their partners and my gaggle of lovely grandchildren, all of whom I promised her she'd get to meet and play with over the coming days. Being an only child, and given the depravities that went on in her own home, I had a hunch she'd be sorely lacking in normal play dates.

'In fact,' I told her, 'I thought I'd have Riley bring the children over today. So you can have someone to play with. Would you like that?'

She nodded, seeming ever so slightly cheered up by the news. A temporary respite from the fear and bewilderment, at least. Which would still be there – how could it not? – but at least she'd be distracted. 'So,' I said, 'after breakfast, we'll run a nice bath for you, shall we? With lots of bubbles and ducks and mermaids, and then we'll get you dried and dressed. I've found some lovely outfits for you to choose from –'

'But not high heels and lipstick,' she said, pouting now a little.

'No, sweetie, of *course* not. Not high heels and lipstick. Just nice little girls' clothes. I think I have a princess jumper – would you like to wear that? It has Rapunzel on the front, and someone else on the back, and I've got some lovely pink leggings to go with it. They'll just fit you.'

'But not high heels and lipstick,' she said again. It wasn't a question. 'I don't want no high heels and lipstick today.'

Since Riley was climbing the metaphorical walls just as much as I was plumbing the metaphorical depths, she was only too happy to bring the kids over to play, seeing it as something of an unexpected bonus.

'How's she been anyway?' she asked, when she arrived and had disgorged her small three-person wrecking crew into my festive front room.

'Up and down,' I said, 'as you'd expect, but mostly up for the moment. Forgetting everything else – which I am trying *extremely* hard to do – I think she must have led a pretty lonely life. So this is a blessing for both of us, even if it does mean my to-do list will have to go hang.'

And, as I so often did, having adult sensibilities, I watched them all shouting and laughing and pulling out the dressing-up clothes, and found myself marvelling at just how quickly Darby was assimilated into the crew; not to mention happily taking Leo's orders. 'You'd never even know, would you?' I mused to Riley, as Darby, in her turn, began organising Marley Mae's toy buggy for her. And you really wouldn't. She seemed a world away from the distress of having been dumped with strangers. Children, particularly young ones, really were astonishingly adaptable, their ability to shut off parts of their brain and compartmentalise never failing to impress me.

Perhaps the placement wouldn't turn out to be as traumatic as I'd predicted. Perhaps Darby would be resigned, in the short term, distracted by the children, and we'd manage to do all we could under the circumstances – give her a peaceful and as-happy-as-it-could-be kind of Christmas, and see what was what in the New Year. We were due to return to full-time fostering then, after all.

Which just goes to show that, when the situation seems to need it, adults are good at compartmentalising as well.

Chapter 5

The next day, to my undying gratitude, Riley brought the grandchildren over again and babysat Darby for a couple of hours, so that Mike and I could dash into town and get the poor girl some presents.

Darby had come with nothing, of course, but that wasn't to say that some familiar things couldn't be collected for her. So I'd called Katy and double-checked, and she'd even managed to get a message through to Darby's parents on remand. And it turned out that they'd not done their Christmas shopping yet (no surprise there), so, no, there were no presents to be collected. And no, we couldn't have access to the house, because it was a crime scene – so that was pretty much that.

It felt weird, that; discussing such normal family matters with Katy, about a pair of parents who'd used their own child as a tiny porn star – the toast of the most depraved websites.

I pushed the thought away. My focus was on Darby and Christmas and the business of making sure she had a sackful of presents to open on Christmas morning – an emergency payment was now winging its way into my bank account, and I intended to use most of it on the purchase of things she could unwrap and play with and be distracted by.

This was no wanton extravagance on my part. The grandchildren invariably spent Christmas Day at ours, which was wonderful, and our tradition was for them to open most of their presents once the whole family were assembled. To bring Darby into that mix, with just a very modest number of presents, would only add to her sense of abandonment and distress.

We'd had the odd child, of course, for whom Christmas had to be a non-day, so raw were the memories and the pain, but in Darby we had a child who would appear to gain a great deal emotionally from being in the bosom of a family – of being wrapped in the security blanket of family rituals and love.

I therefore shopped speedily and well. And by the time Mike and I returned we were weighed down with riches; a baby doll, a little pram (she had been very covetous of Marley Mae's buggy the previous day), a selection of doll's clothes, a couple of new outfits for Darby herself, some books, a big jigsaw and, of course, the obligatory chocolate selection box. I was quite sure we'd spent a lot more than would be going into my account the following week, but it would be worth it, I knew, to see her face.

We opted to leave it all in the car, planning to bring it in and wrap it once she was in bed, and headed up the path, gasping for coffee.

'That's odd,' Mike observed as he singled out his door key on the car fob. 'Very quiet in there, don't you think?'

I listened. It was. And the quiet was even more obvious when Mike slipped the key in the door and swung it open. 'That's some magic touch,' he observed as he slung the keys down and shrugged his coat off.

'Either that,' I said, 'or she's got them playing sleeping logs.'

It was neither. They were quiet because they were stuffing their faces with popcorn, watching another Christmas movie (*Elf* this time – just a glance and I could identify them all).

Riley herself was sitting at the dining table flicking through a Christmas gift guide. She looked up then, and I noticed a strange expression on her face.

'Everything okay?' I asked her, as Mike and I went through the living room and into the dining room. 'I see you've got them all settled down. And if that's not a Christmas miracle, I don't know what is!'

Taking off my cardigan, I then noticed Levi glancing strangely at his mother. Riley gestured to the folding doors that we hardly ever used, but which could divide the dining and living areas into two proper rooms.

'Come in here,' she said quietly. 'And close the doors for a minute.'

I did so, a sinking feeling appearing from somewhere in

the pit of my stomach. We both sat down. 'What's wrong?' I asked, half not wanting to know.

Riley glanced at both of us in turn. 'I don't even know where to start,' she said. 'Honestly.'

'What's happened, love?' Mike asked her. 'Just spit it out. Bloody hell, we've only been gone an hour. How bad can it be?'

Nearer two, I thought distractedly. But that was of no consequence. Riley shook her head. 'Bad, Dad, believe me.'

I'm not usually one for regrets in life generally, and, by and large, the same applies to fostering. But sometimes, and thankfully these times have been few, I get this big whump of guilt about the choices Mike and I make, and how it might impact on our children and grandchildren. This was one such time. A moment when I wished I'd chosen differently. Said no. Because the last thing I wanted – in line with every parent everywhere – was to have my cherished grandchildren's Christmas memories tainted. I wanted a Christmas without drama, or trauma, or sadness. I wanted not to have that evil eddying around in my house.

But it seemed it was.

'Levi and Jackson wanted to play in the garden,' Riley told us. 'So I made them put their coats on, gave them the football and let them out the back. And I am *so* glad I did. Which left Darby and Marley, with the toy box emptied out, and as they had no interest in playing out, I was happy to leave them to it while I went and rustled up some hot dogs for lunch.

'Next thing I know, Darby's come into the kitchen, asking if they could have some chocolate spread. Course, I thought nothing of it – I just said no, and that they'd be having their lunch soon, so, after a bit of a pout, off she trotted. And that was that. Or so I thought.'

I felt the sinking feeling resolve itself into a cold, solid lump. We had elected to tell Riley so much, but *only* so much. Much less that we knew or ever wished to know.

'And?' Mike said.

'Go on, love,' I added. 'Then what?'

'Oh, Mum, it was *awful*,' Riley went on. 'It was vile. I didn't hear anything for a bit, but then I heard Marley raising her voice – and sounding a bit weird, you know? So I went in to investigate. And there she was, standing in the middle of the living room with her leggings round her ankles and her hands in her pants.' She lowered her voice to little more than a whisper. 'And she's thrusting her pelvis forward and there's Darby, showing her how to do it, saying, "That's it, pretend you're licking chocolate spread off your twinkle and go 'mmm'," and all kinds of disgusting shit like that. Christ only *knows* what I'd have found if I'd given her the bloody Cadbury's jar.'

It wasn't often that my daughter swore – it wasn't her style. And not often that my husband's face turned so pale. 'You have got to be *joking*,' Mike said, knowing she was doing no such thing. 'No way, Riley!' He turned to me. 'Casey, we can't have this, we can't. Not with the kids.'

I was still taking it in. 'What did you do?' I asked Riley.

'I just picked Marley up, and told Darby that she wasn't to play games like that. Which, of course, made no sense to her at *all*. She was just playing "growd ups" – no, sorry – playing *for* the "growd ups".' Her eyes flashed. 'Just what kind of terrible things did her parents *do* to her? I'm in shock, Mum. No, really. I could hardly believe what I was seeing. Licking chocolate spread off her crotch? *Jesus*! Thank God the boys weren't there, that's all. I don't know how I'd have even *begun* to explain it to them.'

I felt awful. 'Is Marley okay?' I asked. 'Did she say anything?'

Riley shook her head, almost irritably. 'No, she's fine, Mum. Of course she is. She was fine right away. I just told her it was a stupid game and that little girls shouldn't play it. And to be honest she seems to have forgotten all about it. As does your little mada –' She checked herself. 'As does Darby. But, Christ, Mum. What were they thinking, sending a child like that into a *family*?'

And I knew Riley had a point. And I could see Mike agreed, which didn't surprise me one bit. 'You need to phone John,' he said, his jaw set.

'I will,' I said, 'but, you know, Darby won't even know she's done anything wrong, will she? It's not like it's her fault. She's only acting out what she knows.'

'I'm already aware of that,' Mike snapped. And I understood his annoyance, too. We had been here before, sadly. More than once. No, there was no harm done. But there were limits to how much we should expect to have to deal with. Again, that sense of evil visiting us was strong in me. 'Sorry, love,' Mike said immediately. 'But I'm afraid we're not guinea pigs. Casey, abused children can't just come here and carry on with our kids and grandchildren. It's not right!'

Mike had a very good point. As did Riley. None of this was Darby's fault – she'd been abused so horrendously. She'd suffered so much, and not least because she didn't even appear to see it as suffering. An inconvenience some-times, yes – her comment about not wanting to put on high heels and lipstick made that obvious. But she obviously did what she was told on that sleazy 'film set' – perhaps even derived some weird, non-sexual pleasure from her parents' doubtless lavish attention and stage direction. And the worst of it was that she had no idea that what she did, and what they did to *her*, was depraved. That her parents, whom she loved, were so abusing her. For money. The term 'ill-gotten gains' never seemed so apt.

So she was an innocent victim, clearly. But Mike was right, too. Perhaps we weren't the best people for her to be around. In a situation like this, did we have the luxury of putting her needs first? I doubted it. We had to think of the well-being of our own family.

You're right,' I said, my mind made up. 'I will go and phone John and see if there is somewhere else she can go. Perhaps someone who doesn't have any children.'

But Riley surprised me, as she does sometimes. She immediately shook her head. 'You can't do that, Mum,' she said. 'Dad, she *can't*. That would be too cruel. There was no harm done,' she added, as my eyes widened in shock. 'Marley is too young to have understood what was going on, and Darby didn't know any different, did she? No, it would be too cruel to abandon her – especially so close to Christmas. We'll just have to make sure we don't leave any of the kids alone, won't we?'

'Too bloody right,' Mike said, pushing his chair back and standing up. 'Not for a moment,' he said, going to unfold the partition doors. 'It's all right *us* knowing that she can't help it,' he added before he opened them. 'But there's no way our family should suffer for it. No way. And, Casey, you make sure you report it.'

'And now she knows it's unacceptable, perhaps that will be the end of it,' I soothed.

Perhaps. After all, she was only a little girl.

Chapter 6

John Fulshaw was sympathetic when I called him the following morning, obviously. But he was also anxious to confirm that we'd keep Darby for a bit longer, which I assured him we would, because Riley's unexpected words had hit home. She was right. We couldn't abandon Darby. Not at Christmas. Not at all, perhaps. Not once she'd settled in.

About which I was beginning to feel very ambivalent. 'So we'll be keeping a very close eye on her,' I told John. 'And, if you've no objections, I'll have my whole *our bodies are private* chat with her. She's old enough to hear it. Though whether it sinks in or not is another thing.'

'A good idea,' John agreed. 'Because I'm certainly not going to be able to get anything organised with CAMHS before Christmas. Flying pigs being pretty thin on the ground right now.'

CAMHS stood for the Child and Adolescent Mental Health Service. Usually, with foster children, anything that constituted counselling was dealt with by them. Which was the best way – we provided care, and a safe place and routine; matters of emotional health, when it came to the big, complicated things, were best left to those who'd been trained to give such help. 'And I'll stop by tomorrow, if you're around,' he said, 'because some other things have come to light now, and I'd like to put you properly in the picture.'

'Oh dear,' I said, 'that sounds ominous. Is it more bad news?'

'I'm afraid so,' he said.

Visit arranged, I hung up, took a deep breath and joined Mike and Darby in the living room. No visit from Riley today, but Mike being home was a blessing. Though I was only too happy for Tyler to be off round at his friend Denver's, because the events of the previous day had made me doubly cautious about him acting as any kind of childminder either.

Mike was helping Darby do a jigsaw on the coffee table. And the peaceful domestic scene was so at odds with the reality that it sunk me into an uncharacteristic gloom. Darby was beautiful to look at. And clearly a sweet, polite girl. It made me feel sick to know that she had been exploited by the very people who were meant to protect her, and I realised that her exquisite features probably added to the allure that attracted sick paedophiles to seek her out.

'You okay, sweetie?' I asked as I knelt down at the table to help. 'Oh, *The Little Mermaid*. This is my absolute favourite jigsaw.'

'I love *The Little Mermaid*,' she said, inspecting a piece she'd just picked up. 'I'm a little mermaid sometimes, too.'

I braced myself. 'Are you?'

'Yes, sometimes, at bath time. We don't have bubbles, though.' She looked up at me. 'It's all right if you both want to bath me. I don't mind.'

I was going to grab a puzzle piece, but I stopped mid-reach. Mike was growing pale again. He looked horrified. 'No, no,' I quickly answered. 'It will be just me who baths you, Darby. And as you're such a big girl now, I think you're probably big enough to wash yourself. I'll just help you with your hair. How about that?'

Darby shrugged. Then she looked at Mike. 'You can still watch, though. If you want to.'

'No, darling,' I said quickly. 'Mike definitely doesn't want to watch.' This was probably as good a time as any, and Mike was clearly lost for words. 'Darby, you know your body is a very private thing. Do you understand that? Do you know what "private" means?'

'Course I do,' she said, discarding the piece in her hand in favour of another.

'Good,' I said, 'so you'll understand that when something like your body is private, only *you* get to choose who sees it. D'you understand that? And you should never have to feel uncomfortable about it. Do you understand that too?'

She nodded, but I could see that her attention was all on the jigsaw. And even had it not been, this conversation – which, in theory, should be so straightforward – was very difficult. How could I tell a child that she shouldn't allow strangers to see her naked, when I was a stranger myself? Yet here I was, calmly telling her that I'd be bathing her later.

It was all wrong. At her age, I should have been able to explain that it was safe for her mummy and daddy to see her body, but, of course, in this case, I couldn't even do that. Which was why issues around child abuse and grooming were all so fraught in such young children. Bar the usual sanctions about hitting – lashing out and being lashed out upon – they'd yet to have the first inkling that certain types of non-hostile touching were also wrong.

She had no such anxieties, which made it all doubly depressing.

'It's okay,' Darby said. 'A body's just skin and bones. Nothing to worry about.' She attempted to fit the piece into the jigsaw in the wrong place. I looked helplessly at Mike. What a peculiar thing to say. She'd obviously been told it often. Skin and bones. Nothing to worry about. It was sick.

But for Darby herself it was all completely normal. And that was the sickest thing of all.

Darby was still running around in her pyjamas when John was due to arrive the next day – the pyjamas we'd bought for her and which she'd whooped in delight about, and which she was only too happy to allow me to change her into after she'd had her bath and I'd washed her hair. She was an affectionate little thing, but I keenly felt the abuse she'd suffered. And Mike, usually so physical with the little ones we fostered – the king of tickles and bear hugs – was at constant pains to avoid being physically close to her.

And I completely understood that. In fact, when he had offered to take her to the park with him and Tyler while John visited – at Ty's suggestion; he would be playing a game of five-a-side football – it was me who had vetoed the idea. Awful as it sounds, I wasn't sure if it was the right thing to do. Should such a vulnerable child be alone with a male adult? I didn't know, and I didn't want to risk it. I had heard of such things before and knew that, as a precaution against any allegations, it was always better to have two adults around at all times. Instead, we decided that when John got here I would take him through to the conservatory, and Mike and Darby could make a game of preparing lunch.

She was full of beans, too, having obviously – though she never actually voiced it – come to see her little stay as something of a holiday. That worried me as well. I'd have expected her to display more of her initial behaviours, and to keep remembering she missed her mum and dad. But she didn't. Which meant potential attachment issues were a possibility in the mix. And that didn't bode well at all.

'Catch me, Casey!' she yelled as she leapt through the air from the sofa. I held out my arms and almost got knocked over for my trouble. 'Wow,' I said as I placed her down, 'either I'm getting too old for this or you are actually much, much bigger than six!'

She squealed with delight. As with any little girl, age was very, very important to her. 'I *am* six!' she insisted, giggling. 'Look,' she said, lifting her pyjama top right up to her chin. 'See! I don't even got no boobies – only nipples yet!'

I gently tugged the top down. 'Darby, love, remember what I said? Your body is private, and you shouldn't show it off.'

She looked crestfallen – as if upset that she'd done something terribly naughty. But any further exploration of the subject would have to wait, as the knocker went and I heard Mike welcoming John.

Which was good, because at least now I'd have a little more to go on. Though what that might comprise was anyone's guess.

'I'll get straight to it,' John said after we were settled in the conservatory. 'And it's not good, so fair warning, Casey. They found hundreds of images online during the investigation – pictures and videos, even evidence of a pay-per-view operation. And just as many physical photographs were found hidden in the house. All depicting children – including Darby, obviously. And all very definitely being –' He paused and shook his head, as if to try to shake off the pictures. 'Well, you know the drill. Being exploited and abused.'

'Oh no,' I said. 'So it wasn't just her parents then? This was part of a bigger picture?'

John nodded. 'Your regular common-or-garden paedophile ring, I'm afraid. The father's still denying everything

– though what good he thinks that'll do him, I don't know, given the evidence. Not to mention the fact that the mother's admitted everything and is fully co-operating with the police.'

I felt a glimmer of hope. 'What's she said?'

'The usual. That her husband is some kind of monster. That he is violent and controlling and that she was in fear for her life. That she was too afraid of him – and his cronies – to do anything other than exactly what he told her. Says he brainwashed her into doing everything he said.'

Shades of Rosemary West? Myra Hindley? And there were countless cases documented where women apparently 'stood by' and let their men abuse their children, because they were convinced that, if they didn't, the children would come off even worse. Could this be one such case?

I shook my head, even so, because it still stuck in my throat. I understood the notion of a man controlling a woman in that way – we'd even had lectures about it during training – but even so, my instinct was still strong: how could a mother let such disgusting things happen to her child? Wouldn't a mother do *anything* to protect her child from harm? Why hadn't she taken Darby and run away? 'I'm sorry John,' I said. 'But she *must* take some responsibility for this. It was her own daughter, for God's sake.'

'Oh yes,' John agreed, and surprisingly quickly. 'And trust me, she is most *definitely* taking responsibility. Through the courts. She has admitted her part, in detail –'

'*Good*. Well, not so much good, as good for justice.'

He raised a hand. 'And she's been honest. Says she's more than happy to be sent to prison –'

'Really?'

He smiled grimly. 'Oh, yes. Champing at the bit to be banged up, by all accounts. Apparently, she's happy to do anything that will help her get away from him.'

His words began to sink in. So it was really that bad, then. 'But what about Darby?' I asked. 'What has she said about Darby?'

'That – and I quote – she is now in the best place.'

'But doesn't she *care*?' Silly question. Given what we already knew.

'Apparently not. As far as her mother is concerned, Darby seems to be dispensable. She's expressed no interest in seeing her again. Indeed, thinks it probably best that she doesn't.'

'But she's her daughter!' I was aghast. I couldn't believe what I was hearing. So this vile woman had simply held her hands up and said, 'Fine, you got me, now take me away, I want to forget all about it'? But almost as soon as I bridled I remembered that, in all likelihood, you'd go back into Darby's mother's history and find a whole host of abuses had been visited on her too. Men like Darby's father chose their partners very carefully. And evil was invariably not born but made.

I looked out to the fairy lights Mike had wound through one of the bushes in the garden. And which one of us had, that morning, forgotten to switch off. In the daylight, the light coming from them was barely visible. But it was still shining, reminding me of the one thing we could do. Give Darby Christmas – a little light, a little respite from the darkness, by which to see her way into some sort of future.

Chapter 7

'Morning, love,' Mike whispered as he shook me awake. 'Merry Christmas.'

I smelt coffee. Smelt pine. Realised what day it was. '6 a.m.,' he added, obviously anticipating my first question. 'I knew you'd want to be up early to make a start.'

He was right. Christmas Day in our house was the most hectic of the entire year and, because I was a control freak and found it hard to delegate domestically, I always had a ton of things to do. Which was not to say I minded. The day would surely come when I had to hand the reins over. When, as with my own parents, I'd be poured a sherry and told to put my feet up. And I didn't want that happening anytime soon.

First up, I had to play Santa Claus. I had carefully wrapped up all of Darby's presents the night before, as she slept, and then hidden them out of sight just in case she got up during the night. Like all children of her age, she needed to believe that Santa's helpers or, ideally, the great man himself, had delivered the gifts and placed them underneath the tree in the wee small hours.

'What, no eggnog?' I joked to Mike as I picked up my coffee. 'I'll just drink this, then, and we can then take Darby's pressies downstairs.'

Mike shook his head. 'No need. All done,' he said. 'All nicely stacked beneath the tree. And I've even peeled a huge pan of sprouts for you.'

Sprouts were my least favourite vegetable and my least favourite chore. Well, bar the chore of eating six of them as part of my Christmas dinner, which bizarre ritual dated back to when Riley and Kieron were little. On this one day, I had this thing that if I didn't down a few of them, I'd no business making them either.

I grinned at my husband. 'Okay, spill. What are you after?'

He looked pained. 'Absolutely nothing! I did it for love. Well, and as a down payment on a leave pass for the football tomorrow afternoon. But mostly for love,' he added quickly.

And I believed him, because we both knew it would be a particularly busy day. My parents were joining us for dinner, as were Riley, David and the kids, and Kieron, Lauren and their new baby Dee Dee.

And, of course, Darby, who had been much on my mind since John's visit. She'd been absolutely no trouble in the intervening forty-eight hours or so, but neither had she shown very much interest in the coming revels, and I wondered about her family Christmases past. This, too, I understood, because we'd fostered all sorts of children and, difficult as it had been for me to believe it before we became foster parents, there were children for whom it really had little meaning, hard though it was to avoid.

These were kids who really did live on the edges of society. Children who were kept out of school, who had no televisions, who were part of no normal community. Children who had nothing, and no expectation of ever getting anything either; no presents, no parties, no fun. Children whose parents were so poor they actively avoided anything to do with Christmas, and children who'd been so badly abused, scarred and neglected that they didn't really know what it was to be happy. I had a feeling Darby fitted into the latter category.

Which was why it mattered so much that we gave her a Christmas she could revisit as a happy time in her memory in years to come. And hopefully to an extent that it went some way to softening the memory of being taken away from all she knew.

Because the developments with her mother had brought it home to me that she was done with her former life now. That, although she didn't know it, she'd in all likelihood never see either parent again. A clean break. Which, given she was still so young, was probably best. 'Should I go wake her now?' I asked Mike for the tenth time in as many minutes, having finished the bacon and eggs we'd prepared to set us up for the day.

He checked the time: 7 a.m. And, at long last, relented, even if it was while bearing his 'you're a fifty-year-old woman, for heavens' sake' expression. 'Go on then,' he said. And I was straight out of the blocks.

As Mike had already predicted, Darby was still half asleep – there was clearly no 4 a.m. badgering of parents in her repertoire. I shook her gently awake and she started, her eyes struggling to focus. 'Father Christmas?' she asked then, sitting upright, and presumably remembering the carrots, mince pie and sherry that we'd put out for Santa and his reindeer before she went to bed. 'Has he left me stuff?'

'He most certainly has,' I said, pulling back the covers for her.

'But Casey,' she said as she slid her warm little body out of bed, 'I was thinking last night. How did he find me?'

'I sent him a letter, of course,' I said. 'That's what we always do when we have children staying at Christmas.'

'To the North Pole?'

'Of course! Here, pop your dressing gown on. No need to get dressed yet, because it's Christmas!'

Darby pushed her arms into the sleeves of the fluffy pink dressing gown I'd found for her in my just-in-case box, and, bleary-eyed, tied the belt with clumsy fingers. I wasn't sure she was even half as excited as I was, but if I had one aim today it was to instil in her an understanding that family life could be all about laughter and love.

And presents, which, on seeing them, did elicit a response. One of disbelief. 'Did Santa send all these for *me*?'

I was only too happy to answer in the affirmative, and was then able to enjoy the simple pleasure of seeing a small child who had nothing, and whose life had been so brutal, opening gifts that had been chosen just for her.

'Oh, look!' she cried, 'Look, Casey! My very own baby! And she's got a bottle and food and – look – even her own potty!' and, 'Oh, Casey – look – he's sent a buggy! How did Santa know I wanted a buggy? I can take my doll for walks now! Can we take her for a walk today? And – oh – pink fluffy pyjamas! Can I wear them today? Can I wear them for Christmas?'

I grinned at her. 'Yes, sweetie, you can wear them for Christmas if you want to. But not just yet,' I added, forestalling an immediate strip. 'Let's have breakfast first, eh? Don't want to get them dirty, do we?'

Her expression changed then, and she looked up at me with those enormous blue eyes. 'What about after? When I go home? Can I take everything with me?'

Mike and I exchanged glances, both thinking the same thing. That there was to *be* no going home now. 'Yes, of course, you can take *everything*,' I reassured her, and her mouth opened in a smile.

'That's all right, then!' she said, and returned to her raptures.

By the time Mum and Dad arrived mid-morning, Tyler had opened his presents too, and with the pair of them fully occupied with the construction set he'd wanted – to build a remote-control car – my to-do list was shrinking fast, and I had already allowed myself a small glass of sherry to get into the spirit of things.

Mike and I had dressed, but had purposely kept Darby in her nightwear because I knew my mum had bought her a beautiful red velvet pinafore dress with a silver and white striped T-shirt to go underneath it. They had yet to meet Darby, but there was no question of them not getting her something; one of my enduring joys was the support my parents had always given us with our fostering. And not just on a practical level. On an emotional one as well, in that any child who stayed with us was treated as one of the family, which, from chats I'd had with other foster carers, wasn't always the case – leading to children who were already feeling lost and unwanted being treated differently, and so feeling more unwanted still.

Needless to say, my mum and dad found Darby as adorable as we had. 'Oh! Aren't you just lovely,' my mum said after I made the introductions. 'And what a lovely, lovely name!'

'My mummy picked it,' Darby said as she held her hand out shyly to shake. 'And guess what? Casey wrote to Santa so he'd know I wasn't at home. And he found me all by himself,' she explained, warming to her theme, 'and bringed me *loads* and *loads* of stuff. I never had so many presents in my *whole* life!'

'How lovely,' Mum said. 'And do you know what? He must have known we were coming to see you today because he dropped an extra present off for you at our house as well!'

Darby's eyes grew wider still. 'Oh, lady!' she said, as Mum gave her the parcel and she ripped into it like a pro.

'Oh, lady! Another present, all for me?' She gasped then, as the dress tumbled free of the paper. 'This is just like a proper princess dress, like in Disney! Oh, *thank* you!'

But again, in a moment, her expression completely changed. 'I don't have to work, do I?' she said, looking up at me now.

'Work?' I said, confused.

She held the dress up. 'Like Snow White and Belle,' she said. She might easily have added 'stoopid!' 'Like Cinderella did,' she explained, as if Mum and I were clueless. '*Everyone* knows! *She* was a princess, but nobody knowed it and she had to work *all* the time.'

'Of course not,' my mum said. 'It's Christmas, you silly sausage. No one works on Christmas Day. Well, bar Casey here, obviously.' She winked at me and grinned. 'And doctors and nurses and firemen and so on …'

'And me,' piped up Tyler. 'I'll be on plate clearing and washing up, as per.'

'That's okay, then,' said Darby, who, to Mum's consternation, whipped her dressing gown off and started pulling down her pyjama bottoms.

'Hold your horses,' I said, rushing to pull up her pants. 'Tell you what, let's leave my mum and dad to sit down for a minute, and we'll go upstairs to get you changed, yes? I can fix your hair, too. I've got a bow that will match that dress exactly. How about that? Get you looking all Christmassy and pretty?'

Which, being a little girl, Darby accepted without dissent, gathering up the dress, and the dolly – so she could be 'made Christmassy too' – and trotting upstairs with me gleefully.

It didn't take long to get Darby washed and dressed and ready, me pulling her hair into a ponytail and tying the red bow into it, while she did the same with her dolly. The dress, too, fitted perfectly, and she couldn't wait to show it off. Well, till she came down the stairs and saw Kieron in the hall, at least.

Which seemed to completely startle her. She stopped dead on the second to bottommost step, and so suddenly that I nearly cannoned into her and knocked her flying.

'What's the matter, love?' I asked her.

She pointed at Kieron. 'Him! That man!'

The penny dropped. A strange man had come into the house. Was that a regular occurrence at home?

But her response, given the fact that this was obviously her 'normal', seemed a little OTT. Because she immediately burst into tears, and pushed me aside so she could run back up the stairs.

'Darby,' I called after her, pulling a 'what the …?' face at Kieron and Lauren. I then hurried after her, only to have the bedroom door slammed in my face.

It wasn't locked – it didn't have a lock – but she was surprisingly strong, so it took a bit of pushing and a lot of coaxing to get into the room. And as soon as I was in there she was screaming at me and ripping the ribbon from her hair, then pawing at the dress, which did up at the back and, in frustration that she couldn't undo it, yanking violently at the collar.

'Sweetheart, what is it?' I said, rushing over to her, and trying to gather her into my arms. I was at a loss to understand her near-hysteria. 'It's just Kieron, my son. He won't hurt you!'

'Liar, liar, pants on fire!' she yelled at me, her cheeks pink and hot now. 'Liar, liar! You're a liar, and I *hate* you!'

Still at something of a loss, I took a firmer line and gathered her close to me, then sat down on the bed so she was clamped on my lap. 'What do you mean, love?' I asked her. '*Why* am I a liar, liar?'

'Because you said I didn't have to *work*!' she sobbed. 'An' that lady said it too! And then you tricked me!'

'*Tricked* you?'

'You got me a pretty dress and you *tricked* me!' She was gulping her sobs now. 'You're a liar, liar, pants on fire, and I don't want no dress anymore! I want it off!'

'Then you shall have it off,' I told her, loosening my grip on her slightly. 'See?' I said, dealing one handed with the buttons down the back. 'There,' I said. 'Hop down and step out of it. That's the way.'

She did so, and stamped on it a couple of times for good measure. I let her. 'Better?' I said finally. 'Pyjamas again? What?'

'I want my jeans on,' she said pointedly. 'I don't want your dress-up princess dress!'

'That's fine,' I said, getting up and going to the chest of drawers. She stood and pouted, scowling, in her vest and pants and woolly tights. 'But Darcy, can you explain why you're so cross with me?' I asked her gently. 'Because I honestly don't understand.'

'I told you,' she said, crossing her arms across her chest and pushing her lower lip out. 'Because you said I didn't have to work. And you told a *lie*!'

'You don't have to work.'

'But you got a man with a *camera*!'

The penny dropped. What had distressed her had clearly been Kieron's bag of tricks. Being a bit of a techie – not to mention a new dad with a baby – he was keen to record every precious moment of this particular Christmas, and had accordingly brought his super-high-tech camera.

And, with the benefit of hindsight, I could have kicked myself, truly, for being every bit as clueless as Darby herself had already pointed out.

'Kieron? But he's my *son*, Darby. Levi and Jackson's uncle – you already *know* that.'

The ridiculousness of what I'd just said struck me. My son. Somebody's uncle. A succession of men coming round. I cringed inside. Coming round with one thing in mind. To provide material for the delectation of their sick friends, for money. Coming round, to see Darby, to film her playing dress up – then *undress* – as their little princess.

Which meant she must be thinking that *we* had … It didn't even bear thinking about. 'Sweetheart,' I said, dropping to my knees in front of her and taking her hands. 'You do *not* have to work. You will *never* have to work again – not in that way. That's a *promise*. No one will ever make you

dress up, or take your clothes off, or *work* here, you understand that? *Never.* The dress is for *you*. It's for you to wear
because *you* want to. Not because anyone wants you to get
dressed up to *work*. It's ...'

I floundered. How the hell did you discuss such vile
things? How did you begin to explain something so horrible? What words did you use to explain to a six-year-old
that she was not going to have to spend any part of Christmas
Day being photographed and filmed simulating sex acts
with toys for God knows how many men, pay-per-view?

I handed Darcy her jeans, suddenly remembering a
headline I'd seen calling for paedophiles to be castrated. It
wasn't that simple. It would never be that simple. But right
at that minute, I couldn't have agreed more.

In the end, after another bout of tears, and many assur-
ances, Darby decided she did want to put the dress back on.
So I re-dressed her, did her hair again, and listened to her
talking about how work could be *so* boring sometimes, and
how sometimes she got a very sore twinkle, and how at
other times men came round who didn't smell nice and
shouted at her when she didn't play properly.

She had really begun to open up now – which was
distressing in itself, as I realised her former reticence about
telling of her experiences was simply because she'd been
told that if she said anything to anyone, the consequences
would be dire. And that was up to and including her mum
saying if she wasn't good, she'd not be allowed out of the
'pink fluffy handcuffs' and miss her tea.

She talked of 'only ever being allowed to wear pretty clothes for the pictures'. Of not 'minding it so much most of the time, only sometimes', but of being lonely. And of wanting to 'have friends round to play', and not ever being allowed to. Out it all came – all of a chitter-chatter, as I tied her second ponytail. All so much everyday girl talk.

And down we went then, me hoping Mike would have explained just enough that her peculiar outburst would be put into some sort of box, so that we could gloss over it now, ready to welcome Riley and everyone when they arrived, and get on with enjoying our Christmas Day.

And it appeared he had. 'Well, look at you,' said my mum when Darby returned and did a twirl for her. 'You know what?' she said, pointing upwards. 'You look just as pretty as a princess!'

Our little princess. As advertised by devils. I could have wept.

Chapter 8

Had that been the end of it, I imagine we would have carried on over Christmas, doing what foster carers everywhere do – trying to minimise a child's distress by keeping them distracted and as happy as possible under their invariably traumatic circumstances, while at the same time staying mindful of the root of their vulnerability without fixating on the evils of the world and the bleakness of such a damaged child's probable fate.

As it was, though, there was more upset to come.

Once she'd got over her anger about the lies she thought she'd been told, Darby soon returned to doing what any six-year-old would on Christmas morning, playing with her – and Tyler's – Christmas presents, eating too much chocolate, and generally running around in an over-excited fashion.

I was still on edge, even though now she knew she wasn't going to have to 'go to work', Darby was becoming more

63

relaxed and playful by the minute, her initial shyness around Kieron and Lauren having vanished.

'Do you think it's reasonable for me to ask Kieron not to film any of today?' I asked Mike when I managed to engineer for us to snatch a couple of minutes to ourselves, ostensibly while taking bin bags of rubbish and wrappings out.

'No, I don't,' he said. 'I don't see how. On what grounds? He'll think you've gone mad.'

'I was thinking, you know, on the grounds of Darby's privacy, something like that. I don't know ... I just keep having this sense that she *wants* him to film her ... Like she's playing to the cameras, and, after what happened with Marley Mae the other day ...'

'Love, you know you can't. And calm *down*. We're all with her, aren't we? What d'you think is going to happen when we're all sitting around the living room?'

'Yes, but no one but us knows what's been done to her, do they? What she thinks is *normal*.'

'Nor will they,' Mike said grimly. 'So before you suggest it, no quiet words with Kieron, either.'

'That was the *last* thing I was about to suggest, believe me, love.'

'*Good*. Look, try to keep calm. We've both got our eyes on her and I'm sure we can keep her occupied till Levi and Jackson get here – at which point I'm sure she'll want to play with them instead. Besides, Dee Dee'll be down for her nap soon, so Kieron will take a break from it anyway ... Seriously, Casey,' he said, finally plonking all the wrappings in the right bin. 'It's only –'

But I never got to hear what further pearl of wisdom he was about to impart, because the back door suddenly opened, revealing a rather frazzled-looking Mum.

'Sorry to interrupt, love,' she said. Did she think Mike and I had sneaked out for a tryst? 'But there's been a bit of a to-do.'

They say that sometimes it's best to work on a need-to-know basis but, in the case of little Darby, the jury was definitely out. On the one hand, I was glad Levi and Jackson hadn't been there to witness it but, on the other hand, had I taken the decision to be open about the horrors of Darby's grim past, then perhaps it wouldn't have happened in the first place.

Not that 'it' was anything that terrible, not by the standards we were used to, where kids came from backgrounds that made your hair stand on end and would so often scar them for life.

All 'it' was, as I described haltingly to John Fulshaw on the day after Boxing Day (at 9 a.m. precisely), was Darby having started pulling her dress up, more and more, and, with everyone's attention on her, clearly warming to the attention, gyrating around and, just as she'd already instructed my elder granddaughter, stuffing her hands down her tights and thrusting her pelvis in a fashion that left no room for doubt as to what she was enacting. She'd apparently picked up a walnut – it really didn't bear thinking about – and had even been about to demonstrate where she could put it, to a stunned Kieron, when we'd returned to the room.

'I've put it all in the log, John,' I finished up, lamely. 'But the main thing is that I'm all at sea, and I'm not sure I can cope with something like this, I'm really not. And nor can Mike,' I added. 'Not when it potentially involves the grandchildren.'

John was silent for a moment, and I knew he was trying to digest the unlikely scene I'd just feebly sketched out. Funny, I mused, how we dealt with so many domestic horrors, but this particular scenario crossed an unspoken line.

Which was odd in itself, and I'd lain awake the previous two nights, trying to get to grips with it, because I'd thought – indeed I still largely thought – I was un-shockable. I knew all about the depths to which some depraved parents sunk. Sexual abuse, violence, neglect, outright abandonment. But mostly, if not always, I could tease out the factors that went some way to explain, if never condone it. Substance abuse and addiction, for example, were so often contributory factors. Violence meted out due to alcohol addiction, or neglect and exploitation due to a parent being a slave to heroin; a heroin addict, I'd learned long ago, would do almost anything (to themselves *or* their child) to get a fix.

This, though, was different, and I think that was what was troubling me. This sense that these people had so calmly and deliberately used their own daughter as a child star in the worst kind of pornography. I didn't know how old Darby had been when they first started taking pictures of her, or precisely what acts she'd been trained to perform, and, though I usually craved – and invariably nagged John for – more information about the kids we had, I found myself in the uncharacteristic position of not wishing to know more than I already did.

It was quite the opposite in this case, and that was what kept me awake. I didn't want to know. In fact, I wished I could un-know it. Because I knew about the importance of those early impressionable years. Was little Darby already damaged beyond help? Beyond *our* help? The guilt for thinking that pressed down on me.

'It's not that she's not a sweetheart,' I told John now. 'It's just that I don't know what to *do* with her. Not without psychiatric support, and a comprehensive care plan.'

'Which will all be put in place immediately after the New Year,' he said quickly. 'You know you can trust me on that score, Casey, always.'

'I know, John –'

'And that you'll be supported on *all* fronts,' he added. 'You know that too. We wouldn't expect you and Mike –'

'John.' The guilt pressed even more. I thought of little Darby, out with the doll and buggy as I spoke, with Mike and Tyler, the former knowing the call I'd be making in their absence. The latter knowing nothing.

'John,' I said again, speaking quietly, as if that would make the impact less. 'We can't keep her. I'm sorry, but I've got to come clean. Darby's not going to be right for us, long term.'

The words out, I felt immediately that I should retract them. It just seemed so *selfish*. She was *six*, for God's sake!

And we'd coped with worse. We had coped with *so* much worse. But there was a world of difference between this and managing challenging, aggressive, violent, or even suicidal children. We knew how to do the latter; it was what we'd both trained for. But Darby was complicated, complicating psychological territory, and even if I'd felt equal to the task of trying to unravel it, I could only do so if I disclosed the extent of it to our family. And this was a burden I could not expect them to bear.

So I was effectively disowning her, on their behalf, without even consulting them. Riley's words – it's 'too cruel' – were clamouring in my head. I was all too aware that I had no simple excuse; not like with Connor, the lad we'd briefly had, and whom we'd considered keeping longer – till it turned out that he'd waged a war for supremacy with Tyler, assuring him that, soon, he'd be our favourite. That had been easy, in the end. Because Tyler came first. But this was a six-year-old, now utterly alone in the world.

'I know,' John said simply.

'You do?'

'Of course I do. Casey, I knew almost immediately. It's never been never my expectation that you'd keep Darby long term. I was just hoping you could keep her for a few weeks, that's all. I'm expecting a call today about it, as it happens. Darby's being pushed through immediately for adoption.'

'What, just like that?' I'd never heard anything of this kind move that fast.

'There have been developments,' he explained.

'What, over and above what we already know?'

'Over and above. *Way* over and above, as it turns out. Darby's one of hundreds. *Hundreds*. Sickening, isn't it? And there's no question of her being placed with other family members, either. I've already been told of other relatives who are in the frame. No, she'll be escaping *all* of it. And good bloody job too. And in the meantime, can you just keep on doing what you're doing? Just continue to remove her from situations where you think she will react badly and keep pointing out to her the right way to behave? You can't do much else, can you? And you're doing a fine job.'

'I'm not sure I am,' I said, feeling terrible that I was so keen for her to leave us as soon as possible.

'Oh, you are,' he said. 'Never forget the alternative she'd be faced with. And I'm sorry ...'

'John, for God's sake, don't apologise!' I said.

I heard him chuckle. 'Well, that's rich. You flipping started it!'

Chapter 9

True to his word, John was back with news just forty-eight hours later. Of a couple – the Burtons – we'd had dealings with four or five years previously, while they'd looked after one of our foster children on respite. I remembered them well, principally because they were 'posh', for want of a better word, and lived in the countryside on a farm. Somewhere far enough away, in every respect, to give Darby a chance of a future in a different world.

But they didn't want another foster child. They were looking to adopt now. To focus all their energies on a single child, like Darby, about whom they'd already been briefed. Because, according to the psychologists, they would be perfect for her too.

They were an older couple, childless, and after several years of short-term placements had decided the time had come to give up fostering and create a 'forever home' for one lucky child. An image floated into my mind, and, for once, it was a decidedly pleasant one; of a teenage girl in jodhpurs, riding a horse. As if it were going to be that simple.

But apparently it might be. 'There's no question of Darby having any contact with her biological family going forwards,' John confirmed on New Year's Eve. 'The mother is the only child of a long-absent single mother, and the father's brothers have both been charged with the same crime. It's one big unholy mess, but, in one sense, this is better. Because it will be altogether less messy just to place Darby out of harm's way. She's still young enough ...' He didn't finish. We both knew what he meant. That there was still a fighting chance that she could be, as it were, rewired. Have that part of her life, and the resultant impulses, whittled away to a few fragments of memory. How much did any of us remember of our lives before we were six, after all?

'And in answer to your next question,' John said, 'both Darby's parents have agreed to the adoption unreservedly. Not that we needed it, given everything.'

'I should hope so,' I said, though actually I would have preferred the word 'reluctantly'. But now I was living in la-la land. Though I couldn't say it professionally, nor would, privately was a different matter and, as far as I was concerned, Darby's parents were animals themselves.

I felt the weight of guilt lift as I ended the call. I could see Darby running around the garden, chasing Tyler and shrieking. Her cheeks were a lovely deep pink, and with the new red coat, tartan scarf and smart black boots we'd bought her in the sales, she looked the picture of happiness and health. Nobody would have guessed that underneath that rosy glow and joyful laughter there lay such a deeply skewed and abused soul.

Because I wasn't naïve, any more than was John or Mike. There would be years of counselling ahead for Darby; because of what her parents had subjected her to, and the emotional distress she had suffered, she'd probably continue to suffer, one way or another, for years to come – both because of the abandonment and the inevitable consequence of getting older and understanding more.

As John had concluded when he'd called just that morning, she would doubtless get worse before she got better. Which made it doubly good that there were people like the Burtons to take care of her. Without anyone to consider but the child they were adopting, they could ensure they had the best chance of seeing her through, out of the darkness and on to a better life.

I glanced at the clock on my mobile. A process that would be starting now. All being well. This was to be Darby's first introductory visit with the Burtons and for all that they'd intimated that they already felt committed, I was also aware how much a part instinct played. If things didn't feel right, all the rationalising in the world wouldn't help make a placement 'stick' – and that held true for both parties.

True, from Darby's perspective this was all going to be fun. A visit to a farm, where there'd be sheep and cows and chickens. 'And horses!' she'd enthused when she returned from her briefing the previous day with Katy Morris. 'And a sheepdog called Socks. But no dressing-up clothes. I don't have to work, no more never,' the words running together as she'd gabbled them out, and Katy's and my eyes meeting. My sense of relief.

My relief once again, when we'd laid Darby's clothes out, all ready for the trip out to the country the following day, and she'd grabbed me and kissed me and thanked me for having her. 'I've had the best Christmas *ever*,' she'd said. And then, very solemnly, 'Will you let Santa know where I'm going to be next year? Because the country is a *very* big place.'

I felt Mike's hand on my shoulder as I rapped on the conservatory window. 'Come on you two,' I called. 'Time to get off!'

'It's the best thing,' my husband said, reading my mind, the way he always did.

'I know,' I said, nodding, but feeling the same pang I always did. That, for all that it *was* best, that I had nevertheless failed. In the misguided business of trying to be all things for everyone.

But there were Tyler and Darby now, running across the garden towards the back door, and Tyler veering off to squish his nose against the conservatory glass. And I thought of my kids, and my grandkids, and of this cherished adolescent, and I thought there was possibly another way of putting it. That, for Darby, now, thankfully, there *was* someone.

I never needed to be all things for everyone in the first place.

Epilogue

Children come into and out of our lives all the time and, particularly with those who are only with us briefly, there will always be that sense of unfinished business; of just dipping into and out of a child's life. Moreover, because such children are with us for so short a time, we often lose track of what happens to them.

We took Darby to meet the Burtons and, happily, the bond was mutual and immediate; indeed I don't know why I worried in the first place. How anyone could fail to warm to such a sweet child, I do not know. And a week and a half later – John was as good as his word – Katy picked her up and she moved in with the Burtons.

It's a bitter kind of pill, a child being okay with leaving. Not because we hanker after immortality in a child's memory – we already knew Darby would keep a place in her heart for us. But because a lack of care in a child also means a lack of attachment, and that's a serious business when it comes to their emotional health. But, as we reminded ourselves constantly, she *was* only six and, once taken away from the hell of her early childhood, she could, with the support and love and patience of her adoptive family, re-learn the 'rules' of our much nicer world.

And, at the time of writing, it's a case of so far, so good ...

No Place
for Nathan

No Place for Nathan

'Aha!' a strange little voice said from behind me. 'Mish Mannypenny, I preshume?'

I was sitting at the desk in the corner of my classroom at the time, so I spun around in my swivel chair (a recent and welcome addition) to see a young boy I didn't recognise standing in the doorway. He looked to be about 11, with bushy black hair. The sort of hair that always looked like it hadn't seen a brush in some time, even if it had. Judging by the rest of him, however, I decided it probably hadn't. Way-too-short trousers (so often a give-away) and a shirt that, though clearly once white, was an unpleasant shade of 'old washing-up water' beigey-yellow.

I stood up and extended a hand, happy to play along with his air of formality. 'Well, hello,' I said. 'I'm Mrs Watson. Who are you?'

'The name's Bond,' he replied, giving my hand a gentle shake. 'Jamesh Bond.'

Ah, I thought, *Sean Connery – that explains the strange attempt at a Scottish accent.* 'Okay, James,' I replied, 'it's very nice to meet you, but do you have a school name that I could use?'

He seemed to consider this for a minute, inspecting the hand I'd just shaken. 'Well,' he said finally, 'I'm called Nathan as well and I'm 11 but I have a birthday soon and then I will be 12.' He smiled proudly at me. 'Are you my new teacher, Miss?'

'Indeed I am,' I confirmed, ushering my new recruit in properly. The deputy head, Donald, had already told me he'd be sending a boy called Nathan down after lunch, and by the looks of this little lad, I had the correct one. I also noted that his Scottish accent had now disappeared, to be replaced by a slightly high-pitched, excitable chatter. 'That's a lovely name, Nathan,' I told him, having sat him down. 'And, as I say,' I added, pulling out the chair opposite to make it better to chat to him, 'I *am* going to be looking after you for a bit, though not in the same way as a regular class teacher. I'm going to be looking after you because you have been getting into quite a bit of trouble lately, haven't you? That's why you're here.'

I'd been running the Unit for just over a year now, so I already knew a fair few of the more 'memorable' kids, but with Nathan only being 11, and it only being late September – just a few weeks into the autumn term – he was a boy I hadn't come across before. All I knew so far was that he'd already managed to get a bit of a name for himself as a troublemaker. A boy who kept getting into fights, even though he didn't look the type, he had also variously been described as 'a bit odd', as having learning difficulties and, most damningly, as a child who threw the most outrageous tantrums and was in danger of permanent exclusion.

And all this in a matter of less than a month, I thought grimly. His reputation must have preceded him and then some.

He lowered his gaze to the floor in recognition of his misdemeanours. 'But I'm going to try to help you be a good boy now,' I added. 'That's the plan. Are you going to try your best for me?'

'OK, Miss,' he said, brightening, 'I'll be good for you, I promise. I think you're gonna like me, too, because I like you.'

Running the Unit, as it was called, in our local comprehensive school, was something of a dream job for me. I'd been in youth work for some time and was very experienced, but applying to manage it – 'it' being the place where kids were contained when they couldn't be in mainstream school, for whatever reason – had been something of a long shot for me. I had no education background or formal teaching qualifications, so no one was more surprised than me when I got the call after the interview to tell me the job was mine if I wanted it. They even told me I could work towards whatever qualifications they or I thought might be useful 'on the job'.

And the Unit soon became an integral part of the fabric of the school. Indeed, within just two terms, the head had realised that it was becoming a victim of its own success, the numbers slowly and surely increasing to a point where it would soon risk getting out of control. And perhaps that was inevitable; once the teachers realised I was happy for them to hand me their most disruptive children, they were understandably eager to refer them to the Unit rather than try to find a way to manage them in their classes. Which was not a criticism; I'd have been inclined to do the same myself, not least for the benefit of the other pupils.

I was also, I soon became aware, my own worst enemy. And after realising that I was the kind of gal who just couldn't say no, the head of the school, Mike Moore, informed me that he was hiring another behavioural manager, Jim Dawson. This, he said, was so that one of us could be permanently in situ in the Unit, while the other was free to wander the corridors and sit in on classes where a teacher had reported major disruptions. It also meant I had additional time to do more home visits with parents or guardians; something that was proving really constructive.

Jim and I had soon become an efficient team. We would alternate who did this, and also work with the teachers, to show them different methods of handling disruptive behaviour, so we could at least partly stem the incoming tide. I got along great with Jim. In his fifties, he was diminutive like me, but also stocky, with a friendly face and a no-nonsense attitude. Having him around made my job so much easier.

And it was a great job, no doubt about it; something I could really get my teeth into. Together with Jim, I looked after kids from all kinds of backgrounds, sent to the Unit for all sorts of reasons. They could be the bullied or the bully, the distressed and dispossessed, the lazy, the hyperactive, the angry, the apathetic or, in what seemed to be this case, the complete misfit. One thing united them and informed everything I did: they were kids who had troubles and couldn't cope with school. We currently had 40 of them on our list, too – and usually around 10 in the Unit at any given time.

Needless to say, no two days were ever the same, and each one – day *and* child – brought a different set of problems. And though, right now, little Nathan seemed completely sweet and biddable, you didn't join our numbers for nothing. So, initially, my job would be to observe and assess him, slotting him into the routine and watching him carefully, to see if there were any obvious triggers or situations that would make him flare up and kick off.

This, in the first couple of days, proved difficult. True to his word, Nathan had obviously taken a shine to me and wanted to be constantly at my side, using any excuse to leave his table and come to sit by me instead.

Sometimes it would just be to come and smile at me or touch my arm, at which point I'd just acknowledge him and steer him gently back to his group. But at other times, he'd want to linger and I'd have to become firm with him, and it was during these exchanges that I'd get a glimpse of a darker side, as he clearly didn't respond well to being spoken to sternly. It would be then, having been told in no uncertain terms that he must do as he was told and stay put at his desk like everyone else, that he would stamp his foot and glare and, having returned to his chair, treat me to a look of pure hatred – his lips tight against his teeth, like a dog about to growl, and his eyes narrowing, changing his face completely.

He'd snap out of it almost as soon as he adopted it, but as we reached the end of his first week it was beginning to become clear that this was a strange and clearly complex little lad.

He had other, quite arresting behaviours, too. He seemed to have a compulsion to touch and stroke certain women. I couldn't exactly categorise it – there was no particular type or trigger that I could see, but he was very particular about which women he was drawn to. He also seemed to like disrupting other children if they were playing or working quietly. To do this, he'd usually cry out that someone had just called him a name, then proceed to hit out at or kick the unfortunate victim, who almost always, I quickly established, had not said a word.

He was also without fear; he had no anxiety about tackling his bigger, stronger classmates. He'd take on anyone, regardless of their size. He'd provoke the boys, too – never a good idea, if you're in a behaviour unit – by stroking them as he passed, fluttering his eyelashes and pouting his lips, and saying things like 'You think I'm sexy, don't ya?' and 'Ooh, I know you want me!'

Needless to say, this went down badly. The other lads I had in with me at the time, particularly James and Dillon, would swear at him and threaten to batter him, which of course caused disruption, and I began to realise why he was a difficult boy to have in class. Nathan himself, at this point, would become seriously distressed, and it would be a good 30 minutes – with him mostly sobbing hysterically – before I could quieten him down and get the group back on track again.

That was the most interesting thing, I decided – this abrupt change in mood. I'd catch him out, give him detention, perhaps, and get the evil eye from him, but within a moment, he was usually back to being angelic, particularly if there was no one else around. It just didn't appear to sink in with him that he may have annoyed me or upset me. It would be an interesting process, I decided, getting to understand what made him tick and, if I could manage to do so, to help him gain insight and control over his behaviours.

Interesting, and perhaps something of a multi-faceted challenge, as I was to realise that Friday afternoon. It was a couple of minutes before the final afternoon bell went – home time for the kids and finishing-up time for the staff, before a much-looked-forward-to break over the weekend. I'd had Jim with me for most of the afternoon and we'd been working on conflict resolution with the group; a drama-based lesson where they would act out various scenarios that could lead to an argument, and we'd look at solutions that wouldn't end in a fight or an exclusion.

The going-home routine was the same every day, just as it tends to be in schools everywhere. And today it was Jim who was directing operations.

'Right,' he said, as the bell sounded. 'Stop what you're doing, tidy your area and put your things away quietly, then get your coats and line up by the door.'

Pens began going into pencil cases and chairs started scraping back – so far, just an ordinary end to the day – but then we both became aware of Nathan, who'd moved only in as much as he'd sat back and folded his arms across his chest. 'Do you have a problem with that, Nathan?' asked Jim.

I saw the strange look come across Nathan's face even before he spoke. 'Yeah, I do, you ugly motherfucker,' he said, grinning nastily.

I was used to his kamikaze approach to dealing with bigger, tougher boys but was genuinely aghast to hear him speaking like this to Jim.

The other kids started to giggle and nudge each other as they prepared to leave, and Jim took the sensible step of dismissing them. 'Okay, you lot, you can go now,' he told them. 'Have a nice weekend, and we will see you on Monday.'

I added my own farewell, herding them out, aware of their disappointed faces at being asked to leave just as the entertainment was about to begin. If that had been Nathan's plan – to grab some attention – it had backfired.

I shut the door then, turned back and, after exchanging a glance and some raised eyebrows with Jim, asked Nathan gently if something was troubling him.

He didn't look at me. Instead he put his hands in front of his face, as if to create a barrier between us. He then turned his face towards Jim. 'It's *you* I'm talking to!' he shouted. 'You God-damned cocksucker!'

Jim calmly placed a hand on each hip. 'I'd be grateful if you didn't speak to me like that, young man,' he said mildly.

Nathan glared at him. 'I just did!'

'Or,' Jim continued, 'I might have to ring your dad.'

'Ha!' Nathan threw back. 'You wouldn't dare! My dad is seven foot six and the last teacher that rang him got thrown out of a window and beaten up, you stupid prick!'

I was obviously not meant to take part in this conversation so I simply stood by and watched, bemused. As, I suspected, was Jim. It wasn't as if Nathan had been disciplined for anything. This outburst seemed to have come entirely out of the blue. The question was, Why? Where had it come from?

'Why are you mad with me, Nath?' he asked quietly.

'That's not my fucking name, arsehole,' came the response.

'Sorry,' Jim answered, 'I should have said "Nathan", shouldn't I?'

Nathan shook his head then. 'I said that's not my fucking *name*!'

'Oh,' said Jim, as if enjoying a normal conversation, 'so what *should* I call you, then?'

Nathan uncrossed his angry arms and pushed himself back away from the desk. 'Call me what the fuck you like,' he said. 'I'm off home now anyway. And what *you* can do is stick this up your arse!'

With that, he stood up, stuck his middle finger up to Jim's face, kicked his chair over and walked casually out of the classroom.

We stared at each other, stunned, as the sound of Nathan's footsteps faded, both of us wondering if what had just happened had really taken place. It wasn't that the exchange itself was anything shocking – we'd both heard much more colourful language – it was just the completely random, unprovoked nature of it that flummoxed us, so much so that for a few minutes we could manage nothing more grown-up than a five-minute fit of the giggles. 'Well,' observed Jim, when we finally pulled ourselves together, 'nice to know I've made a good impression, anyway!'

Though I wrote up the notes I'd made on Nathan over the weekend, I returned to work on Monday morning still at a loss to understand my new charge, who seemed to have no clear triggers, or continuity, to his various behaviours. Often it *was* clear – the attention-seeking bully with the minuscule self-esteem, or the child who lacked empathy due to never having formed solid bonds. But in Nathan's case it seemed such a rag-bag of different issues that it was difficult to know where to start.

But wherever I did start, it seemed I'd be starting early. I arrived at my usual time – a good 45 minutes before the children were due to be there – to find him waiting in the corridor outside my classroom. Having the children in school early wasn't unusual – one of the new initiatives Jim and I had put in place being a breakfast club – but Nathan obviously wasn't interested in eating food.

He looked his same dishevelled self and seemed very pleased to see me. I smiled at him. 'Morning, sweetie,' I said. 'You're early.'

'Morning, Miss,' he said brightly. 'You look beautiful today. And I *love* that,' he added, pointing to the jade-coloured glittery scarf I had threaded beneath the lapels of my black jacket.

'Thank you, Nathan,' I said, unlocking and opening the classroom door. 'That's very nice of you. And now you're going to have to find something to amuse yourself with as I have to get some work organised for you all for today.'

'Could I make something?' he asked. 'You know, from the art box?'

I told him he could. 'But only on condition that you tidy everything away nicely before the others get here, okay?'

I thought of bringing up his inexplicable outburst at Jim the previous Friday, but decided against it, something telling me that now wasn't the moment. To start the week the way the previous one had ended, with a flare-up and acrimony, didn't seem the best way to proceed.

Instead I left him to it and went to my desk to start preparing the day's activities, but after around 10 or 15 minutes I became distracted by Nathan, who'd previously been rummaging around and cutting things up in silence, beginning to chatter to himself.

At first I thought he was just providing himself with a running commentary, but the rhythm sounded funny, and

I pricked up my ears. Yes, I was hearing right, he was engaged in a conversation – a two-way conversation he was having with himself. And using markedly different voices, as well: one high-pitched, the other lower. I wasn't sure what he'd been making, but he was bent over his desk and appeared to be putting something on and off his head.

I got up from my chair and walked over to him so I could get a closer look, but he was side-on to me and obviously so engrossed in what he was doing that he didn't seem to notice my approach. It was now even clearer that his dialogue was between a male and a female, who seemed to be involved in some sort of argument. And as I stood and watched – he still seemed oblivious to my proximity – I realised that every time the female character was speaking, he was putting whatever he'd made on his head. The penny dropped shortly afterwards – he'd made himself a wig. It was a band of white card to which he'd attached several long strips of yellow sugar paper, and which he was now balancing on his head as a crude hairpiece.

'Are you okay, Nathan?' I asked, wondering what the discussion was about.

He turned to me and smiled, holding the wig so it didn't slip off. 'Yes, Miss,' he said. 'Everything is fine, thank you.'

'What's that on your head?' I asked.

'Oh, it's just my hair, Miss. I think I have to be Jenny today and she has long blonde hair.'

'Ah,' I said. 'Was that Jenny you were just talking to?'

He giggled girlishly. 'No, Miss. I told you. I *am* Jenny, can't you tell?'

'Ah –' I began.

'– and I was speaking to Jack,' he explained. 'He wants to be my boyfriend but I told him I am not a dirty girl. So I won't be his girlfriend and that's that.'

I was confused now. 'So where has Nathan gone?' I asked him.

He giggled again. 'Oh, Miss, you *are* funny. I'm right here!' He beamed at me then. 'I love you, Miss, and I am *so* glad it's Monday,' he announced, jumping up then and throwing his arms tightly around my waist.

I hugged him briefly, then gently prised his arms from around me, crouching down as I did so to talk to him. 'Good,' I said, 'but listen, it's time to tidy these things away now.'

'Okay,' he said, and duly began gathering the paper and scissors and glue up.

'And Nathan,' I added, 'you'll need to put your hair in your drawer as well.'

'But I want to wear it, Miss! I told you, I need to be Jenny today.'

I began helping him pop things back into the box. 'Nathan, I'm sorry, but you can't wear your hair in school. I mean, it's fine if it's just you and me, but not when the others are around. The big boys might laugh at you, mightn't they? And we don't want that, do we?'

He spent a few seconds considering this, and I wondered if I should be braced for a small explosion. But it seemed not. 'Okay, Miss,' he said, 'I'll take it off as soon as I've finished tidying up.' Which he duly did, clearing the desk and putting the box back in its corner, before taking his wig off and placing it very carefully in his drawer.

With such a lot to think about, I took the opportunity to go and grab a coffee from the staff room and see what else I could find out when Jim arrived and was able to take the reins in the Unit. Did Nathan have some mental health issues or did he just have an overactive imagination? I was no psychologist, but there was clearly something psychological going on. He was clearly inhabiting multiple characters – so did that mean he had multiple personalities too? It would certainly fit in with the sometimes inexplicable about-turns in his mood and behaviour – was he acting out different people? Playing different roles as a coping mechanism? There was obviously a lot I needed to learn about this child if I was going to be in a position to get him back into the mainstream.

Coffee in hand, I went along to visit the special needs team, where I knew the head of department, Julia Styles, would probably be able to tell me more.

'Well, not much,' she confessed, when I explained about 'Jenny' and the wig and wondered if she knew more about it. 'He's kind of fallen off the radar a little. You know what it's like, Casey. It's mostly been fire-fighting. Everyone who's taught him has been too busy running around trying to stop fights breaking out because of his incredible talent for offending right, left and centre.'

'What about the educational psychologist?' I asked.

'Oh, he's definitely been referred. In fact, I'm sure he's been seen ...' She went to a filing cabinet and flicked through some papers. 'Yes, he has. He was seen whilst still at his primary school, and we're still waiting for the report to be sent on to us. That's one of the reasons he's with you – to manage and contain him till we've got something concrete to go on. I suppose we'll decide what best to do with him then.'

'Can you chase it up, d'you think?'

Julia nodded. 'Already on my to-do list.'

'And do you have anything else on him that might be useful? What about his family circumstances? Anything significant there?'

'I'm not sure,' Julia said, scribbling another note on her pad. 'But I can certainly find out ...' She stopped and frowned at me guiltily. 'Sorry, Casey,' she said. 'This should have been chased up for you last week, shouldn't it? You must think we treat your Unit like a kid-shaped black hole sometimes, mustn't you?'

'No, not at all,' I reassured her. *Yes, exactly*, I thought.

It was frustrating, sometimes, waiting for information. We hadn't received anything at all on Nathan up to now, barring a few short notes on his behaviour. We did know he was statemented as having special educational needs, but without the report from his last school, we didn't know exactly why. I knew these things took time, of course, sometimes as long as months, but I also knew that if somebody didn't push for information, it could take even longer.

My little nudge, however, quickly paid dividends. By the middle of that week I was suddenly awash with information about Nathan – child-protection files that might be key to unlocking the mystery surrounding the odd and worrying behaviours of this lonely, troubled boy. I learned that social services had already been involved with Nathan's family on a number of occasions.

But as I delved into the paperwork I was to be disappointed once again, as there was very little that enlightened me. An only child, Nathan apparently lived with his mother and stepfather (he no longer had contact with his dad) and there had been indications of neglect. It had been neighbours who had first alerted the authorities about the family, when, as a younger child, Nathan had so often been left at home alone. And action had been promptly taken. It was recorded that the mother and stepfather had undergone family therapy, but the notes were vague, only summarising that following the intervention no further action had been deemed required.

I was still awaiting the report from the educational psychologist, of course, but, in the meantime, it wasn't much to go on. And as the days went by, it seemed that, now he was based in the Unit with me and Jim, Nathan was a child very much out of sight, out of mind. For Nathan this was obviously something of a welcome development, because away from the many challenges of trying to fit into the mainstream, he was relaxing into being the person he really wanted to be.

And it seemed it was me who was the catalyst. He'd

particularly latched on to me and held nothing back now; he'd arrive early for school more often than not, and pop his wig on completely unselfconsciously. He'd also started accompanying me into the dinner hall every lunchtime – which I allowed – and it became clear that he had some odd food issues too; he would only eat pale-coloured food: rice, pasta, chicken and cheese. If there wasn't anything the right hue, he simply wouldn't eat. And over the next couple of weeks it became clear that there might be a pattern forming in one of his behaviours, because on the next two Friday afternoons we had the same inexplicable end-of-day meltdown; mostly with Jim but also now including me.

'You know what?' I said to Jim after Nathan's third week in the Unit. 'This tantrum-throwing – have you noticed how it always happens on a Friday? No other day, just the Friday, and you know what I'm thinking? I'm wondering if it's almost like he's setting down a marker. Giving us a good reason to keep him in the Unit for another week. What do you think?'

I'd been pleased with my little theory, so I was even more pleased when Jim seemed to think I'd hit the nail on the head. 'That fits,' he agreed, 'because I do think that's something he's worked out since he's been here. That kids come and go – that there's always talk about behaviours that will get them out or keep them in here. And let's face it, there's not much for him back in the mainstream compared to this, is there? It's not like he's missing a great bunch of friends, is it?'

I shook my head. The truth was that Nathan didn't seem to have a friend in the world.

The reality was that it might not just be regular school that Nathan found difficult. As I mulled things over during the following days, it occurred to me that there might be somewhere else that he found traumatic currently: the home he returned to every night and weekend.

Nathan lived fairly close to the school, on a street that was almost on my own route home, and with it still being quite balmy, it was a route I often walked – it was a good end-of-day 20-minute de-stress. On one occasion, I'd even seen him, sitting on a front-garden wall on the corner, nose buried in a comic. He'd not seen me – if he had, I knew he'd be over like a shot – but it had made me wonder what was happening behind his own front-garden wall. And perhaps there was a way to find out.

The next Friday, I casually suggested that as I had to get home early and would be leaving school promptly, perhaps we could walk home – as far as his at least – together.

Nathan was, as I expected, thrilled with this development, and was chattering ten to the dozen as we left the school grounds. It was only when we neared the road that joined his that he stopped talking abruptly, stood still on the pavement and said, 'Oh, God, Miss – I need my hair!'

'Your hair? You don't normally take your hair home, do you, Nathan?'

He looked stricken. 'I do sometimes,' he admitted, as if he'd been caught out in a terrible crime.

'You'll be fine without it,' I reassured him. 'Look, we're not far from home now.'

But he didn't seem to be listening. He'd thrown down his backpack and started tearing at his school sweatshirt. 'Can you help me get this off, Miss?' he asked, holding his hands up like a toddler would, so I could haul it over his head. He looked quite desperate by now, so I obliged.

Once it was free, he immediately tied the arms round his head, bandana-style, knotting it at the front so that the body of it hung down behind his head. 'That's better, Miss,' he said, immediately looking calmer. Then he smiled. 'Did you see anything on Nathan's back when you helped him get his top off?'

He was talking in a higher pitch now and I ran through the words in my head, realising he was now being Jenny. 'No, I didn't,' I said. 'Should I have seen something?'

'Just look at these bruises,' he said, suddenly pulling up his school shirt. 'And no, he *didn't* do it falling off his auntie's washing machine!'

I looked at his back. There were indeed some bruises on it. Yellow-purple. Large. And some nasty scratches too.

He pulled down the shirt again. 'How did this happen, sweetie?' I asked him as he picked up his backpack.

'His no good fuckin' stepfather did it,' he said, in his strange squeaky girl's voice, 'cos the poor lad didn't want no shitty curry for tea, that's how!'

I stopped on the pavement myself now. 'Sweetie, can you take off your hair now, d'you think? Then you can talk to me as Nathan, can't you?'

He looked at me for a moment, then dropped the bag on the ground again and started undoing the knot. He'd started crying. 'You can't tell anyone, Miss,' he sobbed. 'It was only a play fight. My daddy loves me, he does. We were just playing.'

This was clearly something he'd needed to get off his chest for a while. But now he finally had, I could see he was terrified. 'Shush, darling, it's okay,' I soothed. 'And, sweetie, you know you can tell me anything. But there's one thing – sometimes I do have to tell someone, because it's my job. But I will make absolutely sure you don't get in any trouble for telling me, okay?'

I had to say this. It was one of the fundamentals of my job. When a child confided in me it was crucial that they knew I couldn't keep secrets. That there could be no 'don't tell anyone this, but …' with me. And it was of vital importance that I made this clear from the outset, so there would be no loss of trust down the line. I was anxious, though, because for all my reassurance, this was possible evidence of abuse, which I was duty bound to report. And it might end up taking us down a path where my reassurances would be worthless. One thing I did know was that abusers, on the whole, didn't take kindly to being found out. And the best way to ensure meddlesome social services didn't sniff around was to terrify the abused child into silence.

I made a decision, then. To make a detour with him, to a little café just round the corner, where he might open up more or, if he didn't feel he could, at least return home feeling a bit calmer.

And, as it turned out to be the latter, I decided that once I'd dropped him at his house, I would hotfoot it back to school and have a chat with Gary Clark, our child protection officer, who was invariably on the premises beyond five.

'Here we are, then,' I said brightly, as we stopped at Nathan's front gate – a sad affair, listing forlornly on one hinge. I'd made no more mention of his bruises and neither had he, and I didn't want to bring them up again now. 'I'll see you on Monday,' I said, as he headed down the short path, upon which he turned back.

'It's okay, Miss,' he said. 'You can go now. I'll go inside in a minute.'

'It's okay,' I said, 'I'll wait till you get in.'

Nathan looked slightly agitated on hearing this. He shuffled from one foot to the other. 'There's no point you waiting,' he admitted finally, 'cos no one's in yet.'

'So what will you do?' I asked.

'Wait on the wall,' he said, nodding towards it, 'Or sometimes I go to the library to play on the computers.'

'Do you do that every day?' I asked him.

'Yeah,' he said. 'Mostly. So I just go to the amusement arcade, or the library, like I said. Till it's time to go home for my tea.'

Hmm, I thought. Maybe Gary could wait. 'Well, you know what?' I said, making the sort of split-second decision that I knew could work for or against me. 'I'll wait on the wall with you, shall I? Then you won't be on your own.'

And not for too long, I hoped, now that we'd already made the detour to the café. So perhaps I'd finally get a glimpse of the stepfather who was so keen to play-fight with his stepson. And I was right. No more than 20 or 30 minutes had passed before a man who Nathan identified as his stepdad began walking up the street.

He was a small, skinny man, in his late thirties, I'd have guessed, wearing what looked like dirty jeans beneath an even dirtier overcoat. He didn't look particularly menacing, but then I wasn't 11, was I? And there was also something about his expression that unsettled me. As he approached I stood and smiled, the better to greet him, but no sooner had I extended my hand and begun to introduce myself than he brushed past me, quite roughly, scowling and grunting as he did so. 'I know who you are,' he said, even though he couldn't have, surely? 'And the kid knows his way home,' he added rudely.

To say I was taken aback was an understatement. He'd swatted me away as if I was an irritating fly. He'd also grabbed Nathan's wrist and was now frogmarching him up the path to the front door.

'Bye, Nathan,' I called out. 'I'll see you on Monday, okay?' Upon which he turned and gave me a wave and an apologetic little smile, looking every inch a lamb going to the slaughter. I just hoped I hadn't made everything worse.

As it was probably too late now to return to school and find Gary, I headed home myself, mulling over what best to do. There was probably no point in making a direct referral to the emergency duty team at social services. My previous experience, both in school and before that as a youth worker, had taught me that unless it was what they deemed a 'real emergency' then nobody would do anything until after the weekend anyway.

As it was I spent the next day and Sunday worrying about Nathan. I walked into town a couple of times hoping that I might see him hanging around the arcades or something, but this proved to be pointless. And when my husband Mike wanted to know what I hoped to achieve in doing so, I didn't really have an answer for him anyway. In the end I decided that there was no more I could do until Monday, apart from writing up the usual incident report.

The bruises and scratches kept playing on my mind, though – particularly the thought that my presence at Nathan's gate might have caused more to have been added over the weekend. So Monday morning saw me in school even earlier than usual, and straight up to the child protection office. Happily, Gary was there, so I could hand my report over, which he read then and there, very intently.

I liked Gary, and also had great respect for him. He'd been at the school for a good few years now and had helped me out with extra information on quite a few occasions. He was also big on protocol. He knew just what to do when there was a possibility that a child might be at risk. And I knew that he was passionate about the children in his care. It was no surprise, therefore, when he picked up his telephone and immediately rang social services. He explained the situation and said that he would fax them a copy of the particulars; he also said that he would like the matter to be followed up.

'Thanks so much,' I said, relieved that action had now been taken. 'I can't tell you how much of a weight that is off my mind.'

'No problem, Casey,' he said. 'Only too happy to –'

He was about to say 'help', but the word was drowned out by a sharp rat-a-tat on his office door. Since I was closest I went to answer it, only to find myself face to face with the headmaster.

'Ah,' he said, 'Casey. That's handy. Can I have a quick word?'

'Of course,' I said. 'Shall I come to your office? I was just leaving Gary's …'

'No, no,' he said. 'No need. I want to speak to you both anyway. Nathan Greaves,' he continued. 'Just had his father on the phone. Odd phone call. Says he's unhappy with you having out of school contact with Nathan – specifically, walking him home on Friday afternoon. Says it's upset him, and that you ask too many questions about his family situation, which apparently confuses him' – he put the word 'confused' into finger quote marks – 'and supposedly makes him misbehave at home.'

My eyes had been widening as he'd spoken, but not that much. A rearguard action by the sound of things, and Gary clearly thought so too.

'Hmm, you'll probably want to read this, sir,' he said immediately, passing the headmaster the report I'd already given to him.

The head took the report and began to scan it. 'In a nutshell,' Gary continued, 'it highlights some child protection issues that came to light *on* Friday afternoon. I suspect Nathan's father managed to establish some of the things he'd said to Casey and he's now concerned about how much more we might know.'

The head read to the bottom then handed Gary the file back. 'I suspect you're right,' he agreed, 'so I'll leave it with you. Though, as a precaution, I think you'd better not walk Nathan home again, Casey – not until this is investigated, at any rate. Safer not to go against the father's wishes at this point, I think.'

'Absolutely,' I said. 'I'd already come to that conclusion myself anyway. The last thing I want is to make life more difficult for the poor boy. On which note, I'd better get down to my classroom before he and the rest of them arrive, hadn't I?'

The headmaster shook his head. 'Nathan's not coming in today, apparently. He's ill. Or so his father tells me, anyway.'

'Really?' I said, my anxiety now increasing a notch or two.

'Don't worry, Casey,' the head reassured me. 'If what your report suggests is true, I suspect the last thing the father's going to do is play into our hands.'

'I agree,' said Gary. 'If he has been hurting him I'd say keeping him off school will be more about having those bruises heal before he lets us near him, wouldn't you?'

I saw his point but I was still worried that I'd precipitated something, even though, in walking Nathan home, I'd given him the opportunity to voice something that he might not have found the courage to in school. And when the end of the day came around, I was even more dismayed to take a call from the social worker who'd apparently seen my report.

His name was Martin and he'd had dealings with the family for some time, and was keen, it seemed, to reassure me that all was well.

'I need to explain a couple of things,' he said, having introduced both himself and his credentials. 'And they are that, first of all, I don't believe that Nathan has any psychological problems really. In fact, we believe that he is attention seeking, as does his stepfather.'

I took this on board, resisting the urge to ask him if he'd had sight of the overdue psychologist's report. My guess was not, since I hadn't seen it yet myself and it had been the primary school rather than social services that had ordered it.

'Secondly,' he went on, 'we don't believe Nathan's telling the truth about his dad hurting him. He's a clumsy child – I've witnessed this myself when I've visited the family. You might well have noticed that yourself.'

I told him I hadn't, but, in fairness, I'd not known Nathan long. It wasn't my place to presume I knew more than he did, after all. 'So what are your thoughts?' I asked, braced for the sort of response that what he'd told me already seemed to be hinting at.

'We think the family have poor social skills, basically,' he said, 'and that because neither parent works, they do live very poorly. They're not the brightest of people, clearly, but we feel they're essentially coping – doing their best in unfortunate circumstances. So, as I'm sure you'd agree, we really don't want to go wellying in, guns blazing, though if you feel strongly that we need to have some continued input in this situation, then we'll obviously do so,' he finished.

Which left me at something of a loss. Of course no one wanted social services 'wellying in', as he put it, making pariahs of poor, innocent parents. But something stuck in my craw. If they weren't earning then why weren't they ever at home? And another thing – weren't there grounds for accepting Nathan's words as truth? It was hardly as if he'd been eager to broadcast it to the world, was it? He hadn't told me it at all – that had been Jenny.

But perhaps that would be lost on the man I was currently speaking to. He clearly had his own views on the subject. I took a deep breath.

'Yes,' I said, 'I *would* like social services to take some action, because though I obviously respect your views, I don't share them. I have a strong gut instinct that something isn't right here. I'll obviously continue to work with Nathan and support him while in school, but yes, I'd be grateful,' I said again, 'if you could as well.'

He promised he would, but his tone seemed to suggest differently, and when I put down the phone I realised my hands were shaking.

* * *

By the time I reached the staff room, in search of caffeine and solace, my dismay had worked itself up into anger. Fortunately, Julia Styles, the special needs co-ordinator, was one of my soulmates at work and as she was already in there I cornered her and offloaded all my angst.

When I finished she was smiling sympathetically. 'You remind me of a little pit bull,' she observed. 'You get your teeth into something and you won't let go, come hell or high water.' Her expression changed then. 'But, you know, Casey, all you can really do is *your* job. Be there for Nathan, report any single thing that makes you uneasy and trust that, ultimately, social services will also do theirs.'

'But what if they don't?' I asked. 'What if they're not seeing what I see?'

Julia shrugged. 'Then the same still applies, Casey. Report, be observant and keep passing it on. At least then, whatever happens, no one's going to be able to accuse you of not doing your job.'

Which was a fair point and, no, I couldn't do social services' job for them – she was right. All I could really do was trust in the system and hope that trust wasn't misplaced.

'Okay,' I said. 'I feel better already. Well, sort of. I'm sure if I head home and take my frustrations out on Mike, I'll feel 100 per cent better by the morning.'

She laughed. 'Exactly. What else are husbands for?'

* * *

In some ways, the business with Nathan couldn't have come at a better time. Or a worse one, depending on your viewpoint. Either way, by the time he returned to school on the Wednesday, I was busy setting up shop in another part of the school and, apart from an early visit to pick up all my files, didn't go down to the Unit again all day.

With the need for behaviour-management support strategies having grown since I'd joined the school (which, I suspected, along with others, was mostly due to my post having been created), it had recently been decided that, now I'd gained my level three counselling qualification, Jim should be mostly classroom based and I should be promoted to 'office-occupying' status. The plan was that, with an office and some private space, I could spend time supporting the kids that most needed intense one-on-one therapy, without the distraction of other kids and their own problems. It also meant that all the kids who had been referred to the Unit could have the opportunity to spend time with me in private.

Though I'd still be spending time doing group work within the behaviour unit itself, I would now be based in my new office, so Wednesday was mostly given over to customising it, Casey style – i.e. making it look as unlike an office as possible. I spent the whole day setting up new files and sorting out the old ones, as well as having a proper sort-out of the variety of games, art materials and work sheets I'd amassed over the past year, and had trolleyed over.

I was also keen to extend my personalisation by getting some artwork up on the walls, but thought I'd wait and get the children themselves to design and make some for me. That way they would soon feel some ownership of the room and it would help them to settle into the new environment better.

I spent practically all of the next day on it too – walking around the school, tracking down all of my past and current students, and letting them know where my new room was. Some of these were regulars, and some were kids I'd not seen in a while, but one thing I'd learned very quickly since I'd joined the school was that, for some kids, knowing where I could be found was key; it was like a security blanket for them to know where they could find me.

This wasn't just an assumption on my part, either. Some of the kids I'd spent time with even kept copies of my timetable in their school bags so that they knew my exact whereabouts at any time. And I respected this. So, if I had to make unexpected location changes, I would always leave a note pinned to my door detailing where I *could* be found.

Which was no hardship, even though, early on, I knew my attention to these sorts of details marked me out as perhaps a little over-zealous. Which was fair enough, I supposed, because I felt very zealous. The time might one day come when I grew a touch more cynical and a bit less soft about the kids, but I couldn't see that happening anytime soon.

It was Thursday afternoon, then, before I next saw Nathan. Having caught up with my move via Jim down in the Unit, he came rushing in during afternoon break, in a flurry of excitement. 'Ooh, Miss, this is lovely!' he gushed, running around like a wild child, touching everything in sight and stroking all the surfaces. 'I can't wait till it's my turn to come see you in here. When is it my turn? Will it be soon?'

'It will,' I said, consulting a timetable of which I already knew most of the contents. 'I'll be back teaching in the Unit twice next week anyway, but, yes, you're with me tomorrow afternoon, sweetie. And every Friday afternoon from then on.'

He clapped his hands together in delight. 'Oh, I can't wait! Do you want me to do you a picture for your wall? It's very bare, Miss.'

'You read my mind, Nathan,' I told him. 'I'd like that very much.'

He smiled one of his funny little smiles then and looked at me from under his black lashes. 'And I might even get Jenny to do one for you too.'

In the event, it was early on the Friday morning that I next saw Nathan. He was waiting outside my office for me, sitting cross-legged in front of the door.

'You're early,' I called as he pulled himself to his feet and yanked at trousers that were already in conversation with his lower shins.

'I thought I'd come early in case you had any jobs that needed doing,' he explained. 'I'm good at jobs, aren't I?'

I unlocked the door and agreed that he was. Not that I could think of one on the spur of the moment. 'Give me a minute,' I told him, parking my handbag and coat. 'I'm sure I will, but in the meantime why don't you sit and chat to me instead?'

'Actually,' he said, as if he'd been waiting for just such an invitation, 'I have something to tell you, Miss. A secret.'

My ears pricked up instantly. Though so did my training. 'Nathan,' I told him, 'we don't have secrets here, remember? You can tell me anything you like but I can't promise to keep it a secret, remember?'

'Okay,' he conceded, 'but I'm going to tell you anyway, because it's so lovely.'

'Is it, now?'

'It is,' he said. 'I had sex with my girlfriend last night and it was nice, Miss.' He leaned towards me. 'We did *porn*.'

For all his colourful language in the Unit from time to time, this one brought me up rather short. The child was 11, after all. 'Nathan,' I scolded gently, 'I don't think you should be saying things like that unless they're true. Is that Nathan talking?' I added, wondering if we'd strayed into a persona.

'Yes, it is,' he said, nodding. 'It's always Nathan now. I can't use my other people any more, Miss, because my daddy'll get mad with me – like, *really* mad. But if you don't believe me,' he went on chattily, 'I can tell you what I did. I stuck my thingy in her thing and we jumped up and down.'

'You did?' I asked.

'I *really* did,' he said. 'So *there*!'

Somewhat uncomfortable at this revelation, not to mention a little stumped at what to do with it, I repeated that he shouldn't be talking like that unless he was telling the honest truth.

'I am telling the bloody truth!' he said dramatically, 'I know what porn is, Miss. It's when a boy does it with *lots* of different people and nobody tells anyone. I got another secret as well.'

'Which is?'

'I'm partly gay, Miss. I just found out. I found out because me and William did it together yesterday, in the toilets. We touched willies together and kissed and everything, Miss. Cross my heart and hope to die.'

There was a knock on the open door then – the school secretary dropping off some paperwork – and Nathan's hand flew to his mouth. She'd not heard anything, I was sure, though she'd heard enough in her working life not to have batted an eyelid anyway, but it signalled the end of Nathan's confessional session, because he jumped up then and told me he had to be going and that he'd see me that afternoon as planned.

I decided I'd investigate further. I knew William was a friend of Nathan's so it would be sensible to alert their head of year in any case; even if he didn't know anything, he could obviously keep an ear out. I'd also make a copy for Gary in child protection, as it would be him who'd pass it on to social services.

And was Martin right after all? Did Nathan simply have an overactive imagination? Or was there more to it? Nathan had spouted it all out to me so matter of factly that he might as well have been telling me that he had just learned how to ride a bike! Curiouser and curiouser, and not in a good way.

It didn't take me long to do the report, and I duly printed two copies and took them to both of my colleagues' in-trays. When I returned to my office, via a coffee stop, and found Gary there waiting for me, my first thought – and comment – was, 'That was quick!'

'I must have missed you by moments,' he said, following me inside and shutting the door. 'And I'm afraid that at least some of this *is* true.'

I groaned, but, at the same time, felt a small spark of vindication. 'It is?'

'We had William's mother here last night. It seems that something *did* happen in the toilets yesterday and, according to William, Nathan initiated it. Forced himself on Will, by all accounts – the boy's apparently quite traumatised. He was going to keep it to himself, though, by all accounts, but apparently Nathan was keen to tell pretty much anyone in earshot that Will and he had sex and loved each other.' He sighed a weary sigh. 'So, of course, everyone began calling Will names, so he told his mum and – well, you can imagine. She's not very happy.'

'I don't doubt it,' I said. 'You know, we really need that report from the psychologist. In fact, maybe he needs a formal re-assessment anyway. It's already clear that Nathan isn't able to be mainstreamed without full-time supervision, and this just adds weight to that, doesn't it? And you know, Gary, I *still* think that there are underlying factors at home. I just don't accept this "peculiar child" tag he seems to have been saddled with.'

Gary concluded that – thankfully – he was inclined to agree with me and would address the matter with the educational psychologist at once. 'I'll put another child protection referral through,' he added. 'Given the explicit nature of Nathan's revelations, they can hardly *not* act, at least in some way. Fingers crossed.'

'Duly crossed,' I said. 'And toes, too, for good measure.'

That afternoon, as planned, Nathan attended his appointment with me. The buzz phrase at the time was 'life space interviews', where I would simply encourage a child to talk about anything and not interfere with their flow. I would use prompt words to keep them on track if it helped achieve that, but in the main it was all about active listening and the making of (very) discreet notes.

I was determined to make the most of this opportunity with Nathan, who breezed in as usual, thankfully oblivious to the waves he'd set rolling, and came around the back of my desk to stand beside me.

'It's good to see you, Miss,' he said, as if we'd been parted for many months. 'Do you bring your make-up to school? I really love your lip gloss.'

'No, sweetie,' I said, 'I put it on in the morning and just hope that it lasts.'

'And does it?' he asked, scrutinising me. 'Right till bedtime?'

I told him no lip gloss in the world would last through fish and chips and mushy peas, upon which he rolled his eyes and flapped a wrist. 'Could you bring it next time, Miss, maybe, and I'll bring mine too? Then we could have a girlie time putting make-up on, couldn't we?'

I was finding it difficult to know where to go with him in this mode and wished I knew more about the reasons why children adopted such mysterious ways. In the meantime, though, I'd just have to apply common sense. 'Boys don't really wear make-up, do they, Nathan? Just girls and ladies, mostly. Anyway, you look very nice without it.'

He drew a hand across one of his eyebrows to tame a stray curl. 'Do you know,' he said suddenly, 'that we have a parrot in our house? It talks to me all the time; it's *so* funny.'

At last, I thought, *a safer subject*, even if I wasn't quite sure I believed him. 'I used to have a parrot that talked, too,' I told him. 'What do you call yours?'

'It's called Peter,' he said, moving around to the other side of my desk and pulling out the chair. 'And it says "Get the lazy fucker out of bed" and "Fuck off to school" and "Don't dare talk to that Mrs Watson".'

He hadn't sat down and as I looked at him I watched his expression change. He was staring at me intently now. 'Why do you think your parrot says that?' I asked.

'I don't know, Miss,' he said. 'And do you know what else he says?'

I shook my head.

'He says "And don't fucking tell social services that you and your dad sleep on a mattress in your bedroom".'

Nathan's expression was now mask-like – as if he really was just parroting words at me. It was so strange and unsettling that it made me shudder.

'And *do* you and your dad share a mattress?' I asked him, conscious that, as he had already told me this, I wasn't leading him.

He looked me in the eye but his lips didn't move. Instead he shrugged, then said, 'Miss, can I go and read in the Unit now? I'm tired. I don't really want to chat anymore.'

I hesitated, wondering what I could usefully say next, but in the end, unable to come up with anything that wouldn't feel as if I was pressing him, I let him go. I then pulled my chair under my desk, ready to write up yet another report, but thought better of it. Perhaps I'd just go straight to Gary, or, better still, speak to Martin in social services myself.

Martin was, once again, lightly irritable. Well, at least, that was how his voice sounded when I outlined Nathan's latest comments and he explained that he had already visited the family – by appointment – and had concluded that there was nothing amiss.

I told him again that I disagreed; that I felt Nathan was suffering some form of abuse; that I was no psychologist but that it seemed to me he'd developed these different personas as a way to both distance himself from the trauma of what was happening and to enable him to tell someone about it.

In return, I was told – and in no uncertain terms – that the situation had been dealt with; that they were a family that were doing their level best to cope with a child with behavioural problems – one who he understood was about to be reassessed through the school. Perhaps then we'd all be in a better position to help him.

I went back to my office and typed up my report. I wasn't sure quite what else I could do. 'Mattress,' I typed. The word lingered.

I had lots of kids to help support and an invariably full timetable, so I didn't see or hear anything of Nathan till the following week, when he arrived for our session with a big grin on his face, having got through the intervening time without causing any trouble.

'No fights,' he said proudly, 'and no bad language, neither. So, Miss, do I get a reward now?'

I told him he did – I'd already had the heads-up from Jim – and presented him with a big cardboard box full of art stuff, explaining that his treat would be to make a big castle and that on each week that he was good and caused no one any trouble, we would make characters to live in it – princes and princesses and so on.

He was soon sprawled on the floor, planning his model, happy enough to lie there and draw while I got on with some paperwork. It went like this sometimes; kids just needed space and time out from peers. It was at these times when they were often most inclined to open up to me.

Nathan was no exception. After about 20 minutes, he looked up and casually told me that he was doing his castle to be like 'the place me and Jodie sometimes go to'.

I'd not heard the name – not in connection with Nathan. 'Jodie?' I asked. 'Is she your friend?'

He nodded. 'Yeah. We go to a flat to see this man and his dog, and he showed me and her how to do sex.'

I placed my pen down but didn't turn to look at him. 'Oh,' I said mildly. 'And this is a real flat, is it, Nathan? Not part of your castle story? I mean, it's okay if it is. I just wondered.'

'No, I swear, Miss,' he said. 'His name is Michael an' he stinks. But it's fine because he gives me and Jodie money and sweets if we go there and do stuff.'

Now I turned to look at him. 'What stuff do you do?' I asked evenly, aware that I was not allowed to ask leading questions.

He glanced at me. 'I can't say, because you always tell and I get done for it. It's okay, though, Miss,' he added. 'I was just saying.'

And that was that. Nathan went back to drawing his castle ramparts and, with my professional code meaning it would be inappropriate to press him, I went back to my paperwork.

By now, my file on Nathan was beginning to read like a horror story, but once he'd gone – without further mention of flats or men called Michael – I dutifully wrote up the details of our session and got it into Gary's in-tray before the day was out. Of Gary himself there was no sign, sadly – he was out of school, at a meeting, but at least I could start my weekend secure in the knowledge that I'd done *my* part, even if nothing happened till Monday.

* * *

But when Monday came, it seemed something further *had* happened, as explained excitably by Nathan himself. He had obviously been waiting for me to arrive for some time, because he was fit to bursting with the need to share his news.

'Miss, Miss!' he enthused as soon as he saw me.

'Hi, babes,' I said, intrigued. 'What brings you here, then? You look like a cat on a hot tin roof!'

I passed him my key so he could open the door for me, struggling as I was beneath an armload of books. 'Miss, guess what happened this morning?' he said as he unlocked the door. 'I was just going up the road from my house on my way to school and I saw a police car, and so I stopped and then it stopped at my house, so I stood and watched and the policeman went up to my front door and knocked on it, an' my dad answered and the policeman asked if he could talk to me – I even *heard* him, Miss! And my dad said that I wasn't there, but he could see me, Miss – he could *see* me! I was stood right there up the road but my dad said I'd gone to school!'

'So what did you do?' I asked, while Nathan got his breath back.

'I just ran off and came to school. I'm scared of the police, Miss. My dad says they lock people up all the time. Even good boys and good dads, sometimes.'

Not knowing what had gone on, I sent Nathan off to the Unit when the bell sounded, and I went up to see if I could find Gary. His door was open and he was on the phone but as soon as he saw me he gestured that I should come in and wait.

'That was the police,' he said, replacing the handset. 'They're on their way. And yes,' he said, correctly interpreting my expression, 'I did get the report you left for me on Friday. So I called the emergency duty team at social services, as I couldn't get through to Martin, and they told me to report the disclosure to the police.'

'That's good to hear,' I said.

'Well, yes, it is, if we can make it happen. They're on their way now. Coming up to talk to Nathan about this man he called Michael – he was already on his way here when they called at home, apparently. Have you seen him yet?'

I explained that I had, and what he'd told me. Gary nodded. 'That figures. We've just been saying as much ourselves. The father is, potentially, the fly in the ointment. We don't know what he knows or doesn't know about this character, but they're worried that if he *is* involved, he'll try to get to Nathan before they do.'

'What about the mother?' I asked. 'Nathan never talks about his mother. Do you know anything more about her?'

'Only that she's going to be no help to anyone. She has severe learning difficulties and, according to Nathan's old primary school, she's barely ever been a presence. Hardly in the house at all, apparently. Just wanders around the town centre all day and often doesn't go home till Nathan is already in bed. She did turn up at parents' evenings, occasionally, which is something, but rarely, if ever, spoke – left all that to her husband.'

I was just thinking what a sad and depressing state of affairs it all was when, as if on cue, my mobile phone rang. It was the school office to say that Mr Greaves was on his way to the school to collect Nathan because he had a doctor's appointment.

I told the secretary I'd bring him down and Gary and I both rolled our eyes. It seemed to be playing out exactly as we'd expected.

'I'll stall him,' Gary said. 'Keep him talking for as long as possible. But why don't you take Nathan up for a trip to the library anyway. And take your time about it. It's a bit of a way to get back from; know what I mean?'

It was a little unorthodox, admittedly. But, then, allegations of abuse required decisive action and, though we had no right to stop Nathan's father from collecting him, if Nathan wasn't brought down till the police had arrived too, we could perhaps achieve more and, crucially, achieve it quicker. Who knew, after all, now he was aware we might be onto him, whether Nathan's father would bring him back to school at all?

It wasn't to be, though. I hurried back to the Unit, while Gary headed down to reception, and though our little ruse did the trick in that the police arrived shortly after – and before Nathan's father showed up – it proved to be pointless in any case.

Yes, we managed to get him in a room with the police officer, but that was all. As soon as Nathan saw the uniform, he clammed up completely, apart from saying to me, in a voice that was 100 per cent Nathan, 'I'm not telling nothing, Miss. I told you.'

Where was Jenny when we needed her? I thought, as I sat there, unable to do anything, while Nathan remained stiff-lipped and terrified – he wouldn't even speak to confirm his name. I felt utterly frustrated, but I knew that Nathan would have to speak freely and without coercion, otherwise nothing he said could be used anyway.

Mr Greaves arrived shortly after, angry to see the police there and generally stroppy, but without evidence or testimony from Nathan himself, we could do nothing. And as I took Nathan to him I felt again like I was delivering a lamb to the slaughter, especially when Mr Greaves grinned at me.

He spoke to me as well, just as he took Nathan's hand. 'Never mind, Mrs Watson,' he said. 'Better luck next time.'

It was in the nature of my job that children came, we did what we could with them and then they moved on with their lives. Sometimes they moved back into mainstream classes – our best-case scenario – and sometimes they moved on in other positive ways. To new homes and new schools or to other, specialist ones locally; ones better suited, where appropriate, to their needs. Sometimes – the worst-case scenario – they did neither. They just disappeared – were excluded, or were taken out of school – leaving us frustrated and wondering if we could have done anything differently to achieve a more positive outcome.

This looked like being one of the latter. Nathan didn't appear in school for the rest of the week and a phone call eventually established that he was 'ill'. It wasn't until the following week that the headmaster called me and Gary into his office, where he let us know that Nathan's father was removing him from school, on the grounds that we weren't meeting his needs at the moment and that they were looking into 'other options' for him.

'Can he do that?' I asked him. 'Surely the truancy officer would step in, wouldn't they?'

'Yes, in theory, in time,' he said, 'but, as you know, Casey, these things *take* time.' We all exchanged looks. He didn't need to say more. We all knew what we thought was the problem with Nathan, but with him apparently no longer a pupil, there was nothing we could do to help him. It was now going to be in the hands of social services.

'So that's it?' I asked, experiencing a leaden, sinking feeling that would come to be so familiar in the following months and years. It felt all wrong, somehow, to just walk away and try to forget him.

'That's it,' the head agreed. 'I'm sorry, Casey, but that's the nature of the beast, sadly. We can only do what we can do during the time we can be of influence. That's the bottom line. You both did your best.'

'We can only do what we can do during the time we can be of influence.' Those words stayed with me all day.

And all evening, and the next day and the next evening too. So much so that even Mike had to start some counselling training – with me as his very first patient. 'The headmaster's right,' he said. 'There's only so much you can do, and you *did* it. Try to be positive. Social services are aware of the allegations, and even if you can't do anything more to help the boy, they can. They won't have just dropped it, love; that his father's taken him out of the school so suddenly will have rung alarm bells for them too, don't forget.'

But I couldn't let it go and, at the end of the following week, I couldn't resist making a very slight detour on my journey home. I knew I shouldn't – I could hear Mike's voice ticking me off even as I walked – but I knew I wouldn't rest till I'd at least taken a look, even if I had no idea what I'd do when I got there.

I needn't have worried. I didn't even need to think. Because I'd only just started walking up the front-garden path when a voice behind me made me stop and turn around.

It was a woman's voice, and when I turned it was to see a lady who looked in her sixties, perhaps, carrying a plastic carrier bag which she was lobbing into a wheelie bin. 'There's no one in, love,' she said, nodding her head towards the house. 'I just saw him off up the road not ten minutes ago.'

'Nathan?' I asked hopefully.

'Their lad?' She shook her head. 'No, love. He's run off. I meant his dad.'

'Run off?' I said, startled at her matter-of-fact manner.

'So I've heard. So his father says, anyway. Run off to some auntie or other somewhere.' She flipped the wheelie-bin lid down. 'Not surprised,' she added drily. 'Funny kid, that one. Weird boy.'

She ambled back off up her path then. I hurried home.

This development did nothing to quell my conviction that Nathan could, and probably would, now slip through the net. Was it true, even, what I'd been told? I wondered. A big part of me doubted it. Could it not just be some line the father was spinning to get people off his case? And even if it was true, what would happen about following up on his disclosures? Would that happen? In theory, it should, but what if he'd left the area altogether? If that were the case, he would presumably come under the jurisdiction of a completely different social services office. How efficient were one lot of social services at communicating with another? I didn't know, but I didn't feel very positive. I had been around the block too many times.

So when a note from the head arrived in my pigeonhole a couple of days later, I read it with interest but not optimism. '*Could you pop in and see me later? News on Nathan Greaves*' was all it said, and though I was keen to hear the news, I didn't expect it to be good.

But, in fact, it was the best news. Well, under the circumstances, at least the most encouraging. 'He's been temporarily taken into care,' the headmaster told me, without preamble. 'When they began investigating his disclosures to you regarding the Michael character, it came to light that he lived just down the road and is a convicted paedophile. Out now, but obviously breaking the terms of his discharge. So we have some progress.'

'Oh, poor Nathan ...' I murmured. 'But progress is good.'

'Anyway,' he continued, 'as I was just saying to Gary here, the other reason I asked you to pop up was to see what your timetable is like. As the teacher who's spent most time with Nathan over the past couple of months, his social worker wondered if you'd be able to spare a couple of hours this week to attend a pre-placement meeting with the pair of foster carers they've found for him. He's already with them, but Nathan's social worker felt it would be useful for you to see them – to give them some insight into his somewhat complex emotional needs.'

'How about tomorrow?' I said.

Nathan was being Jenny when I visited. He squealed with delight when he saw me, throwing his skinny arms around me and telling me, in his high-pitched Jenny voice, how much he had missed me. 'We're making Christmas decorations, Miss,' he said excitedly, 'and I shall make one for you specially. You can put it in your posh office then, can't you?'

His foster mum, a lovely middle-aged lady called Caroline, agreed that they'd do exactly that and, having promised him that they'd go up to school and deliver it personally, told him that we needed to have a chat.

Nathan skipped off without argument and we spent a productive 20 minutes comparing notes about her singular little charge, and the various challenges he might bring in the time he was with her while social services waited on the psychologist's assessment and decided what best to do in the short term.

'I'm going to miss him,' I said. 'I've been so anxious about what might have happened to him. I still am. It's that horrible not-knowing thing, isn't it?'

She smiled. 'I've racked up a fair few of those over the years, believe me, Casey. Sometimes it works out fine, and sometimes it doesn't. Sometimes you know that, even though you can hardly bear to think about it, they will, in the end, go back to the same sort of lives they had before – and, in some cases, even do it willingly.'

I thought about Nathan going home and nothing having changed. 'I don't know how you do it,' I said. 'Not once they've got under your skin and you've started fretting about them. I'd be a nervous wreck, I think.'

But the foster mum shook her head. 'It doesn't get any easier,' she admitted. 'Some kids, especially the longer-term ones, you just can't help but fall in love with them. Then it's *so* hard – it breaks your heart. But I wouldn't change a thing. I've done all sorts of jobs over the years, but as soon as I started this one, I just *knew*. I can't imagine doing anything else now,' she said, 'no matter how challenging the child. You can't change the world – sometimes you feel you've hardly changed a thing, to be honest – but, well, if you can do *something*, that's the best feeling *in* the world, believe me.' She grinned. 'You should try it yourself sometime.'

I left the foster mum's house – and Nathan – with mixed feelings. On the one hand, I knew I would continue to worry about what might happen to him, but on the other, I felt much lighter of heart. As the head had said, you could only do what you could do while you were of influence; a feeling that seemed to be shared by the lovely lady I'd just been chatting to.

Though, as for trying if for myself, that was a whole other matter. *Hmm*, I thought, as I climbed into my car, *maybe not …*

Afterword

Though it was never proven that the man called 'Michael' had ever touched Nathan and Jodie sexually, he was returned to prison anyway for breaking the terms of his discharge, in inviting the children into his flat. As for Nathan's father, though he admitted to having perhaps being 'heavy-handed' with his discipline, no charges were ever brought against him for either violence or sexual offences, and Nathan's bruises remained unexplained. He did admit when interviewed, however, that he and Nathan did both sleep together on a mattress in his bedroom, while his wife slept on the floor in the other. For this reason, though Nathan was returned home some months later, he remained on the 'at-risk' list, and his mother and stepfather were ordered to attend parenting classes.

As for Nathan himself, he was moved to another school, the educational psychologist's report having made the recommendation that a specialist unit might be better suited to his complex mental-health needs. It would be eight years before I next saw him. By that time, aged 19, he had come out as gay and seemed happy; he had a job in retail and was living with his boyfriend. I didn't ask him about his father.

And, as for me, well, I learned some valuable lessons. That you really *can* only do what you can do, when you can, and that real life is different from stories. Sometimes you have to accept you won't get all the answers. The main lesson I learned, however, would take a while to filter through: that a new career, down the line, had started beckoning …

Daddy's Boy

Chapter 1

Mike groaned as he heaved our bulging suitcase from one of the carousels in baggage reclaim at our local airport. 'Back to grim reality,' he moaned. 'Goodbye sunshine, hello grey British skies.'

'Oh, stop being so melodramatic, love,' I said, laughing, shaking my head at his hangdog expression. 'It's not even June yet. We still have the whole summer to look forward to! Just be grateful we've been able to have this little break.'

I took the laptop bag from him while he tried to guide the misbehaving case through the 'Nothing to Declare' area without looking shifty. Personally, I did feel grateful – enormously so – for our impromptu mini-break in Minorca, which had been a last-minute bargain, courtesy of my mum and dad, who'd just sold their caravan and treated us as a surprise.

'It's all right for you,' Mike grumbled. 'There's Tyler off to another footie camp, and you'll be doing fun stuff with the grandkids … And there I'll be, as bloody per, nose to the grindstone at work, while you guys have all the excitement.'

I grinned as we emerged into arrivals. I knew he was only trying to wind me up. Though he was right, of course. Tyler *was* off to his football camp – his second one this year, in fact. He was becoming quite the little footballing superstar. Or, as he put it, the 'next Gareth Bale', whoever he was.

And, no, I didn't have any 'proper' job to go back to, not in that sense, because my job was being a foster carer (and Mike's second job as well, if we were going to split hairs), so there were times when I was between jobs, and this was one such.

I knew it wouldn't be for long – it never was – but he was wrong about the 'excitement' part. Yes, it was true. I had time to indulge the grandkids. We had four now, all living close by (my daughter Riley's three, plus son Kieron and his girlfriend's brand new baby daughter, Dee Dee), so there was never a dull moment in that regard. But much as I loved being a nana, there was always a part of me that didn't feel quite right when I wasn't fostering. Yes, I could keep myself busy, and time with grandkids was always to be cherished – but I was still only 49 and when I didn't have a foster kid in, I very quickly felt very old and very useless.

And 'having a foster child' no longer included Tyler. Yes, that was what he was, officially, because that's how he had come to us, but it no longer felt like that – couldn't feel *less* like that, in fact – because, for one thing, we were committed to care for him permanently now and, for another, it just didn't. He felt like ours.

And, as Mike had pointed out, he'd be off on Monday morning anyway, in pursuit of footballing greatness. No, all things considered, I decided as we headed in search of our car, I rather hoped we'd get a call sometime soon.

Because it had, by now, been quite a while. Our last long-term foster child, Flip, had left us a couple of months ago, and apart from a brief and eventful placement involving an eight-year-old boy called Connor, it had all been a bit quiet on the western front. I knew that was partly because of the mini-break (it wouldn't have been appropriate, or even workable, to book a holiday abroad with a new foster child just installed), but now we were back I had ants in my pants.

No, I thought, as we made the short journey home, much as I couldn't wait to see my family, I was also crossing my fingers that a call would come from our link worker, John Fulshaw, pretty sharpish. I said as much to Mike.

'Glutton for it, you are,' he said. 'You do realise, Casey, don't you, that most women would love a nice long break from looking after kids?'

'Oh, give over,' I said. 'You miss having a rowdy house just as much as I do.'

'I'm just *saying*,' Mike said. 'Be ca–'

'Yes, yes, I *know*,' I interrupted. 'Be careful what you wish for.'

Which made us both laugh, because those half-dozen words had been said by one or other of us *so* many times now, and, almost without exception, they'd proved to be the right ones, as well.

When you spend a fair few of your waking hours in the company of little people during the school holidays, it's odds on that, when a phone goes, it'll be one of them that answers it. And so it was that, come the Sunday morning – the beginning of the late spring half-term – Marley Mae, Riley and David's youngest, aged two-going-on-seventeen, sashayed to my smartphone, and also managed to unlock it, before I'd even properly heard it ring.

There are few things more arresting than being at the wrong end of your forties and realising that your grand-daughter can work your technology better than you, despite being only just properly out of nappies. And what she couldn't quite manage, her older brothers certainly could. Though, on this occasion, their help clearly wasn't required.

'Gangad! It's me, your cheeky monkey!' Marley Mae shouted gleefully into it. 'We're having yoghurt and crisps!'

I gently removed the phone from my grand-daughter's iron grip. 'Hey, love,' I said. 'How are you doing? Bearing up?' Mike had not only to go into work, but had to do so a day early due to staff sickness. About which he wasn't terrifically happy.

'Hey, love, yourself,' came the response, along with a chuckle. 'And – hmm – Gangad? Is there something you're not telling me?'

Not Mike then. 'About blinking time, too,' I said,

mouthing 'It's *John*!' at Riley. She raised a thumb. Then another. 'Tell him he's a lifesaver,' she added, loud enough so he could hear. She knew exactly what I was like.

'No, that'll be *you*,' John corrected. 'Well, you and Mike, to be more precise. And before you ask, I mean it. Well, if you're up for it, that is. It's another emergency one, so I'm rather putting you on the spot here. A boy that needs a berth by tomorrow.'

'What, you mean respite care?'

'No, not quite that. He's not coming from another foster family. He's coming straight from the family. Currently with an aunt ...'

'Oh. Not in care at all, then?'

'Not *quite* yet in care, no. Well, actually, yes, in care, unless something radical happens in the next few hours, which, frankly, I doubt. And, yes, I know this isn't really one for you two, but you know what it's like in the school holidays   horrendous. What with carers on holiday and one thing or another, and it's sod's law that we always get emergencies in.'

'I suspect the two might be related,' I observed, eyeing Levi and Jackson, just at the start of what looked like being fisticuffs over what game to play next.

'I suspect you're right. And it does leave us in the rather unfortunate position of not always being able to get the matching quite right.'

'Which means you want to send us someone you wouldn't normally send us? *Again*?' I added, in case he'd already forgotten that our last child had been one of those as well. Only for a weekend, to be fair. But it was something of a full-on weekend. When what we really wanted – well, to be accurate, *I* really wanted – was a new child with whom I could try to 'add some value'; one of the last-chance-saloon kids we'd been originally trained to foster.

'It's *fine*, John,' I finished, already intrigued despite myself. 'You know me and Mike. Always up for a challenge. Something different doesn't scare us. Bring it on.'

'I know that,' he said, 'which is obviously why I called you. And it *is* something rather different. He's only five.'

'Five?' I said. 'Wow. You're right. That *is* different.' In fact, I couldn't recall when we'd last taken in a child that was so young.

'And it's not just the age, Casey,' John went on. 'Oh, and his name is Paulie, by the way. And he's no ordinary five-year-old. Not by a long chalk.'

With the boys upping the decibels I took myself out to the garden. 'Go on,' I said, as I sat down on one of the patio chairs, the better to hear him.

'Well, for starters, don't worry – this is going to be a very short placement. Few days or so. Couple of weeks, tops.'

'How can you know that for sure?' I asked. Because it's always prudent to ask that.

'Because there are only two outcomes happening here,' John explained. 'He's either going home, back to his family, which is what everyone is hoping, or to a longer-term placement, possibilities for which are being looked into as we speak.'

I understood that and my heart sank a little. That meant

they weren't even considering us for the job. Which was understandable, I supposed. This wasn't our sort of placement, as he'd already mentioned, and our role would be to simply provide a stopgap. Which was fair enough. Mike and I *were* specialist carers, after all, employed to look after a very niche set of children. Usually older ones; kids who'd been through many placements before us, and were now deemed to be 'unfosterable'. This was an extremely hard tag for them to carry, but it existed nevertheless. And, sad to say, it was a tag that was beginning to fit an ever growing number of kids in care. Which meant carers like Mike and me – carers who'd been trained, at some expense, to know how to handle such challenging children – would be somewhat wasted if they routinely sent us sweet, biddable five-year-olds.

And even though I then remembered what he'd also said about 'no ordinary five-year-old', I couldn't imagine a five-year-old who would require specialist carers like us anyway.

Except today, when there was a crisis. And we did have a bed. 'I see,' I said. 'And that's fine. Yes, of course. We're free. Why not?'

'So you won't mind me bringing him with me tomorrow morning? I mean, I could come on my own first, run everything by you ... But, to be honest, it would help a great deal if I could just bring him with me, and you could take him ...'

I laughed. 'Sight unseen?'

'Kind of,' he said. 'And no commitment to buy, obviously.'

And though we both laughed, we also both knew that sort of stuff was all nonsense. The intention was to bring him and leave him with us, end of. And that was fine too, because I couldn't imagine *any* five-year-old child who could be so difficult that I'd feel obliged to slam the door in their face. Except there was something in John's tone ... And I knew John very well now.

'You say like no ordinary five-year-old,' I said. 'John, is he really *that* bad?'

'I'm afraid so,' he said. 'At least, let's say I have a strong indication that he might be. And, look, I know we usually have time – time for you and Mike to make your minds up and discuss things. But in this case we don't. The pressure really *is* on. He's with an aunt for tonight, as I said – the mum's sister – but she already has five children and will *not* keep him beyond that. And he can't go home. Or *to* a home. So you really are our only hope.'

'Flatterer,' I said. And I smiled as I agreed. After all, for heaven's sake, he was *five*.

Chapter 2

Belatedly, I worried slightly about Tyler. Now we had Tyler permanently, who was thirteen and a half, any fostering decisions we made had to include him, even though it had always been understood that we would continue to take in children for our programme.

But, in fact, he was very relaxed. 'I'll be gone tomorrow anyway,' he pointed out, 'so I'll barely even see him, will I? And he's only five,' he added, echoing my own thoughts.

Mike, perhaps predictably, was slightly more cautious. 'If John says he's trouble, then I imagine he *is* trouble,' he said when he did phone, later on that afternoon, to let us know he was on his way home. 'But it's up to you, love,' he added. 'And like you, I'm struggling to imagine just how bad a five-year-old can be. Anyway, I won't be able to be there if John's bringing him round tomorrow morning, so I'm going to have to trust your judgement on this one anyway – well, such as it is.'

At which we both laughed. Well, he laughed, and I made a note to punch him later, but what stayed with me was what he'd said just before that. That if John had said that, then it *had* to be true.

In the short term, however, I had to think of practicalities. Although my house was, of necessity, pretty well geared up for my very young grandchildren, the spare room we kept for foster children didn't really feel like a home from home for a child that was so young. Back in the day – before Tyler – we had two rooms for fostering so, me being me (i.e. ever the little house elf), we had one done up to be very boyish and one very girly to cover all eventualities. Since Tyler had moved in permanently, however, that was no longer an option, so the one spare room was neutrally decorated, to suit boy or girl. Surveying it, however, it was clear that it suited neither that well.

But I wasn't short of books and games and toys and character bed sets so, once Riley and the kids had gone and Mike, Tyler and I had finished our makeshift, just-back-from-holiday Sunday tea, I went up and did what I could to make the room right for a little lad of five, down to the rather elderly Bob the Builder duvet cover that hadn't seen service since Kieron was young.

I was just finishing off when John Fulshaw called again, to let me know that, assuming we were still happy to help him, he'd be round with Paulie around nine the following day.

'Epic,' Tyler said, looking in on his way to bed. 'I can give him the once over and size him up for you before I go. Make sure he's safe.'

I laughed. 'Size him up? Safe? Ty, he's *five*, not 15. I don't think size or safety will be much of an issue here, do you?'

'Yeah, well,' he said, narrowing his heartbreaker eyes. 'You just never know.'

And, given some of the stories I could tell about some of the kids we'd been asked to care for, I had to concede I knew what he meant. It was true. You just didn't ever know.

I couldn't help but think back to that when John's car pulled up the following morning. And, in doing so, found myself grinning. There was nothing to worry about here. In fact, far from it. And it seemed Tyler was having a double take as well.

'Whaaaat?' he whispered, as we stood in the front window and watched as John unbuckled the child from his car seat. 'Casey, are you sure that's even a *him*?'

John carefully placed the child on the pavement, then, as if handling fine china, and I had to accept that Tyler did have a point. The boy was tiny! He barely looked more than a toddler, and a somewhat androgynous one at that. I knew that long hair was currently fashionable with both sexes, and that some mums liked letting their little boys' hair grow. But this child looked not so much like Little Lord Fauntleroy as Little Miss Muffet. Indeed, with his blond ringlets, it was only his outfit – denim jeans, trainers and a baseball jacket – that gave any clue to his gender.

Telling Tyler to close his mouth, I made my way to the door to greet them. 'Hi, John!' I said brightly before squatting down in the hall and smiling at the child before me. 'And this must be Paulie. Hello, sweetheart,' I said warmly. 'I'm Casey. And this is Tyler,' I added, gesturing behind me. 'Gosh, you're a big boy, aren't you? What are you, six or something?'

Lame, I know, but it was mostly instinctive, my hunch being that his diminutive size was probably one of the things he routinely got teased about. I then decided to stay down where I was for a response. And, boy, did I get one.

Eye to eye, as well, because, of course, we were at eye level. He looked me straight in the eyes and, had he not been the age he was, I would have been convinced he was sneering. 'Are you stupid?' he wanted to know. 'I'm *five*!' He then looked up at John, who was obviously squirming. 'I told you I'm not stopping with no bloody woman,' he said. 'They're all thick. Where's the daddy?'

Now it was my turn to have my mouth hanging open. I stood up again, not knowing quite how best to answer. This kid was just *five*? Was he being operated by robots? 'You'd better come in,' I said, raising my eyebrows – both to signify my surprise at his unexpected point of view, and to let him know that, actually, we weren't eye to eye at all. 'If you mean my husband Mike, love,' I said mildly, while Tyler still gawped, 'he's at work. He won't be back till tonight.'

I led them through to the dining room, trying to process what had just happened. The child had just spoken to me like an angry, petulant teenager. Where had his vocabulary come from? It just felt so incongruous coming from some-

144

one so small. And could a five-year-old child even *think* like that?

John started helping him out of his little jacket. 'Remember what we said about not being rude to grown-ups, Paulie?' he was saying gently. 'What you just said to Casey was very rude, wasn't it? So now you need to say sorry to her, don't you?'

John used the gentle, calming tones of a man long used to dealing with challenging, traumatised children. And this was clearly one such. He looked anxiously towards me. 'Am I going to get a smack?' he asked. 'Is the lady going to hit me?'

I could see Tyler shaking his head out of the corner of my eye, clearly as bemused as I was. 'Don't be daft, Paulie,' John said. 'Remember, we talked about that too? Grown-ups don't smack children.'

'Some do. My mam does. My stepdad does.'

'But Casey *doesn't*. Of that, you can be very, very sure. But you *do* get into trouble if you're rude to her. Of course you do. I think Casey has a naughty step in this house,' he said, glancing at me. 'Isn't that right, Casey?'

I didn't, as it happened. I was from the wrong generation. But Riley certainly did, and I knew how she used it. As time out for naughtiness, upsets and transgressions in pre-schoolers. And I remembered the rule, too; one minute for each year of a child's life.

I nodded. 'Indeed, I do,' I said. 'Though I don't need to use it very often. And I hope I won't have to while you're with us, Paulie.'

Again the look. The adolescent-seeming sneer. The expression of derision. 'I'm not going on no fucking naughty step!' he shrieked at me. 'I'm not going on no scary fucking step!' Then he burst into tears.

Wow. I really could not believe my ears. I'd been around kids from every walk of life, with all kinds of problems. But, try as I might, I could not recall a time when I'd heard such words coming out of so young a mouth. Yes, I'd seen behaviours in children who weren't a great deal older – early sexualisation, from being groomed practically from birth – but I'd never seen a child so young use such language in anger. They might be able to parrot the words, but this felt different; this really did feel like an older child trapped in a younger one's body. It felt too bizarre to be true. But true it most certainly was. This angelic-looking, tiny child was right here in my dining room, yelling obscenities at me as if it were all normal.

John looked as helpless as I felt, but was clearly disinclined to pick him up or otherwise physically comfort him. Knowing almost nothing about the ground on which I was treading, I followed John's lead. 'Tyler,' he said calmly, 'Paulie likes cartoons. Do you think you could get him settled in front of the telly for ten minutes while me and Casey talk?'

'Sure,' said Tyler, nodding his head towards the snivelling Paulie, whose sobs, it seemed, responded well to this news. He certainly showed no hesitation in meekly taking Tyler's outstretched hand.

Within moments, he was installed on the sofa, apparently happily, with control of the remote and a cushion to cuddle, with Tyler – for the moment, at least, since he'd be leaving in half an hour or so – remaining close by in case he was needed, bless his heart. So far, I thought, so bizarre.

'What on *earth*?' I whispered to John as I led him into the kitchen and set about making him a caffeine fix – he was as manic a coffee-addict as I was. 'Come on then, what's his story?' I smiled. 'And, trust me, nothing you could say now would surprise me. What a singular kid!'

John shrugged off his own jacket and ran a hand through his hair. 'It's hard to know where to start really, and most unusual. You're right. He's a funny kid.'

'Funny doesn't even cover it. Perhaps I'm out of touch,' I said, conscious that I was of pre-naughty-step vintage, 'but I can honestly say I never realised there were five-year-olds who could speak like that.'

'It's obviously all he knows,' John said. 'It seems completely second nature, doesn't it? I honestly don't think he has any idea that the language he uses is inappropriate.'

'Which begs the next question – what sort of world has he come from?'

'A complicated one,' John said. 'That much I do know. Though, in truth, we need to know so much more.'

'So what *do* you know?' I asked him, keen to form a picture. 'Like, how come he was brought to social services by his mother?'

'How come indeed?' he said, then explained that it had been something of a drama – that she'd brought him in, kicking and screaming and crying, and all but dumped him on the floor of the reception. 'She was certainly a bit hysterical, by all accounts,' he told me.

'And just dumped him? But look at him! He's hardly more than a baby! A baby with a potty mouth all right, but still a baby.' I shook my head. 'It beggars belief. Does she have other kids?'

John nodded. 'Just a couple,' he said, his tone slightly sarcastic. 'Three girls, aged – I think I remember right – 14, 12 and 11. Then Paulie. Then an 18-month-old baby boy.'

'Okayyy …' I said, finding the picture forming all too easily. 'And Dad?'

'Dads, plural,' he corrected. 'Dads in triplicate, in fact. The girls are the children of a partner who died in a motor-cycle accident seven or eight years back –'

'Oh, that's so awful,' I said, immediately regretting the thought that had only just formed.

'I know. Then it's Paulie, who she had with her next partner – who's apparently ex-forces. And the little one – Alfie – is the child of her *current* partner. So as you see, complicated.' He grinned. 'You keeping up?'

I nodded. 'Yes, I think so. Well, sort of. So it's obviously not the Waltons, but that still doesn't explain why she's flipped out over the little man' – I indicated with my head – 'sitting in there.'

'I'm not sure we've gotten to the core of it ourselves, even. The only thing I know for sure is that she's adamant there's something seriously wrong with him; that he's different from her other kids –'

'Well, he would be. Different fathers.'

'Yes, but more than that. She thinks he's psychologically damaged. Well, "brain-damaged" was apparently her term. And there would seem to be some corroboration of that, as he was apparently asked to leave his nursery school a couple of months back. For aggression. Fights various. Meltdowns. You know the sort of thing. Since which, he's been at home full-time, and she doesn't know how to cope with him any more ...'

''Specially when she's already coping with a toddler.'

'Exactly,' John said. 'But the reason it's such a problem – more of a problem than it should be – is that she's absolutely adamant she doesn't want him back.'

'What – *never*?'

He shook his head. 'Apparently not.'

I sat back, trying to get my head around that. And couldn't. Then a thought came to me. 'Perhaps she's suffering from depression? Post-partum psychosis or something? Not thinking straight?' I was speaking my thoughts aloud. 'Perhaps she's anxious that she'll lose her rag and hurt him, perhaps. Something like that?'

John shrugged. 'Perhaps all of it. I just don't have the facts yet. We'll be digging – well, social services will, and will report back to me as soon as they have anything more to tell me – but in the meantime, that's pretty much all I can tell you. Except for one thing – I got this from the sister this morning – that this has all been brewing for a very long time. Since he was born, or so the sister says; always crying, always a handful, always at odds with his siblings ... She doesn't know all the facts, but her take on things is that he's out for his baby brother. He's attacked him more than once and, if I were to put money on it, I'd say that was probably the crux of it – that an attack on the little one was the straw that broke the camel's back.'

I tried to digest it all. A simple case of sibling rivalry gone mad? 'And all this from such a tiny little thing,' I said at last. 'Anyway, so what's the plan? Mike and I have him for a couple of weeks while you do all you can to get him home again?'

John nodded. 'That's about the long and short of it, Casey. I can't lie to you – I suspect he really will be a handful, so I won't pretend it's going to be easy. But as you said yourself, he's only five, so I'm sure there's nothing he can throw at you that you won't have already dealt with a million-fold.'

'Well, that's certainly true,' I agreed, glancing over into the living room. 'So I suspect we'll probably manage, don't you?'

And I believed it. After all, he was just a traumatised little kid. I just hoped he'd soon be back in the bosom of his family; that stuff could be put in place, a support package, to help them all sort it out. And in the meantime, it would simply be a few days of babysitting, of the kind Riley seemed to enjoy when she and David did bits of respite – a far cry from the profoundly damaged older kids we usually had, even if with the side order of four-letter words. No, I told myself, we'd be fine. Why ever would I think anything else?

Chapter 3

I always say that you can tell a lot about a foster child by the possessions they bring with them, and the fact that Paulie had a little teddy bear in the bag John brought in for him gave me hope. Call me fanciful, but I chose to believe that a teddy bear signified something good; it meant that some-body, somewhere, loved, or had loved, this child. It could have come from his parents, his aunt or someone else alto-gether – perhaps a grandma or grandad. The whys and wherefores didn't matter. What mattered was that it was cherished, which was why he had brought it with him. And by extension, in most cases, it meant the person who gave it mattered to him too.

The teddy also told me that Paulie, scared, angry child that he was, was capable of giving love as well. This was important, even if it was only to a soft toy, because it meant that underneath the glares, the bad language and the atti-tude, there was something in this child that I could work on.

It was with this very much in mind that I spent the next couple of days trying to get beneath Paulie's surface, grabbing at any opportunity to tease out what made him tick. Yes, it was true that he was only going to be with us for a few days, but if I could return him even one tiny bit happier, and more able to function than when he'd come to us, then that was what I'd set out to do. At the very least, I could try to help him to understand that there were ways of interacting with other people – particularly grown-ups, particularly those in authority – that would serve him so much better than his current *modus operandi*, which obviously wasn't serving him well at all, not given that he'd been asked to leave nursery and his own mother had delivered him to social services.

Of course, it could well be that there were things going on in Paulie's life that I couldn't possibly know about. Indeed, there almost certainly were. But that was true of almost every child we'd fostered, and it changed surprisingly little; however tragic or evil or destructive were the influences on a child, all that child had to fall back on, in the end, was themselves. And it was how they chose to handle the future that mattered more than anything.

'Gawd, you're not off philosophising again, are you?' Mike moaned, for the second night running, as I ran through my training notes, and plundered the internet for insights into aggressive, disrespectful, precocious five-year-old boys. Because, in reality, I'd not got much further with Paulie, except to establish that I alternated between being a 'stupid woman' and 'nice Casey', depending on what his needs were at any given moment. He really was a strangely mercurial little thing – more like a two-year-old or a 14-year-old.

All I had established with any certainty in the first 36 or so hours was that there seemed to be only one love in Paulie's young life, and that was his father. His biological father, who was apparently no longer around.

There was nothing unusual in that, of course – children whose parents have split up do sometimes do that: cast the absent parent in the role of much maligned hero, to some extent, while the one close to hand bears the brunt of the flak; all complex psychological territory in itself. But it was becoming clear that in Paulie's case this was happening to a massive extent – he talked about him endlessly – causing me to wonder if, with a young brother taking his mum somewhat away from him, he'd focused on his biological father even more.

Everything certainly seemed to revolve around him, even though I hadn't managed to establish whether he even saw anything of him. 'Come on, sweetie,' I cajoled as I tried to get him to eat the scrambled eggs I'd cooked for lunch that Wednesday. 'You just said you liked eggs. That's why I cooked them.'

'Not these eggs!' he ranted. 'I want eggs like my daddy cooks! Real eggs with yellow on them! Like they do in the army!'

He pushed the plate away, sending half of if bobbling across the kitchen table, like a load of runaway yellow marbles.

I removed the plate from the table and Paulie to the newly inaugurated naughty step, which he accepted without argument because, to use his own phrase, he wanted to get away from my stinking kitchen anyway.

And as I cleared up blobs of scrambled egg, I wondered about fried eggs. Would fried eggs be what he meant? Probably. Which made me ponder about the army. And the father. And the mother. *And* the stepfather. And the whole 'complicated' nature of it all. I also considered what a curious business it was having children come and live with you whom you knew so little about. It just made every tiny thing so, well, *complicated*.

And, much as I was warming to at least *some* aspects of our little tyrant's personality, I found myself hankering after our next placement already – the sort of child that came with a file half as thick as a phone book. Which was, by any yardstick, just a little bit bonkers, because such files usually spelt just one thing: trouble.

But for all my surmising and pondering and wondering, I probably couldn't have anticipated the contents of John's email, which came in that same afternoon.

He couldn't phone, he explained, because he was in a place without a signal, but once I'd had a read-through of what he'd established – and this had all come from the mother's sister again – he'd be happy to chat to me later.

And as I started to read, though my interest was piqued, my expectations were low, as it was really only expanding on what I already knew. I certainly didn't think I'd need to phone him. It seemed Paulie's biological father was indeed retired from the army. But what we also now knew was that he was retired SAS and had been discharged early on 'medical grounds'. It also seemed it had been something of a quick liaison, Paulie's mother and he having apparently met only months after her bereavement, with her falling pregnant very quickly. Things hadn't worked out, though; according to the sister, the father – who was called Adrian but known as Adi – had had ongoing mental health issues (ah, *those* kinds of medical grounds) and it seemed taking on a mother, her three daughters *and* a new baby son was all too much – another proverbial straw that broke the camel's back.

So that had been that. The couple split, and in time she found someone new. And although contact between infant son and father still happened sporadically, according to Paulie's aunt (who, John had noted, thought *very* little of Adi), a new home was established and a further child born; the Alfie for whose safety they now all feared.

And then something else. A something else that made me prick up my ears. *The crisis apparently came*, the email finished, *just before the assault on the baby. It appears it was directly related to an incident the previous week when Paulie had killed the family's pet rabbit by bludgeoning it to death with a rock.*

I know! John had signed off, echoing the words on my very lips. *I can hardly believe it either. We'll talk later. J.*

* * *

Him and me *both*. As I'd been party to this bombshell for a good couple of hours before Mike returned home from work, by the time he arrived it was all I could do not to jump up and down and bundle him off into the utility room, so badly did I want to tell him this new information. But, of course, I couldn't – not till Paulie went to bed.

Though, ironically, it had been an uneventful afternoon in the end. Once both the fried eggs *and* the email had been digested, I was too full of pent-up energy to contemplate having a quiet afternoon in, so I'd suggested that Paulie and I take a walk to the park at the end of the road to feed the ducks, and, once there, he'd seemed to enjoy himself. But all the while I kept hearing the word 'bludgeoned' in my head. Forget the bad language – that had suddenly become something of a side issue. How could such a tiny slip of a child do such a thing?

Oh, I wasn't stupid; I'd seen kids lash out at siblings, playmates, animals. Toddlers mostly, in that unthinking way that toddlers do – and woe betide the mum who lets them wield the 'bash-the-shape-into-the-slot' game's wooden mallet. But this wasn't a toddler. This was a child who was sentient and articulate. What kind of things could have possibly been going through his head to make him capable of such a barbaric act?

But keen though I was to address all these questions to Mike, it would have to wait a bit because, as had been the case the previous night (something I could now see fitted a pattern) seeing Mike was the highlight of our young visitor's day. And as I watched him clamour to be picked up, to be tossed around, to be talked to in a deep masculine voice, I wondered if in Mike he saw something of the father in whose shadow it seemed his stepfather must live.

Not to mention his mother; Paulie clearly didn't have much time for women either. And though he tolerated me – thrown together as we were, he pretty much had to – he so obviously bonded with Mike so much more. Which was interesting in itself, but suddenly not quite so interesting as what I'd read about in John's email. *Bludgeoned*, I kept thinking, as I watched Paulie and Mike playing. *He'd bludgeoned the rabbit to death.*

Chapter 4

'I want my army pants!' screamed Paulie as he kicked and thrashed on his bed. It was early on Thursday morning and I'd been trying to get him into the bath for a good half hour, but he'd refused point black unless I assured him I'd found his 'army' pants first.

And had been doing so ever since, increasingly hysterically. Trouble was, I didn't know what or where his army pants even were. 'Paulie, I told you, they aren't here, sweetheart,' I told him for the umpteenth time. 'There was nothing like that in your case. Look, I'll phone my boss as soon as the office opens – which won't be very long now – and I'll ask him if he can find out about getting some other clothes for you – those included – but for now, I've things that I need to do today, which means I need you in the bath first, okay?'

'Not wearing your shitty stuff!' he continued to rage. 'They're not mine, those horrid ones,' he said, pointing to the ones I'd put out for him. 'They're rubbish!' He sat upright on his bed and tried to kick out at me. 'Go away!' he screeched, his cheeks growing pink. 'I hate you! You're a big bitch an' I don't want to see you!'

'Big bitch'? I may have been packing a few extra holiday pounds, but I was also five foot nothing, so that was a first. I tried to file away the thought – one to laugh about with Riley later – but for now I had a close-to-hysterical five-year-old on my hands and, much as I preferred not to, this was an occasion that called for only one course of action. I decided I would just shout right back at him.

'Right!' I snapped, digging my fists into my hips for good measure, in the time-honoured, power-pose, don't-mess-with-me tradition. 'Stop that silly shouting *right* now, young man!'

To my delight and surprise it immediately had the desired effect, perhaps because he wasn't expecting it, and I wondered if he'd had way too little parental authority in his life. It could happen so easily. Once a child is painted as a little monster (and this one was very much painted as that now) it's so easy to forget that, actually, they're not – it's just the *behaviour* that's monstrous, the behaviour every time – and that tiptoeing around them, as if they were dangerous sleeping dragons, was the wrong route to go down.

Mike had been less stunned than I'd been about the rabbit. Not to mention more sceptical. 'It's hearsay, apart from anything else,' he'd pointed out, once Paulie was tucked up in bed the previous evening. 'Do we *know* he actually did that? I mean, know for a fact? You have to think about where the information's coming from as well, don't forget. Which is the mother's sister. And has she got a vested interest in all this? She obviously didn't want to take him in, did she? I'm sorry, but I'm not sure there can be many five-year-olds capable of doing something like that. Not on purpose. I'd like to see some hard evidence before taking it at face value. And let's be honest, isn't it all a bit *convenient*, all this stuff? Come on, love – I know he's got a gob on him, and has picked up some slightly unsavoury attitudes. But can *you* see it? I'm not sure I can.'

And, in the end, I hadn't wanted to bother John in the evening just to go over the same questions; he might very well be of the same view as Mike anyway. The bottom line was that we had our little visitor for a week or so, and our job wasn't to psychoanalyse him, draw up a report and make recommendations – it was to keep him safe from harm and as stress-free as possible, while the powers that be took on the business of sorting everything out.

Including the matter of 'army' pants, which seemed harder to rustle up than 'army' eggs. Hence the firm military line I was now taking.

And it certainly seemed to be working, because Paulie had stopped thrashing about and instead stared at me, his mouth hanging open in surprise. He soon regrouped, however – I could see his brain and mouth both kick in again, ready for another onslaught. 'And don't even *think* about swearing at me!' I snapped at him, my tone emphasising that, yes, I could – and *would* – give as good as I got.

Worse in fact. 'I've *told* you about your clothes,' I added. 'And you haven't listened, have you? Now, I'm going downstairs and you're staying in this room for five minutes to calm down. And *then* Paulie, you *will* be going in the bath, even if I have to get in with you myself.'

I turned and left the room, closing the door behind me. As I walked down the steps I tried not to listen to the abuse that was being hurled from behind it.

When I sat down at the dining table with a coffee in my shaking hand (shaking after a stand-off with a five-year-old!) I started to think more rationally, and put the whole rabbit business to one side. This wasn't actually the poor boy's fault. I tried to imagine being so young in a stranger's house and not even having the familiarity of my own clothes. It wasn't as if I hadn't asked, either. John had given me the name and number of Paulie's assigned social worker – a man called Phil Thoresby – and I'd already been on the phone to him to try to get hold of some more of Paulie's belongings, but it seemed that wasn't as easy as it sounded.

'I know it's important, Casey,' he'd said the day before, 'and I have asked, I promise. But even trying to get past their front door is a nightmare. They've put me off twice, and when I turned up unannounced this morning I was practically shooed away.'

'Because they're worried what you might find?' I asked.

'No, I don't think it's that, to be honest. More like they've passed the problem to us now, so job done.'

'Surely not?'

'Well, maybe not quite,' he conceded. 'But there is definitely a reticence. I suspect his mother worries – not to mention the stepdad – that if they let me come in, I might pressure them into having him home again.'

'But surely that's what you *do* want to do, isn't it?' I asked him, flabbergasted.

'No,' he said. 'Not just like that. The genie is out of the bottle now. Now Paulie is in care, *we* have a duty of care, don't we?'

It was a question I'd reflected on well into the previous evening, and as I reflected back on it again now, it still confounded me. Not so much as far as the clothes went – though I certainly got why Paulie was upset, because a child's clothes could be so bound up with their identity – but how it could be so incredibly hard for his mum to just stuff some in a bag for him? Just how hard *could* that be? Or was she really washing her hands of him that thoroughly? I decided I would ask again – even though I had already been pestering Phil for answers. Did she have learning difficulties? Was she under the cosh of the step-dad? Was it that she really *was* struggling psychologically, and it wasn't being picked up? What? Because how the hell did a mother – one who was fine with her four other children – discard her little boy like that without a backward glance?

Having given Paulie what I considered long enough to make a more judicious decision re the bath – ten minutes, rather than five, in the end – I went back upstairs, ready for round two. And was taken aback to see him now kneeling on his bedroom carpet, still in his pyjamas, a colouring book on the floor in front of him, and clutching a thick crayon in his chubby hand. In every respect, what looked just like a normal five-year-old boy. As I opened the door further, he stopped colouring and smiled up at me. 'Look, Casey! A fire engine. I done it for you! I'm gonna do Mike one next. Of a racing car!'

Looking into those big blue eyes, I felt a prickle of emotion behind my own. 'That's so good, sweetheart,' I said, smiling back at him. 'What a clever boy you are. I didn't realise you could colour like that.' I leaned in closer to make a more detailed inspection. 'Look, you've kept inside the lines too. All the way round. It really is like you're six and not five. Wow!'

His chest puffed out in pride, he threw the crayon down and scrambled to his feet. 'Should I get my bath now?' he asked. 'I can finish my pictures after, can't I?'

Without really even thinking about it, since it was something you'd do so naturally, I held up my arms out to scoop him up and carry him. And it was only when he launched himself up at me – settling against my hip like a baby panda, head nuzzling into my neck – that it occurred to me that this was something of a first; a connection. One he'd so far made with Mike, but definitely not with me.

'Are you really going to get in the bath with me?' he asked shyly, as we crossed the landing and went into the bathroom.

'Not today,' I said. 'Today you get it all for yourself. Bubbles and all.'

His eyes widened. 'I can have bubbles?'

'Yes, indeed you can have some bubbles.'

He sighed happily. 'This is the bestest place *ever*.'

Because that's just the way life works out sometimes, now that the army pants had been forgotten along came the call from Phil to let me know he'd managed to procure them. Well, the promise of them anyway. It seemed he'd arranged to visit the family again and this time he'd told them he wouldn't leave without some more of Paulie's clothing. 'Though her term was "rest of", I'm afraid,' he added.

I explained what I thought Paulie must mean – 'You know, camouflage trousers, probably' – and, true to his word, Phil had called again just as we were sitting down to lunch to let me know that he had another bag of stuff and that, assuming it worked for me, he could drop them round in 20 minutes.

'Not that man!' Paulie said, looking up at me fearfully as I ended the call and put the phone back on the counter.

I turned around, surprised. I hadn't even thought he'd been taking any notice. I'd popped the television on and as far as I'd known he'd been eating his spaghetti hoops while engrossed in the antics of four teenage turtles.

'That man?' I asked.

'*That* man. That man on the telephone. He's a bad man an' he'll tell you about the rabbit.'

'About the rabbit?' I asked, sliding into the chair across the table from him and trying to keep my expression neutral.

Daddy's Boy

Paulie put down his spoon and pushed his bowl away, tears running down his cheeks now. 'Don't let him come! Not that fucking Phil man!'

I spent half a second wondering if I should point out the 'F' word, but decided to let it pass. He seemed genuinely upset. And, naturally, I was keen to hear what else he might have to say. I pulled my chair round so I was closer to him, and stroked his head.

'Sweetheart, Phil's one of the good guys,' I told him. 'He wants to help you. He's the one who's got your clothes for you, isn't he? And you know what else he just told me? He's bringing your Power Rangers too. So you see,' I finished, 'he *is* a nice man.'

Paulie shook his head violently. 'No, he's not! Don't let him in! Just get my stuff and bang the door shut! He made me tell him lots of stuff and I don't like him!'

He pushed his chair back from the table and, once he had sufficient room, wriggled down from it. Then he ran off into the hall and up the stairs.

I followed. 'Paulie, sweetheart, don't get upset,' I soothed as I went. 'He wants to help you. There's nothing to be frightened of, I promise you … He's going to bring your favourite clothes, so you can start wearing them – your army pants, remember? I bet you can't wait to put them on again, can you?'

By the time I'd reached his room – only a scant few moments behind him – he'd already dived for his bed and burrowed right under the duvet. All that was visible was a hump in the bed. In this, I thought, my heart going out to him, he did seem like a five-year-old. If he couldn't see the nasty social worker man, then the nasty social worker man unquestionably couldn't see him either.

I sat down on the bed and tried to tug the duvet from what I assumed was the head end.

'Go away!' came the response. So I had the ends right, at least.

'Silly monkey,' I said gently. 'Social workers have a job to do, sweetie, and part of that job is to talk to girls and boys about their life.' I tugged at the duvet again, and this time he let me reveal his head and shoulders. 'That's all it is, love, I promise,' I said, reaching to stroke his hair again.

He brought his arms out as well and rubbed his eyes with his fisted hands. Then his nose. On the sleeve of his jumper. Then he sniffed what was left up and sighed heavily. 'It wasn't s'posed to happen.'

This threw me. 'What wasn't s'posed to happen?' I asked, thinking I might be about to hear the truth now. Perhaps Mike had been right. Perhaps it hadn't been on purpose.

Paulie's chin was wobbling again now, as if the enormity of his situation had just struck him anew. 'I told him about the rabbit. I told *everyone* about the rabbit. And they said –'

'Who's they?'

'Everyone!' he huffed at me. '*They* said if I 'fessed about it – about deading it – everything would be okay. But it's *not*, is it?' Then he burst into tears again.

With impeccable mistiming, the doorbell then rang. Damn. The shortest 20 minutes in the history of the world.

Perhaps Phil Thoresby had miscalculated the distance to where we lived. Paulie flung the duvet back over his face again. 'Send him away! Don't let him take me!' he sobbed from beneath it.

'Take you? Paulie, he's not come to take you anywhere. He's come to bring you ...'

But there was little point in finishing the sentence because it was drowned out by the volume of his screaming.

Chapter 5

There's nothing normal in what most foster carers do. And that's understandable. Because there's little that's 'normal' in many of the situations that mean kids need to be fostered in the first place. Even in the most loving, committed, fully functional families, it's invariably a sudden crisis – the antithesis of normality – that leads to a child having to be looked after by the state, even if only for the shortest of periods. A parental car accident, perhaps, where there's no friend or relative to take the child in, or a sudden serious illness that means hospitalisation. Though much more frequently (in Mike's and my experience, anyway) it was one of the side-effects of a breakdown of some kind or other; be it the breakdown of the family unit, a breakdown in relations between child and step-parent or, as in the case of so many of the kids we fostered, a simple breakdown in any fragile, optimistic, hopeful progress made by parents locked into a world of substance abuse.

So the events that happened next, though certainly a first for me, were in hindsight just another reminder (as if one were even needed) that our fostering always has the potential to take us into very abnormal, and often challenging, situations.

Right at that moment, however, I patted the hump in the bed again, oblivious to what was coming, and simply went down to answer the door.

I had a good feeling about Phil Thoresby straight away. In his mid-thirties, or so I guessed, he looked professional and smart. Although his shirt sleeves were rolled to just below his elbows – as to be expected on such a hot day – it was a pristine white shirt, worn with smart black trousers, which, along with the leather messenger bag over his shoulder, lent an air of authority and confidence to his warm smile and firm handshake.

He'd also come prepared, having had the foresight to bring a 'play worker' with him, a similarly aged woman who introduced herself as Cathy. Not that I'd heard of a play worker before, so while Cathy took the bold step of going straight up to Paulie's bedroom (which I was more than happy to sanction, since they were apparently already acquainted) I asked Phil if hers was a newly created role in social services.

'No, not at all,' Phil said, as I ushered him to a seat at my dining table and put down the large refuse sack of Paulie's stuff that he'd brought with him. 'They've always had them – well, all the while I've worked for them, anyway. Ah, but, you might not have needed them, I suppose. You usually foster older children, don't you?'

'That would explain it,' I said, feeling a little silly. 'But, listen, while they're still upstairs, can I ask you about something?'

'Of course,' he said. 'Fire away.'

'It's about the family rabbit,' I said.

'Ah.'

'John Fulshaw emailed me about it yesterday, and I assume you probably know more about it than I do,' I added. 'And it's just that Paulie was talking about it himself, just before you arrived. Anyway, it's true, then, is it? He did kill it?'

Phil had already pulled the messenger bag from over his shoulder and now delved into it, pulling out the obligatory A4 manila file, which I could see had little in it. Well, as yet.

'I'm afraid it seems that way, Casey.'

'Only seems?'

'Well, pretty much. I mean as in, yes, the rabbit is dead and, yes, Paulie was out in the garden directly before the pet was found. But it's also true that everything other than that is a little bit "he said, she said" – you know, circumstantial evidence rather than "caught red-handed" stuff. Both he and the rabbit were found by the stepdad, who demanded to know what had happened, and by all accounts – and this is the one thing everyone seems to agree on – Paulie didn't waste a lot of time in coming clean and confessing to what he'd done.'

'He's just said as much to me. That he killed it – and told everyone about it – so that "everything would be okay. Except it's not." Those were his exact words, and I can't for the life of me work out what they mean. I thought you might be able to?'

He looked thoughtful. 'Well, only in so much as perhaps he thought they'd be more likely to forgive him. You know, more likely than if he tried to deny it, anyway. And it was a pretty elderly rabbit … I don't know. Perhaps he got rough with it? Maybe in a temper about something? They don't have the strongest hearts, do they, rabbits?'

I agreed that they didn't. 'But everyone's pretty sure he definitely did it? As in killed it intentionally?'

'Well, given that's what he's told all of us, well, yes, I suppose he did.' He sighed. 'But I guess all of this is going to come out in the wash at some point, isn't it? So though I'm keener to believe he *didn't* kill it – not intentionally, anyway – it's really not the main concern now, anyway. The main problem is the family breakdown and what's going to happen to him next. Believe me, I saw no softening of human hearts back there earlier.'

Since all was quiet upstairs, and there was no rush for them to leave (Cathy was likely to feature significantly in Paulie's life in the coming weeks if no resolution could be found, after all), I made a pot of coffee and, while I did so, Phil filled me in on what else he could.

It seemed Paulie's mother Jenny had had quite a few different men in and out of her life since losing her husband. The children were always reluctant to get along with any of them, always wary that if they got close, they might wake up one day and they'd be gone, something that was particularly true of her daughters. It was especially hard with the girls because, lacking a biological father, they had themselves become something of a handful.

And it seemed the family were already very well known to social services, after all. 'Family support has been in place for about a year,' Phil explained. 'But up to now mainly to help with the girls – get them through school without exclusions, and so on. It's only very recently that little Paulie's come to our attention, and that seems to have coincided with his real dad, Adi – John's told you about him? – making waves about having his son go live with him.'

A tickle started up on the back of my neck. 'Really? But I thought he had major mental health issues?'

'Yes and no. He's adamant that he's fine now and on medication that controls his violent episodes, but of course the danger is that when he *doesn't* take his meds – which apparently does happen – then he wouldn't be fit to take care of Paulie, would he? Which leaves us at something of an impasse – well, more a mess, really – because we're now doubtful whether mum and stepdad are going to be able to give him the upbringing he deserves, even if they *could* be persuaded to have him back and accept more support. Of course, as it stands, they've washed their hands of him, say they can no longer cope, and have a real fear – not without grounds – that he'll harm the baby. He's recently threatened to choke him, did you know that?'

I shook my head. 'And Dad's not an option because he's also potentially dangerous ...'

'Exactly,' Phil agreed. 'Terribly sad situation all round, isn't it?'

It was indeed. A child so young, and so vulnerable, apparently killing the family pet, just so it would 'make everything okay'. Although in what way he thought it might, I couldn't fathom. His dad was mentally unstable, and his mum and stepfather – well, partner – were busy pushing him out of their lives like he was a broken toy. No wonder little Paulie was so angry and messed up.

As if on cue, Cathy and Paulie came down to join us at precisely that moment, the latter pink-cheeked and red-eyed but seemingly feeling much happier, and keen to replicate a magic trick Cathy had just taught him, involving a handkerchief and a disappearing coin. 'Look, mister,' he said to Phil, having apparently forgotten he was the hated grand inquisitor, 'the coin will vanish, an' I swear it's real magic, not bullshit or anything!'

'Paulie,' I said on autopilot, 'please, love – *without* the swearing!' before getting up to make Cathy a cup of tea.

It was just about then that my mobile phone rang (I had to write everything down afterwards, and I remember writing: 1. My mobile phone went), which I picked up from the table and took into the kitchen with me.

The display told me it was Mike – probably calling for a Paulie update in his lunch-break – and I was just giving him exactly that, telling him what Phil had told me, about Cathy coming, about Paulie's magic trick, when a commotion, in the form of Paulie suddenly shrieking at the top of his tiny lungs, started up in the other room.

'Christ! Love, I'll have to call you back,' I told Mike, cutting him off and throwing the phone down. I ran back into the dining room and on through into the living room, where Paulie was yelling 'Daddy! Daddy! Daddy!' and jumping up and down.

I had no idea what was going on, but quickly took in the elements of the scene – which involved Paulie wriggling free of Cathy, who was frantically trying to restrain him, while Phil peered anxiously out of the window towards the road.

And then I did a double take, as I realised what was really happening. There was a man – a very big man – standing not only in my front garden, but actually in the flower bed directly in front of the window. And, as if to ram the point home, he now pounded heavily on the glass.

'Oh shit!' I said, before I could stop myself. 'Phil, is that –'

He nodded briskly. 'Yes, it is. Stay here. I think I'd better to go out and talk to him.'

'I want my daddy!' Paulie was screeching. 'I want my *daddy*!'

'Phil, are you sure you *should*?' Cathy asked him. 'I mean, *look* at him!'

'I'll be fine,' he said. 'Come on – what's he going to do in front of all of us, in broad daylight?'

'I'm not sure you should,' I said. 'I agree with Cathy. Why don't we just call the police?'

'Do that anyway,' said Phil, already heading towards the hall. 'I think on balance it might be better if we can talk him down before they get here ...'

'Daddy, Daddy!' Paulie was still screeching, endlessly. 'I want my *daddy*! Let me go! Let me *go*!'

Presumably seeing that Phil was coming out, the man had now moved away from the window and, before Phil could even get to it, there was now a loud rat-a-tat-tatting on the front door.

'What if he barges his way in?' I said, panicked now. Was the side door locked? I couldn't remember. 'Hang on tight to Paulie,' I said to Cathy, rushing to check if it was, trying to recall if I'd left the key in it and, if not, where I'd put it, and seeing the front door slam behind Phil as I did so.

Thank God for that, at least, I thought, dashing to secure the other door. Then it occurred to me that our courageous social worker had now effectively locked himself out there. And with a mad man? I was starting to feel very scared. I'd not seen much of the man but I'd certainly seen all I needed to. He was here to get his son back and he seemed to mean business. *Did* mean business, I realised as I glanced through the kitchen window, which also looked out over our small front garden. The body language of the two men was unmistakeable.

I grabbed the phone again, going back in just as Cathy was manhandling the still writhing five-year-old back into the dining room. 'Tell them his name is Adrian Selby,' she told me, as I punched out the three digits. 'Who he is. Why he's come.'

'Get off me, you fucking bitch!' Paulie yelled as he bucked and kicked against her. 'My daddy wants me! He's come to get me! Let me go or he'll kill you!' And at such a volume that I returned to the front room to make the call, for fear of not being able to make myself understood.

Similar levels of aggression were very much in evidence out the front. It was like witnessing a real-life hooligan movie. 'Get my fucking son out here *now*,' Paulie's father was screaming at Phil, 'or I'll rip your fucking throat out, you fucking nancy boy!'

To my horror – because real-life violence is *nothing* like a movie – he then shoved both his hands, flat-palmed, into Phil's chest, almost knocking him off his feet. He kept his balance, however – just – and held his own arms out in front of him, connecting with Adi's shoulders and trying to keep him at the proverbial arm's length. 'Adi, listen,' he said calmly, 'this isn't helping your case. Paulie will see all this and he'll be scared. Is that *really* what you want?'

By this time Cathy had shut the doors between the living room and dining room so that, in fact, Paulie was seeing nothing – well, as yet. Although what the cost to her might be was anyone's guess, because he was screaming like a banshee and presumably still attacking her.

But if I was horrified already, I was about to be more horrified still, as Adi lifted him arms, batted Phil's from his shoulders then drew a fist back and smashed it into the side of Phil's face. And this time he did fall down. Like a stone.

'Shit!' I said, wondering quite what the hell to do next, as I watched Paulie's father calmly step over the moaning social worker, intent, presumably, on resuming battering down our front door. Did I go out and try to face him down? Was Phil badly hurt? God, where *were* the police when you needed them?

In fairness, this had all taken the space of ten minutes. They'd be here soon, I told myself, as Phil rolled over and started getting up onto all fours. He glanced across and up at me, and I frantically gestured to him to get away. To go round the side, where I could let him in – well, if I was quick about it – so that we could leave everything, including Paulie's father, in the hands of the police.

But I wasn't sure I was making sense, and Adi was back in my line of vision again, though now he suddenly turned away and seemed to look up the road. *At last*, I thought, *thank God!* But then my eyes widened in shock. It wasn't a police car. It was *our* car that was coming down the road.

Chapter 6

If I had been frightened before, I was terrified now, watching in mortification as the car slowed to a halt, half up on the pavement, and Mike leapt out, almost before it had even fully stopped.

'No!' I cried, standing up from the chair arm I'd been perching on. I banged at the window as hard as I could.

Mike barely gave me a glance, though I knew he could hear me, because he thrust a finger in my general direction and barked, 'You stay inside!'

Which, of course, immediately made him the new focus of the ex-SAS man's ire, and I knew – I just *knew* – what was going to happen next.

If Phil, fit lad though he obviously was, was a simple standing target, I could see – in that way you can't help but see if you're married to a big, well-toned man – that Adi had Mike sized up straight away as someone who might require a little more effort. And when that happens – again,

I knew this from experience – it makes any would-be adversaries go in even harder, thinking they'd best make a good job of it first chance they got, as, should they fail, there might well not be a second.

I burst into tears as his fist met my poor husband's nose – as I said, real violence if not *remotely* like the pretend stuff on screen, and I also felt a kind of sick, primeval fury; it was almost as if I'd been punched myself.

Mike apparently had no such concerns; he seemed keener to redress the balance and, though I wasn't sure exactly what series of events caused it, within seconds, and amid much pulling and shouting, they were both rolling around together on the ground, while Phil, back on his feet, tried manfully to separate them, his pristine shirt not so pristine any more. Never has the sound of police sirens been so welcome, and when I heard them I almost crossed myself in gratitude.

'What's happening out there?' It was Cathy's voice. She'd poked her head between the double doors. I couldn't see Paulie but I could still hear him wailing, and the way Cathy was positioned I concluded that, if not in a head-lock, she certainly had him in some sort of body-lock; perhaps firmly wedged under her arm. He had no fight left in him, evidently – that was the main thing.

'Police,' I mouthed, not wishing to inflame Paulie into another burst of energy. Then I motioned towards the hall, miming that I considered it safe to go and open the front door now, a decision helped in part by the sight of two burly constables bearing down on the tangle of limbs on our path that was Mike and the luckless former soldier.

It was all over, then, in a moment. By the time I'd gone into the hall and opened the front door, both men were back on their feet, Mike shaking his head, while Adi, safely held between the two grim-faced officers, was scowling his defiance even now.

'He's my fucking *son*!' he was ranting at Phil. 'You have no right – no fucking right – to keep him from me!'

'Keep this up, mate, and you'll have a lot more than a caution,' one of the officers was saying to him. 'Just come with us, quiet, like, and let's get in the car, shall we?'

'He has no fucking *right*!' Adi persisted. 'That's my kid in there, don't you realise? My fucking *kid*! And he needs me!' He turned back to Phil again. 'How would you like it, eh? *Eh*? You got kids, have you?'

'Come on, Mr Selby,' the other officer said, trying to coax him to turn around and go with them. But he was having none of it.

'Can't you give me a fucking *minute*, here? *Can't* you? You got kids?' he almost spat at him. '*You*?' he asked the other. 'Yeah, I'll *bet* you have. Tucked up all nice and safe at home, are they? Safe and with *you*. You and the wife? Yeah. I'll bet.' His face contorted in distress. 'Well, lucky old you, mate, because I *haven't*!' With his arms pinned, he had to use his head to indicate. 'My little nipper – he's in there, he is. In there, shut up. Can't even *see* me. While his fucking slag of a mother – *God*!' He seemed momentarily speechless. 'Her and that *shit* of a bloke she's got – they don't love him, they don't want him – they just want fucking shot of him! Shame on the bitch. Fucking *shame* on her!' he was looking at me now. 'Yeah, right. An' what happens? My Paulie's sent here. To fucking strangers! To –'

'Mr Selby!' Phil entreated, 'we need to sit down and discuss all this like *adults*.'

'Yeah, look, mate,' Mike added calmly. 'This is doing you no good, is it? Please just do what the officers tell you. Leave us be. Go with them peacefully. No one wants this …'

Adi looked at him contemptuously. 'Yeah, you know what, "*mate*"?' he said, looking like he'd be well up for round two. 'And you, "*mate*", can *fuck* off, as well.'

'Right, that's enough,' one of the officers said. 'That's it, now.'

Adrian Selby was bundled into the back of their patrol car within seconds. And he was crying. He was sobbing like a baby.

'Well, what else was I going to do?' Mike was saying half an hour or so later. 'No idea what's going on. You slamming the phone down. Some racket kicking off – God only knows what kind of racket. Tell you what – I am *very* glad I turned up when I did. State of your face,' he added, grinning at Phil – and then grimacing at how much it hurt to do so. 'Man, if I hadn't turned up you might have been pulverised.'

Phil's face did indeed look a tad worse for wear. When he lifted the bag of peas I'd supplied to try to help reduce the swelling, it was clear the swelling was winning the battle, for the moment, at least. 'I perhaps *should* have stayed in the house,' he admitted, echoing my thoughts. Then he grinned as well. 'Typical social worker, eh? Always thinking we can perform miracles.'

Mike shook his head. 'I'd have done the same, mate. You weren't to know he'd kick off like that, were you?'

'Well, strictly speaking, yes,' Phil said. 'But you do what you do, don't you?'

'Tell me about it,' said Cathy, who'd just come into the kitchen. She dabbed at her lower lip, which was also swelling badly, as well as cut.

'God, you too?' I said, running the cold tap again so I could moisten some cotton wool for her. 'D'you want some ice for that as well?'

She shook her head and grinned ruefully. 'Only in a large gin and tonic.'

'Well, I have to say, I'm impressed,' I said. 'Do you know any other magic tricks? Though with the one you already have you'll probably be set for life.'

And it was true. By some miracle, Paulie was out for the count currently, having at some stage – between my going outside and the police coming and going – succumbed to whatever dark magic Cathy practised when not being a play worker, and fallen into an inexplicable and extremely convenient sleep.

Not that there wouldn't be hell to deal with when he woke up again, as he would before long. When he woke up and it all came flooding right back to him; that his dad had come to get him and we'd failed to hand him over, which was why, half an hour after that – Phil and Cathy having gone back to their respective offices – John informed me that in all likelihood he'd pick Paulie up that evening, because there was a chance – if Adi wasn't kept in the cells overnight, which apparently he might well not be – of another visitation.

'I'd like to think not,' he said. 'I'm hoping the sensible part of him will prevail. Mental health issues or otherwise, he can't be so stupid as not to realise that another episode such as this will certainly scupper whatever chance he has of getting custody of his son.'

I did a double take. 'You think there *is* a chance?' I asked him, strangely unsure whether to be mortified or pleased.

'There's always a chance,' John said. 'Whatever else is true, this is a man with a distinguished military record. Whatever's happened since ... well, we all watch things like Afghanistan on the telly, don't we? So we all know the toll it takes on servicemen and women.'

'But if he's that unstable, that potentially violent ... *actually* violent, as we've seen ...'

'That's true as well. And my hunch is that if anything *were* to be sanctioned, we'd been looking at the longer rather than the shorter term. But, you know what? I'd like to think there's some hope here, don't you? After all, who's to say that his problems haven't been exacerbated by losing his son? Who's to say that, if Paulie *does* stay in care, and Adi is supported – you know, with regular contact – that he can't get better and be the father he needs to be in order to get him back? There's also a mum and dad – did I tell you? Adi's parents. I'm told they'd quite like to be proper grand-parents again. So that's something too, isn't it?'

It was. And I thought back to the teddy bear Paulie had come with. Someone did love this strange little child. Several someones, perhaps. And John was right. That was something indeed.

Chapter 7

Paulie left our lives almost as quickly as he'd come into them. Within two hours of my putting down the phone to him, John Fulshaw was due back on our doorstep to collect our small visitor, who'd slept for a full two hours after Cathy had put him down, almost as if to give me the wherewithal to deal with the hours of distress I was braced for when he finally awoke.

As it was, he awoke teary and sad and washed out, but Cathy had been right when she'd said he had no fight left in him; he seemed just like a rag doll from a children's playgroup toy box – if not happy, at least accepting that his role, for the moment, was to play dead, so to speak, and let events and words wash over him, and to submit to whatever miseries all the strangers had planned for him. He had, in short, gone into his shell.

Which made it all sadder still, because I knew about the next stage; the stage when a looked-after child, abandoned and bewildered, shuts down all their emotions, increment by increment, as a way of making themselves less vulnerable to emotional attack.

But I also felt hopeful. Just the tiniest bit hopeful, admittedly (I was still a realist), because the ranting of Paulie's father, however awful the prior violence, had held a note of sincerity that I reckoned couldn't be faked. And those tears. Those tears had also been real.

'So you see, you *are* going to be able to see your daddy,' I told Paulie, as I helped him put on his army trousers, hoping passionately that I wasn't speaking out of turn. I had bathed him and dried his hair, and we were all but ready for when John came. 'Not right away, because things have to be organised,' I explained. 'Things have to be worked out and everything. But it will happen soon, sweetheart. And then, well, I'm told you should be able to see him regularly, too.'

Paulie had tears tracking down his face as I spoke, but they were silent tears; less an explosion of emotion than a kind of seepage, as if expressing all the hurt he was carrying around inside him, but more a simple release than anything else.

And as I'd spoken, I'd seen his expression change – hope had crept in and filled the space his tears had left. 'So *will* it be all right in the end, Casey?' he asked me, as I held the tongue of his trainer back for him to wriggle his foot in.

I thought of all the older children I'd had these sorts of conversations with. How much I always agonised over every single word I uttered. How hard I tried never to resort to platitudes and false reassurances. How much it mattered that, in a world full of them, it was my job *not* to lie. I knew I could give Paulie no guarantees on that score. But, then, could anyone? Ever? Without a crystal ball?

But he was five. A boy of *five*. And he needed just one thing now. 'Yes,' I said firmly. 'I think it will.'

Epilogue

When Tyler returned from football camp on Friday evening to find Paulie already gone, his first utterance, perhaps naturally, was 'How did it go?' and his second, also naturally (because he had eyes in his head), was, 'Mike, what the hell happened to your face?'

We were a long time round the tea table that night.

Riley's naughty step dictated that an errant or out-of-control child's time out should run to one minute for each year of a child's life. It didn't escape my notice that we'd managed a similar sort of regime with Paulie – for every year of his life we'd taken care of him for a day, and though it was anyone's guess whether those five days made any difference, I knew they were numbers that would remain in my memory whenever naughty steps were mentioned again.

We found out some facts – John's always brilliant at keeping us updated – and they all made a welcome kind of sense. It seemed Paulie hadn't intentionally killed the family's rabbit. The facts were pieced together down the line by a counsellor who began working with him, when it emerged that he had an extremely high IQ. Paulie, in fact, had accidentally slammed the hutch door on the animal's neck – having been sent outside to feed it he'd acted too quickly when the pet made a bid for freedom and he'd tried to bang the door shut. He'd then incurred the wrath of his stepfather, who, all too ready to believe it had been an act of murder (perhaps unsurprisingly under the circumstances), laid into the child for a confession, and, of course, duly got one.

As Paulie explained to the counsellor, he decided it would be 'better to say I purposely deaded it, because if I did, they'd send me to go and live with my daddy'. Except he wasn't. He was whisked into care, and then off to our house. And, interestingly, no mention of a rock or stone was ever made by him. It was perhaps just a 'figment of the stepdad's imagination', if one wants to be charitable.

Paulie is currently with a long-term foster family, and is likely to remain there for the foreseeable future. He's also in school, and being well supported, having been diagnosed as being on the autism spectrum – something that has now been identified as probably having played a bigger part in his challenging behaviour than anyone had previously realised.

Sadly, this seems to have made little difference to Paulie's future when it comes to his mother. Tragic though it is, it seems he was always destined to be rejected by her, having been the product of a short, and probably ill-advised, liaison – not to mention being affected by the bitter acrimony that followed their split. He was damaged, to put it mildly, by association. The better news, however, is that he has regular contact with his father. It's still supervised at present, while Adi works through his own issues, but sometimes includes, to their joy, Paulie's grandparents.

So, all in all, it's still very much a 'watch this space' situation, but, increasingly, it's looking like the picture is slightly rosier. Oh, and one of the things that needed to happen before Adi was officially allowed to make his case to social services was that he properly displayed remorse for his actions on the day Paulie left us – the memory of which Mike has stashed away in a mental file marked 'When moaning about going back to work and that your wife has all the excitement, be *extremely* careful what you wish for!'

We still have Adi's letter.

The Wild Child

Chapter 1

'How about it?' I asked my husband Mike and our long-term foster son Tyler.

Neither batted an eyelid, because it was the sort of thing they were both used to me saying – Mike because I'd spent most of our marriage persuading him to do things against his better judgement, and Tyler because in the year and a half he'd been with us he'd had ample chance to get to know how I ticked.

I looked pointedly at my watch. 'Only they're phoning back in ten minutes and we need to make an executive decision.'

'I know,' said Mike, equally pointedly. 'And I know the one they'll want. But hold your horses, Superwoman. Let's stop and *think* first. Come on. It's a bit short notice, after all.' He held his hands up then, presumably seeing my expression, not to mention realising the silliness of what he'd just said. Of course it was short notice. It was an emergency placement! 'Okay, point taken,' he said. 'But, like I said, we should still stop and think first. What with John being on holiday, and everything ...'

The mention of the word 'holiday' was like rubbing salt in a wound. It was just what we needed, too, but currently couldn't quite stretch to, our elderly car having recently gasped its last. Yes, we had a new(ish) one, but a car that starts is no match for a week spent on a beach, particularly today, which had dawned hot, dry and sunny but already saw me sweating over a hot stove.

It was Saturday and Tyler had half a football team coming over, not only to go to football, but also to eat the breakfast I'd impulsively promised them *before* going to footie practice: bacon butties, sausage sandwiches, the lot. That was the sort of hare-brained thing superwomen tended to do as well.

'John' was John Fulshaw, our fostering agency link worker, and when it came to taking kids on, everything normally came through him first. 'I know,' I said to Mike, 'and in an ideal world we'd run it all by him, of course we would, but EDT need an answer, and they need it fast.'

'They don't have *any* other options?' Mike asked, probably seeing his weekend disappearing.

I shook my head. 'Nope. Well, they say not. Say there's absolutely no one else to ask.'

'Eight you say?' Mike asked. 'A boy? Eight years old?'

I nodded.

'And just for the weekend?' Tyler asked. 'Because I'm on my soccer skills course next week, aren't I?' He grinned.

'So I won't be here to help you if he runs you ragged.'

I blew Ty a kiss, bless him. I'd forgotten about that. He was right. He was off at some ungodly hour on the Monday morning and, as he'd pointed out, would indeed be unable to provide an extra pair of hands if our potential house guest did end up staying longer.

I glanced at Mike. We both knew there was no such guarantee that he wouldn't be, either. We both knew that 'just a couple of days' or 'just for the weekend' didn't really mean anything in our line of work. The truth was that once a child was out of imminent danger, safely installed in an emergency placement, then, bingo, the urgency was over. Which meant that (sometimes fortunately, and at other times, unfortunately) the child who you'd agreed to take just for the weekend could end up being with you for weeks and maybe even months.

Which was fine. Fostering was what we did. Most placements were long ones. The problem lay in that word 'emergency', which meant little time to consider. No time for preparatory meetings, no chance to see if there was a 'fit'. It was a 'sold, sight unseen' sort of situation, almost. Yes, you'd see the child, but they would be even more of an unknown quantity than the children you *did* get to see before you took them, and they could be complicated enough.

'I think you should say yes,' Tyler piped up. 'Just go for it. Might be fun to have another kid around for a couple of days, mightn't it? 'Specially another boy,' he added. 'Yeah, I think you should say yes.'

Mike rolled his eyes and grinned. We *all* knew the circumstances in which Tyler had come to us. 'So let's be clear,' he said, holding a hand up to tick on fingers. 'He's eight. He's attacked a social worker. And there's an iron bar involved. What could possibly go wrong?'

Chapter 2

We all laughed of course, but taking on such a child was a serious business, even if it was only in theory for a couple of days. That they'd rung us at all seemed to be an indication that we shouldn't take the child on lightly; EDT (the social services emergency duty team) only rang private fostering agency carers like us when they had exhausted all other avenues.

Which Julie Jenkins from the EDT had already confirmed. 'We've tried every single authority carer we could think of,' she'd explained, 'and without success. So I really don't have anyone else to turn to. And I saw in your file that you've helped us out in the past. I know it's not an easy one, but we're pretty desperate.'

'Not an easy one' was something of an understatement.

'He's called Connor,' she explained. 'Latterly of a children's home in Swindon. He's been in children's homes since he was five, by all accounts –'

'Five?' I spluttered. 'Not with a family?'

'No, not with a family,' she confirmed. 'And right now, his current placement is no more.'

She went on to explain that Connor had taken an iron bar and attacked his social worker with it and, as the children's home staff had tried to restrain him, another child – a ten-year-old girl – had ended up in the firing line and had also been hit; she had cuts to her face and a broken bone in her hand where she'd raised it to try to protect herself.

'Wow,' I'd said, shocked. And I'm fairly unshockable.

'I know,' Julie said. 'And I'm afraid that's pretty much all I can tell you. But the manager at the home is ringing me back with more details any minute, so while you have a think, I'll see what else I can find out. And don't worry. They have assured me that after the weekend they have a number of carers who will be freed up and can take him. So it really *is* just till Monday, I promise.'

Although I was slightly stunned by the thought of an eight-year-old who could be so violent, as I'd put the phone down – having promised to talk it through with Mike and Tyler – I reminded myself that a collection of bald facts could sound so much more damning than they might be in reality. Take Tyler himself, for instance; our first meeting was following a phone call from John asking me to turn up at a police station to see about taking on 'an 11-year-old boy who's stabbed his stepmother'. Which he had, but the reality was quite different from the image that series of words first conjured up. Rather than it being an act of extreme violence – a knife plunged into an innocent victim

– it had actually happened by accident. Which wasn't to condone it; the knife should not have been in his hand in the first place, even if it *was* only being wielded after provocation, as an empty threat. But it did serve as a reminder that it was important to see the whole picture with a child, *and* a situation, before jumping to conclusions.

And I knew Mike was thinking that, too.

'So, yay or nay?' I asked again now, as my mobile began to vibrate again. Both Mike and Tyler nodded – as I'd already known they would – so I shooed them into the kitchen to take charge of breakfast as I took the call.

Julie Jenkins couldn't have been more grateful. 'Really?' she said, as if she really couldn't believe her luck; a child with nowhere to go wasn't the sort of headache anyone wanted – particularly on a Saturday morning.

'Really,' I confirmed. 'No, that's fine. We'll take him for the weekend. Well, provided he isn't a serial killer or anything.'

'Oh, Casey, that will be *such* a help,' she said, the relief evident in her voice. 'Honestly, trying to get a carer freed up on a weekend is nigh on impossible. Mind you, I can't lie to you. It hasn't helped that he's a bit of a nightmare.'

Alarm bells began buzzing in my head. Had I got that wrong about her having no prior knowledge of the boy? I'd assumed she'd been reading from notes she'd been given, but did she already know him? Trying not to feel cross – had she deliberately kept that from me till I'd agreed to have him? – I regrouped. 'Oh, right,' I said lightly. 'Do you already know him?'

'Not personally,' she replied, 'but this isn't the first time we've had to find an emergency placement for him, sad to say. I can recall doing it myself on at least three occasions and I know other colleagues have had similar dealings with him, too.'

I felt a mixture of heart-sink and determination when she said that. Much as a child like this could completely derail our weekend, there was always this part of me mentally rolling my sleeves up. Which is undoubtedly why I became a foster carer in the first place. I do love a challenge. 'Is he really *that* bad?' I asked, now I knew there was more she could tell me. 'I mean, how bad can an eight-year-old really *be*? And was it really an iron bar? I know how these things can change in translation. And how on earth does a child get hold of such a thing in a children's home?'

I heard Julie sigh. 'And it wasn't just any children's home, either. It's a semi-secure unit. I don't know where he got the weapon from but, yes, it was definitely some kind of iron bar. And he had no fear about attacking the staff member or anybody else who got in his way.'

I started to waver then, regretting my earlier gung-ho enthusiasm, imagining recounting these minor details to Mike and Tyler. What was I letting myself in for? What were *we* letting ourselves in for? 'Can you be straight with me?' I asked. 'We have a 13-year-old boy here, as I'm sure you already know. I feel daft even asking this given Connor's age but, well, will we be putting Tyler in danger?'

There was the briefest of pauses. 'All I can give you are the facts,' Julie said. 'But if it's any reassurance, what I can tell you is that when it gets to this – when Connor has flipped out so much that he's had to be taken off somewhere else to get himself together, then that's just what he usually seems to do. He usually has a few weepy days away, feeling very sorry for himself and for all the trouble he's caused, and then goes back all contrite and vowing to be better.' She sighed. 'You know how it works, Casey – it only ever lasts for a couple of months, sadly, but there you have it. The one thing I can say with a bit of confidence is that the respite carers don't get to see the worst of him.'

I made a mental risk assessment. What she said did make sense. Then I told her yes for a second time. That she could have him transported to us and that I'd just be extra vigilant on all fronts. The way I saw it, Mike and Tyler would be out at football for half the day anyway and, well, we'd deal with the rest of the weekend when we got to it. If this lad was going to be as wet and weepy as Julie predicted, perhaps a day trip would be in order for Sunday – maybe out into the surrounding countryside for a picnic. Something calming and low key anyway, and then, before we knew it, it would be Monday. Nothing I couldn't handle, I was sure.

'So there's no chance of him going back to where he's coming from then?' I finished.

'Sadly not,' she said. 'But we're already looking at various options. Don't worry. We'll have him fixed up by the time Monday comes around. Oh, and I'll email his files over so you can read more of his background. Well, if you've time. If I make the call now, he's not going to be long. On which note, will it be okay if I give the home manager your mobile number so he can give you a ring and have a chat with you as well?'

There was never a situation in fostering when extra information was a bad thing, so I agreed to that, too; after all, the home manager would know Connor extremely well. Then I hung up and headed off into the kitchen.

Tyler's friends had all arrived while I'd been talking and the decibel level was through the roof, with Mike in the midst of it, wielding the fish slice, asking for orders. Calming and low-key it wasn't, and I was glad our temporary charge wouldn't arrive till the boys had headed off to training.

Mike put the fish slice down and pointed to a fat bacon sandwich he'd just made for me. It was stuffed with crispy bacon and oozing ketchup, just the way I liked it.

'All sorted?' he asked, as I joined him cooker-side to eat it.

'All sorted,' I said. 'He should be with us in a couple of hours. Coming in private transport apparently.' The rest I could (and perhaps should) leave till later on. No point paving the lad's route to us with negativity.

Mike raised his eyebrows. 'No expense spared, eh?' He then checked his watch. 'We might well be back from football by then, too.'

'Yes, do try,' I said, and then glanced around at the scattering of black and white striped football jerseys. 'But just you and Tyler, please. I think that's best, don't you? I think this little lot would be a bit too much as a welcoming committee given the circumstances.'

The Wild Child

Mike grinned. 'I think this lot would be a bit much given *any* circumstances. You can almost smell the testosterone in this kitchen!'

I licked ketchup from my lips and pretended to sniff the air. 'At least it's better than the smell *after* the match.'

Chapter 3

As soon as my house was male hormone-free I made a quick call to both my kids. Both adult now and with their own families (Kieron had not long had his first baby) it was odds on that either or both would pop round at some point. We had a bit of an open-door policy in that way, and what mum doesn't like seeing her grown-up kids?

Today, however, it made sense to ask them not to call round, so that I could give Connor a chance to settle in. And if that went okay, we could all get together on the Sunday. In my experience, something like a big family picnic was one of the best ways to take a troubled child out of themselves – fresh air and exercise being two of the best medicines around.

That done, it was time to go and power up my laptop so I could see what might have fetched up in my inbox. And something had. And it made interesting reading.

It seemed Connor had been born in south London. In his early years he'd lived there with his mum – who was called Diane – and his dad, Connor senior, together with an older brother and sister. These older siblings were, according to the notes, Connor's polar opposites, in that, while they were model kids (if such a thing exists) he'd been labelled a 'problem child' early on; screaming all day for no apparent reason, and violent from the moment he could walk. He had been excluded permanently from every school he had attended in his short life (including nursery, where he was already deemed too aggressive to be around other kids), and by the time he was seven he'd already been tagged 'streetwise'.

I continued to read with a sense of depressing inevitability. Though it seemed no one had commented on or suggested reasons for Connor being such an apparently difficult toddler, one thing leapt out as a factor that might exacerbate the problem; that his father had been in and out of prison all his life. Connor senior was quite the criminal, it seemed; something not usually conducive to family life, and when Connor was five his wife left and then divorced him.

Then came the nugget that I couldn't help but home in on. That she'd left him, taking only two of her three children. She simply left for some village in the north-east, close to Scotland, and as it coincided with a period when Connor senior was at liberty, she left little Connor behind with his dad.

I couldn't help but sigh. I could never do such a thing. I struggled to understand how a mum could leave her kids at the best of times – in all but the most extreme of cases – but to take two and leave one with a jailbird husband? How much more completely could a child be rejected? I read on. It seemed Dad had been happy enough to keep him, but within six months he'd received yet another prison sentence and at that point five-year-old Connor had been taken into care. He'd been part of the system ever since.

It was dreadful reading – starts in life don't come much worse – and I felt genuinely moved, not to mention slightly sickened, thinking of where he'd come from and just how damaged he must be as a consequence. I wasn't alone; various social workers and carers had made similar observations, one noting only recently that, at the age of just eight, Connor truly believed himself to be 'properly grown-up', had seen enough of life to know 'exactly what was what' and that half the adults he'd encountered 'didn't have a clue'.

I closed my laptop. Bye bye weekend. This clearly wasn't going to be an easy one. Though I already knew that – mine was a job that required me to know that – I also knew instinctively that I now had to make a choice. Not about hanging on to Connor – our next long-term placement would be decided in consultation with John Fulshaw – but about how I – or, rather, we – approached the next two days.

I had two choices. I could fill the time with fun things to do, keep Connor happy and act like he was just with us for a little holiday, or I could choose to try to help in some way. That would mean touching on some very painful areas for Connor and 'interfering' in his life, and I knew doing that was tantamount to creating all kinds of trouble. But to opt for simple containment would leave me feeling that I wasn't doing my job. And that, admittedly to my own detriment at times, simply wasn't in my nature.

John Fulshaw was still away, of course, but I could hear him like Jiminy Cricket on my shoulder. He'd have looked at the notes and advised against this particular bit of respite, for sure. I could actually hear him telling me not to take it on, saying that since we'd decided to take on Tyler permanently we needed to take a break before embarking on our next quest. Yes, do a bit of respite, perhaps – for quiet, biddable children who happened to find themselves in unfortunate circumstances – but save our emotional energy for our next long-term challenge; not take on a kid with a dossier of escapades that made for more eye-popping reading than James Bond's.

John would probably have been right, but I'd committed to it now, so it was up to *me* to advise me, and I told myself sternly that I should play things by ear. Much as my instinct was to cast myself as a mixture of superhero and avenging angel, the best thing to do would be to see how things went. In any case, half the day would be gone before Connor even got to us; I'd never been to Swindon but I knew it was at least a couple of hours' drive away, probably more. And he'd be tired, he'd be shaken, he'd be scared; hopefully he'd be contrite. Which thoughts showed just how much I *didn't* know.

* * *

Mike and Tyler arrived back from football at one o'clock, exactly the time I expected to receive Connor, so I hustled them in, ordered them both to the bathroom with a command of 'Get those filthy sweaty things off!' and flew around with a can of air freshener. Only then, with my home feeling fit to receive visitors, did I take up a vigil by the living-room window.

'Is that a security van?' Tyler wanted to know, once he and Mike had come to join me.

'Certainly looks like one,' Mike agreed. He laughed. 'Though I'm sure it's *not*. It's probably just –'

'It bloody *is*,' I said, gawping at what had just pulled up outside our house. 'Look at the writing on it! And it's got those armoured windows and everything.'

'It is,' Tyler agreed. 'It's one of those vehicles they use to transport criminals back and forth from where their trials are. I remember seeing them when we were there. Don't you remember?'

Indeed I did, one of our first outings with Tyler having been to accompany him to court.

'Bloody hell, Case,' Mike observed before I could answer. 'What the hell did he *do*?'

We all watched, agog, as the driver got out. He was a huge man – as tall as Mike and a great deal wider – and when he went round the back to open it he was joined by another man-mountain; they were clearly hand-picked for the job.

Which was what made what happened next seem even more incongruous. Because what emerged from the van was a slip of a boy; if I'd been asked his age, at this distance I would have guessed somewhere around six. They were joined by a third man – three men! Come all this way with him! And all three, amazingly, escorted the lad up our path.

I realised we all had our mouths hanging open. 'Come on,' I hissed. 'Come away from the window. The kid's probably petrified!'

Not, it had to be said, that he looked it. It was hard to drag ourselves away from watching this tiny thing, his head a mass of blond, cherubic curls, who was currently marching towards our front door. Really marching, too. Like you see young boys doing when they're playing soldiers. Arms stiff and swinging in time with their feet, expression blank, head held high. I had never seen anything like it in my life and half expected one of the 'guards' to shout 'Halt!'

I rushed to open the door, closely followed by a bemused Mike and Tyler. Trying to ignore the hard, inscrutable gazes of the three men, I immediately bent down so I could smile at Connor at his level. 'Hiya, sweetie,' I said, touching his shoulder as I spoke. 'I'm Casey, this is Mike and this is Tyler.'

I then stood upright to speak to the men, who returned my chirpy greeting almost as if they were robots. I wasn't sure they were much used to delivering small children to middle-aged women in the suburbs. 'Do you have his things?' I followed up. 'His clothes and the usual paperwork? And how about a cup of tea or something?' I added. 'You've had a long drive. Come on, please do all come in.'

I moved to one side, then, to allow the procession to pass but the men stayed where they were. The one at the back passed the small suitcase he carried to Mike and then a large envelope to me. 'We won't come in if you don't mind,' the front man replied. 'We've got a long drive back and want to crack on.' He then turned to Connor and cracked a smile, too, finally. 'You'll be alright here, son,' he said, patting him on the head, closely followed by the second man. 'And don't forget, you just be good for these people, won't you?'

Connor nodded solemnly. The two seemed to have bonded en route. He then turned and smiled shyly up at me.

'I *am* a good kid you know. I dunno what all the fuss is about really. But like I told these fellers on the way, it's 'cos me dad's a famous gangster from London. They all give me grief about it, but it's alright, I can take it. There's not much fazes me. You got anything to eat? I'm starving!'

I grinned back, delighted by the warmth in his smile and the endearing 'Artful Dodger' way he spoke. I was also aware of Mike and Tyler trying not to laugh. 'Go on in, then,' I said. 'Mike and Tyler will show you your room while I sort you out some food. Cheese sandwich and some crisps? How about that?'

'Sounds safe,' he said, hopping over the step and coming in.

I thanked the men for bringing him and, as soon as Connor was out of earshot, I asked the question that had been on my mind since they arrived. 'This all seems very odd,' I said. 'Do children in care always get transported like this from your neck of the woods?'

The man at the front laughed. 'Nope!' he said. Then his face was once again serious. 'But then again, not all children are like young Connor. Don't let them big blue eyes fool you, Mrs Watson. He's already bitten a chunk out of one of my men, and only ten minutes ago said his dad would slit my throat the minute he gets released.'

He patted my shoulder, just as he'd done to Connor's head. 'Stay safe,' he said cheerily as he led the procession back to the van.

Chapter 4

I stood and watched the huge vehicle turn around and drive away, letting the shocking things he'd said to me sink in. They had just seemed so at odds with the way Connor looked and had behaved – well, so far – that my instincts were all over the place; I really didn't know what to think.

I'd yet to hear from the care-home manager, so I still felt somewhat ill-informed; I'd have liked to know the circumstances around the incident that had brought him here, but right now all I had to go on were the email I'd already studied and the envelope I had in my hand. I ripped it open and had a flick through while Mike and the boys were still out of the way, but there wasn't much more than I'd been told earlier. Well, apart from some further info on how he'd got hold of an iron bar. It seemed he'd acquired it from the grounds of the home, where some repairs were being done to some of the outbuildings. Apparently left behind by a workman, it had found its way into Connor's hands a few days earlier – he'd admitted to having it hidden under his bed.

'For protection' had been his answer when he'd been asked why he'd taken it, but it had certainly not been used in defence. No, it seemed the social worker – a Mr Gordon – had wound him up in the dining room, so he'd gone to his room, retrieved the bar, which was apparently some part of an old window, and then duly caused mayhem over breakfast.

This morning's breakfast. All that trouble caused, and on this very morning, by the little dot of a kid upstairs. Hearing the stairs creak, I stuffed the papers back into the envelope.

It was Mike. 'Told them I'd call them when there's some food ready. Ty's helping him settle in. Anything juicy in there?' he added, nodding towards the paperwork. I paused, wondering whether to try and sugar it. I decided not.

'He does appear to be a *bit* worse than we first thought,' I said, keeping an eye on the door. 'It certainly doesn't make nice reading. I think we're going to have to keep a close eye on him.'

He held his hand out for the envelope. 'Let's have a nose, then. Don't worry. He's busy unpacking and Ty's promised him they can play on his Xbox.'

I handed it over. 'Well, I guess all we can do is treat him as we find him and play it by ear. Julie did say these outbursts invariably follow a pattern. That once he's messed up his placements he goes through a period of remorse. Let's hope he's in reflective mood today, eh?'

'Placements *plural*?' Mike said. 'How many has he been through?'

'More than are commensurate with peace, love and harmony,' I told him. 'So let's make sure he sees some while he's with us. I'll leave them for a bit, then how about we take them both out? Maybe even stay out for tea. We'll just keep him busy,' I added, as Mike finished scanning the notes.

'Hmm,' he said. 'Be the other way around, I reckon.'

He wasn't wrong. After he went into the lounge to watch his Saturday sports programme I quickly made both boys a sandwich, then took them up; if they were settled with the Xbox, I was happy enough. They could get on and get to know each other over some mutual game they liked while I dealt with the laundry, and we could head off on our outing a little later.

I reached the top of the stairs and smiled as I heard boyish laughter coming from Tyler's room. Tyler was routinely great around younger kids, not just because he had his own little brother (whom he still saw pretty regularly, even though he had no contact with his dad or stepmother) but because he spent so much time around my own grandchildren.

I hovered a moment, listening – you could glean lots by listening to what kids chatted about when out of earshot – and, as a result, my smile didn't stay in place long.

'Mate, you're almost a *man* at your age,' Connor was saying. 'Don't tell me you never look at tits.'

I swallowed a gasp and edged closer to the very slightly open door. 'Casey'll go *mad*, Connor, trust me,' Tyler answered, sounding uncomfortable. '*Seriously*. I didn't even know my Xbox could do that.'

I heard Connor giggle – such an innocent sound when made by an eight-year-old – and I could picture his angelic face as he answered. 'Aw, mate, you got a *lot* to learn. You can get pornos on 'em and all sorts!'

I almost dropped the sandwiches in my haste to transfer both plates to one hand so I could knock loudly on the door before opening it. Tyler stared at me, red faced, while Connor smiled sweetly. 'Hi, Mrs Watson,' he said politely. 'I think I'm going to love it here. Thanks for letting me stay, an' that. I really appreciate it.'

I knew at that moment that I could simply pretend I hadn't heard. Get the boys out of the room and then speak to Tyler later. We were only taking care of this pint-sized porn-fancier for the weekend, after all. Or I could make my life a bit more difficult. I chose the latter.

'You're welcome, Connor,' I said, fairly sharply, as I put the plates down on the chest of drawers. 'But I just heard the conversation you boys were having and I'm telling you right from the off, Connor, that I won't tolerate that kind of thing.'

I then looked at Tyler, trying to transmit that we were in this together, while at the same time saying, 'Tyler, I know you were trying to be nice to Connor, but I'm afraid there'll be no more Xbox this weekend. Connor, go to your own room and get your shoes on. You can have your lunch with me downstairs. And then we're going out.'

Tyler nodded, looking embarrassed, then got to his feet and started winding the leads round the Xbox handsets. Connor stood up, too, but his expression had morphed into something like a sneer. 'So I'm not allowed to play *anything* now, then? What kind of fucking house is this?'

I picked up the plate that contained his sandwich and held the door wide open. I then pointed towards the bedroom he'd just unpacked his things in. 'You, Connor,' I told him, 'are the same age as my grandson. I would not tolerate that kind of language from him and, trust me, I won't tolerate it from you either. Do you hear me? And if I hear it again, I'm sure Mike will have something to say about it, too,' I added, sensing what I might be dealing with here, given Connor's early years. I wasn't generally one for the 'wait till your father gets home' variety of disciplining generally, but I knew this boy was used to being disciplined by his father, so might well be more fearful of his wrath than mine. As it would turn out, I was right on the money about that, but for now I was just pleased to see him respond. 'Now go on,' I said. 'Let's not ruin today before we've even started. Grab your shoes, then downstairs to eat.'

Gloves off, then. Still, at least it was good to know where we stood. And it seemed Connor was keen for that, too. 'Tell "Big Mike" if you like,' he said, sauntering past me through the open doorway. 'He's just another one I'll add to the list of men for me dad to sort out.' He left the bedroom actually whistling.

'Oh my God!' Tyler said, his jaw dropping. 'What kind of kid *is* that?'

I groaned. 'The kind that is going to make this a *very* long weekend, I imagine, don't you? Hmm. I think we'll go to the Jungle Pit. Have tea there as well. Yup, that's a plan. Try and help him burn off some energy.'

'Oh great,' Tyler said, rolling his eyes. 'He trash talks you and gets a *reward*?' He then grinned at me. 'I'm only kidding, Casey. Don't look so worried. I know what you're trying to do.'

Bless him, I thought, marvelling at his perceptiveness. Tyler was no angel – he was a thirteen-year-old boy, so could still get up to mischief and give us some attitude from time to time – but it was reassuring that he understood that there were ways and ways of playing things.

I followed Connor back downstairs and while he ate his sandwich – and there wasn't a peep out of him now – I went to tell Mike both a watered-down version of what had happened (leaving out the 'Big Mike' bit) and the plan I had for keeping our charming young visitor occupied for the afternoon.

Despite my telling him he could stay behind and watch telly – he'd had a long and busy week, after all – Mike felt the same as Tyler. 'So, let me get this straight. You're taking him to a play centre to thank him for being rude to you? Good plan, Case.'

I was pretty sure I'd get the same response from Riley if I told her as well, so as soon as it popped into my head that I could ask her to join me instead of Mike, I dismissed it again. No, better if the 'containment' part of the weekend involved only myself.

'I'll come as well,' Tyler said, bringing his own plate back down to the kitchen. 'Keep you company while Connor here goes and plays.'

If Connor noticed the slightly patronizing tone in Tyler's voice, he didn't show it. In fact, I reckoned he was now on a different track with us. Having been denied his 'pornos' and made his feelings known, it was almost as if, having realized he was stuck with us for a couple of days, he'd now made a conscious decision to keep us on side. In any event, I reasoned, he *would* enjoy playing there; I'd never met a kid who didn't enjoy having free rein in a giant warehouse full of ball pits and climbing frames, ropes, slides and trampolines. If he didn't find something to amuse himself he'd be a very strange boy indeed.

Though, by any standards, he *was* a strange boy. Given his early abandonment by his mother, and the frequent absences of his father, it would have been a miracle if he wasn't. I wasn't silly. He was damaged by his upbringing, and I knew all about that because I saw it all the time. But there was more to it than that. And as Tyler went to get himself ready, and Connor meekly offered to wash up his plate and mug, I'd pretty much decided I knew *exactly* what I was dealing with. My guess was that he was on the road to becoming a sociopath.

It's a word that gets bandied about a lot, 'sociopath', but it's important that the condition is correctly diagnosed, because a child with sociopathic tendencies is a damaged and potentially very dangerous child; one who needs a great deal of specialist help and a supportive and firm environment if they aren't to grow up to become a damaged and dangerous adult as well.

I knew a little of what I spoke. We'd fostered a child a few years back, a boy almost exactly the same as Connor in some of his background and ways, and the professional view, given his behaviour, which was often extreme and very entrenched, was that he was a sociopath, too. Thankfully, in that case it turned out he wasn't; he was simply reacting to a situation nobody had known about, much less understood. It had been his father – his charming, personable and apparently bewildered father – who'd been the wolf in sheep's clothing that had so damaged the poor kid.

Along the way, however, I'd read up a lot on the subject and my hunch was that Connor might just be the real deal. His notes certainly seemed to point to it and his behaviour *before* going into care seemed to as well. It's accepted in many quarters now that there are features of brain chemistry linked to sociopathy and psychopathy; that it's a combination of this, coupled with terrible circumstances as a trigger, that brings about the lack of empathy that characterises such people. Sadly, though, once it's part of someone's personality it's extremely hard to treat.

Which made several things clear. That a weekend with us would probably make no difference to what became of him, and that he needed help that the likes of us weren't qualified to provide. So, despite it going against everything

I believed in, I knew then that this mini-placement *was* to be purely about containment. There was simply no other way to approach it.

With that in mind, I knew I should stop floundering about, trying to think of ways in which I could try to help him. I just needed to put lots of things in place to keep him out of trouble and occupied. A sad thought to accept, but obviously necessary.

I wondered if he could read minds as well as he knew his way around an Xbox. Because by the time he'd climbed into the car he had completely lost his attitude. Indeed, as I got into the front seat I felt a hand on my shoulder. It was Connor, with the angelic smile once again in place. 'Sorry about swearing, Mrs Watson,' he said meekly.

'You know, Connor,' I said, swivelling to face him, 'it's fine to call me Casey.'

'Casey, then,' he said, as if finding the familiarity uncomfortable on his tongue. 'I was only having a bit of fun with Tyler, honest.' He glanced at Tyler, who was looking at him as if he really wasn't sure what to make of him. 'We should never have been looking at boobs,' he went on. And I was about to agree that he certainly shouldn't have been, when he finished off with 'not with a woman around the house'.

I swivelled back and switched the ignition on, speechless. I caught Tyler's gaze in the mirror, but decided we'd best ignore what Connor had just said. 'Right, fasten up then, boys. Let's go and let off some steam, shall we?'

Though, in Connor's case – Connor who was *only eight years old* – a cold shower might have been a better choice.

Chapter 5

While I drove, the boys chatted away about more appropriate subjects, Tyler explaining to Connor about what he could expect to find at Jungle Pit, which were the best and worst slides, and the scariest rope swings. I started to relax a little. Perhaps I'd over-reacted earlier. The poor kid was a product of his early environment, after all. Maybe he'd just been testing the water – kids who were shunted around often pushed and strained at the boundaries. Perhaps he was just keen to see how far he could go.

The café area of the Jungle Pit was actually in the same cavernous space that held the play area itself, cordoned off to one side by a low yellow plastic wall. Here it was traditional for all the mums, dads and all the other kinds of childminders to install themselves at one of the various tables, while the kids scampered off to throw themselves about.

Being a Saturday, it was heaving, despite the glorious weather. It was a big draw in all weathers simply because it was so contained. You could sit and read a book or catch up with the papers while your kids ran amok in a corralled and controlled environment, with the safety-conscious staff always looking on.

Once installed, I sent the boys off and told them I'd call them back once I'd got some drinks and then later, if they were hungry, some food. They duly deposited their shoes and ran off towards the big colourful cubes in which the various spills and thrills could be had. Some of the cubes were suspended from beams by thick chains and ropes. These were for older children only, or, rather, children over a certain height, as they purposely swayed to make the activities in them that bit more exciting. Connor was only just big enough, but as Tyler headed off to the area with all the footballs it was to these that he immediately made a beeline, and once he was out of sight I strolled off to get myself a coffee.

It's easy to lose yourself in places like the Jungle Pit. Whether it's because they are so well managed, bristling with young energetic staff, or perhaps just because zoning out is one of those essential parenting skills, I was miles away, reading one of the free newspapers and sipping on a latte, when the commotion by the hanging cubes started up.

I certainly knew it had been going on a while, because it was the activity at the tables around me that first grabbed my attention: the adults who were scraping back their chairs, the various oohs and ahhs, the fact that the area was fast emptying of people. I was sitting in the middle of a sea of abandoned tables by the time I became aware – aware that everyone had gone to look at whatever was happening elsewhere.

I put my coffee down and stood up, too, conscious that all eyes seemed drawn upwards, glancing around as I did so to see if I could see the boys. I tilted my own head – whatever was going on was happening high up in the rafters – or whatever the steel things were that constituted rafters in such a place. Which was when I saw Connor, who was a good twenty or twenty-five feet above us, perching precariously on a dangerously narrow beam; one of several that spanned the building and from which hung the giant cubes on chains.

'What on *earth* ...?' I said in a panic as I rushed across to the play area. Tyler ran across to me then, looking bewildered. 'What the hell's he doing, Casey?' he asked, not taking his eyes off Connor. 'That's *well* high, that is,' he said, with a note of admiration. Then he turned to me. 'I don't think he's allowed up there, do you?'

'He most certainly isn't,' I said, wondering what was going to be done about it. And if so, by whom. I called up to him, all too aware of the heads swivelling towards me. 'Connor! Get down from there *right now*! And be careful about it. *Very* careful. Come *on*!'

Having presumably identified me as the responsible adult, a young girl in a Jungle Pit T-shirt also ran across to me. 'We can't be responsible if he falls from there,' she pointed out. 'It's clearly marked that they shouldn't climb on top of the cubes.'

I didn't doubt it was clearly marked. They'd be extremely

keen not to be slapped with a writ, wouldn't they? And I'd seen the sign myself. Despite the high levels of staff, you couldn't move for firmly fixed notices reminding you that whatever happened it was unquestionably neither their fault nor their responsibility.

'I'm sure he knows that,' I told her. Then I turned my gaze upwards again. 'Connor!' I barked at him. 'You come down from there this instant! You know full well that you're not allowed to be up there!'

'Piss off, you old fart!' came the immediate response. I cringed. I could also feel my cheeks burning as the previous looks – which had mostly been of the sympathetic variety – now changed to ones of disapproval. The young girl who had spoken to me started to edge away now, too, walking backwards so that she didn't miss anything.

'I think I'll go and get the manager,' she said. 'He'll know what to do.'

As she scurried away I looked back up to check that Connor wasn't in any imminent danger. Yes, the place was full of soft structures and crash mats but he was much higher up than he was supposed to be and – to my extreme annoyance – he was beginning to put himself in further danger by acting up for his now captive audience. I had no idea what had inspired him to climb up there in the first place, but there was no doubt that he was enjoying being in the spotlight, walking the beam like a tight-rope act, holding his arms out to the side and whistling a tune as he pretended to trip, eliciting a mass gasp from the increasingly nervous crowd.

'Get down here, Connor!' I tried again. 'Get back down here this *minute*, before we're asked to leave!'

'Ooh! Asked to *leave*!' he mimicked. 'Ooh, I'm so *scared*! Piss off, old lady. I can stay here all night if I want to.'

Tyler's face had blanched now, and I misread it. 'It's okay, Ty,' I said quietly. 'He'll come down soon enough. He's got to come down eventually, after all.'

'No he bloody won't,' Tyler replied angrily. 'He's coming down right now. He's not speaking to you like that and getting away with it.'

He hared off to the nearest cube, from which he could begin making an assault. 'Ty, don't go up there,' I called to him. But he ignored me. 'Get down, you little idiot!' he yelled. 'Get down here now. If I have to come up for you, you're getting a slap, you hear me?'

I headed after him, keen to dissuade him, dodging past the other parents, and, as I did so, Connor sat back down on the beam.

Good, I thought. Perhaps he was going to shimmy down and put an end to it. But I was wrong. He was merely relocating further along, the better to call down and argue his case. 'Well, I'm *definitely* not coming down now then, you fucking idiot. An' if you try to come and get me, I'll kick you in the bollocks and then I'll feed you to the porn queen of Brixton!' he shouted. 'Just you see if I don't!'

I took Tyler's wrist and squeezed it. 'Don't go up there, love,' I said quietly. 'That's exactly what he's hoping. And I'm rather keen to keep you in one piece.'

'I'm keen to keep *everyone* in one piece,' came a voice

from behind me. A male voice. 'That your boy up there?' he asked me.

I turned and nodded. 'Kind of. He's my responsibility, anyway. He's in care,' I explained. 'Between placements. We've just got him for the weekend. His name's Connor.'

This was clearly the manager because he had a whistle on a string round his neck. Perhaps he'd have better luck coaxing Connor down. He blew it, though to what end I didn't know. He already had Connor's full attention. 'Come on down, Connor, lad,' he coaxed. 'It's not safe up there. Get down now and that's the end of it. You'll not be in any trouble.'

As if he'd care, I thought. He'd probably be hundreds of miles away in just over a day. But the manager couldn't know that and I wasn't about to tell him. Though, on the plus side, his intervention had at least signalled a kind of end to things, because the crowd that had assembled began drifting away.

All but a committed core of anxious parents, at any rate. Which was still audience enough to keep Connor astride his rafter, despite further barked commands from the manager. Why wouldn't he stay up there? What exactly could they do? And while he still had their attention he was still having fun. Which gave me an idea. 'I tell you what,' I said, keeping my voice down. 'Can you go with me on something? Let me try another tack?'

'What sort of tack?' the manager asked, looking anxious.

'The leaving tack,' I told him quietly. 'As in Tyler and I

leave – well, pretend to, at any rate. We'll only be outside, but I've a hunch it'll do the trick.'

The man, whose name badge read 'Declan Patterson, Centre Manager', was around Kieron's age, I reckoned, and seemed happy to go with whatever tack I came up with, even winking at me surreptitiously as I sent Tyler off to get his coat with a loud, 'That's it, I've had enough of this! We're leaving!'

I then flapped an arm upwards, before talking as if to a full house in the theatre. 'I'm sorry, but we have to go. Can I leave my phone number at the entrance? Would that be okay? Then if he decides to come down – or if he falls or anything – just give me a ring, will you? Though there's a thought,' I added, turning back just as I was about to sweep Tyler out of the place, 'can you make sure it's not between six and seven? Only that's when I watch *Emmerdale* on catch-up.'

I doubted Connor could have seen Mr Patterson's uncomfortable expression or, indeed, Tyler's monumental struggle not to laugh. But he could certainly hear me, and must have had the proverbial bird's-eye view of our departure through the security barrier and then out of sight.

'We're not really going anywhere, are we?' Tyler wanted to know, once we were back out in the building's entrance.

'Don't be daft,' I said, pulling him against the wall by the double doors, the better to keep an eye on developments. 'Just using toddler-taming tactics, that's all. Give it five minutes – ten, absolute tops – and my hunch is he'll be shimmying down and following us through those doors;

behaving like a clown's only fun when you have an audience.'

Though I wasn't as confident as I sounded (Connor was an unknown quantity, after all) it wasn't even five minutes before he burst through the door and headed back out into the car park – or, rather, would have done if he hadn't caught sight of the pair of us out of the corner of his eye.

He stopped dead in his tracks and did a Tom and Jerry-style slow-motion double-take, before thrusting his hands in his jeans pockets and trying to inject some swagger back into his stance. 'Ha! Had you then!' he crowed. 'Done you both up like kippers! *Oh, Connor! Don't fall, Connor! Oh, Connor, come down!*' He laughed and puffed out his bony little chest. 'You don't know me,' he added. 'I'm like a *pro* at doing high wire. I done circus skills, I have. Sammy the Dwarf an' the Porn Queen of Sarf Landen taught me everyfing they know.'

It was something of a job not to laugh. Not to mention something of a job not to form the bizarre mental picture of Tyler being devoured by the Porn Queen of Sarf Landen while Connor was being coached by Sammy the Dwarf. But this was no time for laughing. The smile I was trying not to crack was born of relief more than anything.

'Car!' I barked. 'Right now. I'm not very happy with you, Connor. You've spoiled the day now – not just for you, but for me and Tyler, too. I'm going to have to think seriously about what to do with you after that little episode. About whether I can trust you enough to even take you out of the house. Is that what you want?' I asked as I frog-marched him across the car park. 'To spend the whole time you're with us locked indoors?'

Connor only shrugged as I unlocked the car and briskly clipped him into his seatbelt. 'Don't care what you do,' he said. 'You can do what you like. Lock me in, leave me out. Makes no difference to me. I'm off to live with me dad soon, anyways.'

'Yeah, right,' Tyler said.

'Yeah, *fucking* right!' Connor growled, swivelling to face him. 'You got a problem with that?'

'And what if I have?' Tyler said. 'What you going to do? Set Sammy the Dwarf on me?'

And it wasn't even Saturday teatime.

Chapter 6

'Sammy the Dwarf?' Mike said as I slid a couple of frozen pizzas into the oven. '*Seriously*?'

I'd regaled him with the key points of our all too brief outing, and, like me, he was inclined to see the funny side. And, to be fair, by the time we were home the mood had lightened considerably, Connor getting over his strop – and the telling off he got for it – by responding to Tyler's comment not by maintaining his aggression but by seeming keen to appease him. Indeed, he'd become very chatty, regaling us with a potted history of his diminutive circus mentors, who it turned out had been quite key figures in his young life.

'A drinking friend of his dad's,' I explained to Mike now. 'Him and someone called Lydia, aka the 'Porn Queen of South London' by all accounts. Seems they used to look after him a fair bit when Connor's dad was out "working".'

'By which you presumably mean "robbing",' Mike observed drily. 'And by the sound of it, he's spent a fair bit of time with that father of his down the years, hasn't he?' He shook his head. 'No wonder he's such a delicate soul, eh? You couldn't make it up, could you?'

But though the situation had been defused and Connor was once again contrite, I still felt a seed of anxiety growing within me about what was going to happen to him long term. What would happen if they *didn't* find a place for him on Monday? Did I ask them to collect him anyway? In reality, were we acting like we were playing pass the parcel? Having torn off a sheet of him, were we simply pushing him on to the next foster carer?

In truth, I hoped they'd have a place for Connor, and coming face to face with that fact really upset me. I'd never thought like that before about *any* child we'd cared for, not even a scrawny eight-year-old with so little going for him. And it wasn't as if I was inexperienced with kids who were angry, disobedient and out of control. They were my stock-in-trade, even when they were trying their hardest to be unlovable. No, there was something else about Connor; something in the core of his being. Something I'd yet to put my finger on.

But if I thought I'd have a minute's peace to mull over my concerns I was wrong.

Once we'd all been fed, I decided I needed to burn off some excess energy as well, and in the time-honoured fashion. So, Mike having elected to slope off and build some flat-pack furniture with Kieron, I told the boys they could have the living room to themselves for a couple of hours.

Satisfied that I'd made myself clear, I then left them to it while I tackled the dinner plates and then pulled my cleaning stuff out of the kitchen cupboard. I smiled as I donned my Marigolds. I was quite looking forward to a spot of 'me' time, even if the 'me' in question was donning rubber gloves and squirting various cleaning sprays.

But I should have remembered that the phrase 'five minutes' peace' hadn't been turned into the title of a book for no reason. Yes, it was probably longer than that, but it certainly didn't feel a lot longer before I heard thumps and bangs and shouts coming from the living room. I yanked off the Marigolds and went to investigate.

We usually kept the big double doors opened fully back so that the living and dining areas merged into one much bigger space, but to create some privacy for all – particularly given this particular fraught weekend – I had closed them earlier, giving us two separate rooms. I opened both. 'What's going on in here?' I wanted to know. 'What's all the noise for?' I had to shout to be heard above the noise of the blaring television.

Which neither seemed to be sitting and watching. Indeed, neither boy was sitting at all. Tyler was standing behind the sofa, both hands gripping the headrest, while Connor was standing in front of it, looking cartoonishly frozen in mid-sprint, as if in a party game someone had just shouted 'Freeze!'

I ignored him and looked at Tyler. 'Ty, what's going on?'

'It's that little idiot,' Tyler replied, jabbing a finger in Connor's direction. 'Just because I wouldn't play his stupid "smack-each-other-round-the-head-with-cushions" game.' He pointed to his book, which was lying open at the other end of the sofa. 'So he ripped a page out of that and then ran round the furniture with it. Idiot! You're gonna pay for that. That's a school book, that is!'

'No I never, you fucking tourist!' Connor yelled back. 'I was minding me own beeswax an' you just belted me one. That's why I ripped your stupid book!'

I could see the rage in Tyler's face. 'He's a liar, Casey!' he yelled, running around the sofa to try to grab his tormentor. But he was too slow, Connor deftly leaping up onto the coffee table and vaulting the sofa in a single bound.

'Right!' I shouted, using an arm to block Tyler from attempting to hurdle it, too. I used my free hand to grab the remote and switch off the racket blaring from the TV. The resulting silence was deafening. 'I warned you, didn't I?' I said, throwing the remote down on the sofa. 'In fact, Connor, you can forget your bath. Go to your bedrooms, the pair of you.'

'What?' Tyler huffed indignantly. 'What did *I* do?'

'To your rooms,' I said again. 'And get your pyjamas on, please, Connor.'

'Ain't got none,' came the answer.

'Yes you have,' I replied. 'There's a pair folded on your bed. Go on. Hoppit!' I finished. 'I'll be up to speak to you both in five minutes.'

'But Casey –' Tyler began again. 'I never *did* anything, I swear!'

I didn't doubt that at all, and felt extremely sorry for Tyler. But at that moment I could see no other right way to act. Not till I'd spoken to them individually, at any rate. To focus my recriminations on Connor now would be to play right into his hands. It was a case of one's word against the other's, after all, and to accept Tyler's without question would be unfair. No, we'd go through the motions and I'd make things right with Tyler when I went to speak with him.

'I'm sorry, love,' I said, 'but until I get to the bottom of it, I need you *both* to go to your rooms. I'll be up in a minute and we can talk.'

Tyler stomped out, his cheeks ablaze, and Connor watched him go, before adopting his usual swagger and following suit. But not before delivering what he'd obviously been preparing as his parting shot. Looking me up and down in a way I can only describe as pitying, he turned in the doorway and rolled his eyes. 'I'm a celebrity,' he drawled. 'Get me outta this dump!'

Tyler had put his own pyjamas on, even though I hadn't asked him to, and looked the picture of gloom as he sat on the bed, a vision in fleecy black and white stripes.

'I'm so sorry, love,' I said, joining him on the bed and putting an arm around him. 'And trust me, Ty,' I said as he leaned into me, 'I know it's not your fault. I just wish you'd have come straight to the kitchen to tell me when he started acting up. That way I could have dealt with him there and then.'

He sighed heavily, all the huff and puff having gone out of him, thankfully. 'I didn't get the *chance*, Casey,' he whispered. 'I don't think you realise just how bad he is. The things he says. He's, like, proper filthy. Honest, you'd never think he was eight. Trust me, he uses words even *I've* never heard of! Seriously, Casey. He's a full-on nightmare, that's what *he* is!'

I supressed a smile at his expression. He seemed right about it, too. 'I know, sweetie,' I said. 'And like I said, I'm sorry. Look, we've only another day to go, and as you've done nothing wrong, how about you get that Xbox back out and have a play on it now? And maybe come back downstairs once me laddo is in bed? Mike'll be home in half an hour or so, won't he? Perhaps you can both watch *Match of the Day*.'

He looked happier. 'Can I now? I'll be extra, extra quiet. I'll be – what's that? You hear that?'

I had heard something. We both listened again, hard. There was another sound. One that was horribly familiar. 'Oh, for pity's sake!' I said, rising and dashing to the window. I scooped the curtain back.

'Was that what I thought it was?' Tyler asked, following.

'Yup,' I confirmed. 'Oh, for pity's *sake*!'

Chapter 7

We've had all kinds of kids down the years, and seen pretty much everything. And there are few things more anxiety inducing than a child with a penchant for absconding. Which will be no surprise to any parent – or foster parent, for that matter. There you are, charged with taking care of a young, vulnerable person, so when that person disappears, you're – in absence of a better word – jiggered.

Not that Connor was showing any signs of absconding, not at that moment. He was down in the front garden, barefoot, having presumably jumped from his bedroom window; or at least, jumped from halfway down the drainpipe that ran down alongside it, as if a character in an Enid Blyton book.

It was an effect that was enhanced by the sight of his red pyjamas, which were patterned with blue, green and white teddies. But neither impression was consistent with what was coming out of his mouth – nothing cuddly or Enid Blytonish about *that*. In fact the only redeeming feature about the string of obscenities he was yelling up at us was that, screaming like a banshee as he was, much of it was incomprehensible.

'Thought you'd lock me up, did you, you fucking lunatics?' he shouted, vaulting the low front flower bed and then spinning on the ball of one foot out on the pavement. Which meant half the street could now witness him. 'Well, I escaped, didn't I? An' now I'm off to the phone to ring my dad in nick. So just you wait, right?' He flailed an arm up. 'Just you wait till I tell him! He'll slit your fucking throats, all fucking three of you!' He then bent down and scooped up a handful of gravel from the roadside and proceeded to throw it towards the house, shouting 'Looo-serrrrs!' as he did so.

They say it's all about the timing, and Mike's just then was perfect. Just as Connor hot (or cold) footed it off down the street, the beams of our car headlights swept round the corner and over him, causing him to jump like the proverbial rabbit.

I knew it was our car because it wasn't quite dark yet. But it soon would be, so I prayed Mike would work out what was happening, get out of the car and stop him getting away.

'Come on,' I said to Tyler 'Grab your slippers or something.' And as we rattled down the stairs, I remembered Connor's footwear too, snatching up his trainers before heading out into the street. Yes, it was warm but he was running barefoot down the street and could easily step on a nail or shard of glass.

Mike hadn't managed to catch him, either, and I was all too aware that we'd soon be having company. There wasn't much on telly at that time of the evening, but there was plenty of entertainment outside our house. Well, around our next-door neighbour's car, to be more accurate, where Mike and Connor were now playing cat and mouse, the latter laughing almost hysterically as he feinted right and left, peppering his jeers with a colourful selection of profanities. Tyler was spot on. Full-on nightmare was right.

'Grab him!' Mike spluttered as Connor darted in my direction, having narrowly missed being downed by a flying tackle. I tried my best, dropping the trainers in order to wrestle him to the ground, but he was as slippery as an eel, even in the fleece pyjamas, yanking the bottoms up as he stumbled and then sprinting off up the road, firing back a 'Piss off, you fucking losers!' as he went.

Mike was breathing hard. 'What's he *on*?' he puffed, rubbing his hands to get the dirt off. 'Look at the state of me!' he added, looking down at the dust and grit on the knees of his jeans.

'Look, he's there!' Tyler shouted from the doorstep. 'Up by Mrs Grey's house! Behind that car! Oop, no he's not! Casey, he's heading that way. I just saw him. Over the road. By that blue car up on the left!'

Mike cupped his hands around his mouth. 'You come right back here this minute!' he boomed. Then, lowering his arms, 'If he's planning on going, why the hell doesn't he just *go*?' He shook his head again. 'What's he *on*?'

'Attention,' I said, cringing as I saw old Mrs Grey watching from her window. And presumably having heard much of the language flying about, too. 'So you know what?' I said, feeling suddenly inspired. 'How about we go back inside and pretend to ignore him, same as I did this afternoon?'

Mike shook his head and smiled, though without a lot of humour. 'He's actually just said that to me – well, as good as – before you came out. No, I'd better chase him down, love, while you ring the EDT. Doubt they'll be able to do much, but we ought to let them know. Right!' he added, raising his voice again and handing me the car keys. 'You've got ten seconds, lad, or there's going to be trouble! You hear me?' he finished, sprinting back off down the road.

'Mike, he's off again!' yelled Tyler. 'Behind the white car! Now the red car! Mike, he's gone down that alley! Oh, what a *shame*,' he finished dryly, as I ran back up the garden path to join him. 'I think he really *is* running away.'

Despite his apparent glee at seeing off his tormentor, Tyler was really keen to get dressed and go and help Mike, but I shook my head. 'Thanks, but no, love. It's not your job to be running around after him and even if it was – even if you managed to catch up with him – I'm not sure you'd manage to get him back. No, you keep an eye out for Mike while I phone the EDT. We need them to take charge of this now.'

Well, would have been, had they answered, which they didn't seem to want to. I was still hanging on the phone, re-dialling and re-dialling, when Mike returned a quarter of an hour later. He was empty handed.

I went to hang up, but he stopped me. 'No, keep trying, love. He's vanished. I reckon he's gone over one of the walls and got through the backs somehow. He's nowhere on the street, and if he's still in earshot he's ignoring me. Though Christ knows where he thinks he's going to go with nothing on his feet and in a pair of flipping pyjamas!'

'To find a phone box,' I told him, 'so he can call his father "in the nick".'

'And get us murdered in our beds,' added Tyler.

'That so?' asked Mike. 'Well, he'll be looking a while then. I think the last time there was a phone box in this neck of the woods it was about 1993. I –'

He stopped then, in response to my hand, which I'd flapped, the duty officer having finally answered the phone. I ran through what had happened, then answered the usual questions: a physical description, plus the events that led up to him running off, step by step, from my overhearing his altercation with Tyler in the living room, to the actions I'd taken, to his climbing out of the window. I was then told, as I'd known I would be, that I must next call the police and go through the whole process once again.

It was a futile business, I always thought, the system we had in place; to have to go through such a rigmarole when in reality they couldn't do anything – well, apart from telling you to phone the police. But it was protocol, and protocol was king, so I had no choice.

'Am I in trouble?' Tyler asked me, as I dialled the local station.

'Trouble?' I asked him. 'Why would you be in trouble?'

He looked anxious. 'Well, I was there, wasn't I? It was me he was rowing with. What if he doesn't come back? What *then*?'

'Ty, mate,' Mike said, putting an arm around his shoulder. 'You are not in any trouble. Not the tiniest bit of trouble.'

'But I called him things,' he said, as I began explaining what had happened to a police officer. 'I told him I'd punch his lights out. That's, like, assault, isn't it?'

Mike put his mouth to Tyler's ear and whispered something I couldn't catch. But could guess at. And at least it put a smile on Tyler's face.

Needless to say, there wasn't much the police could really say to me, because at this point there was little they could do. Except mount a manhunt, which given he'd been 'missing' precisely 20 minutes, felt unlikely. Though, given Connor's age and the background I'd sketched out for them, they at least promised that, assuming he didn't turn up in the next half hour, they'd send someone out to get some more information.

'So that's it?' Tyler wanted to know. 'No one's going to look for him? He can, like, just disappear?'

'Well, not disappear, exactly,' I told him. 'Given how far he is from home, that would be fairly difficult. I mean, where would he go? He has no friends here, no shoes and no money. I suppose he *could* find a phone box and make a reverse charge call, but even if he has the number of the prison memorized, he's not silly enough not to know what would happen next. They'd tell him to go home, wouldn't they? Tell the police.'

'Trace the call, even?' Tyler asked.

'I doubt that,' said Mike. 'You know, perhaps I'll jump back in the car, have a drive around. See if I can spot him. He's going to be difficult to miss in those pyjamas, after all.'

'Can I come with you, Mike? *Please*?' Tyler asked him. 'Two sets of eyes are better than one, after all.'

'I don't know, mate. It's not your problem ...'

'*Please*, Mike.' He turned to me. '*Please*, Casey? I know he hates me, but you never know. I might be able to talk him down, mightn't I?'

'Talk him *down*?' said Mike. 'Blimey, I hope it's not going to come to that, mate! Go on, then,' he said. 'Go and dress again, while I grab the torch.'

'Yess!' Tyler said, doing one of his trademark fist pumps.

'Hates you?' I went to ask him. 'Where on *earth* did you get that from?' but he'd already thundered up the stairs.

Chapter 8

Eight o'clock came and went and, alone in the house, I re-donned my Marigolds and set to work with a vengeance. There wasn't much that needed cleaning – almost nothing, in fact – but it filled the time I'd have otherwise spent pacing up and down, fretting about something I could do absolutely nothing about anyway.

We'd been here before. A few years earlier we'd had a serial absconder; another lad with a grim start of indifference and neglect behind him. And I thought of that phrase again: 'five minutes' peace'. It was one that had a lot to commend it, but at the same time it had a lot of uncomfortable connotations; was it a craving for five minutes' peace that led Connor's mother to give up on him the way she had?

I was also concerned about Tyler. He clearly felt responsible for Connor running off, and I prayed that it would be him who would spot him and return him. At the very least

I needed to make clear to him that Connor behaving as he'd done was absolutely not his fault.

As for fault itself, as a concept, where it concerned a child like Connor, where did you start in apportioning blame? And where did it end, more to the point? What would happen to him next? Another children's home? Then another? Till the heart was completely ripped from him? Assuming that hadn't already happened long before.

In the short term, the 'crisis' (as it would be described in my log when I wrote it up later) came to an end just over an hour later. The promised officer had arrived and had just left with all the particulars, when the doorbell rang again, several times in quick succession. I thought it might be Mike and Tyler, in too much of a rush to use either of their keys, but I opened the door to reveal a man from the end of the road – one whom we had up to now been only on waving terms with – clutching an irritable-looking Connor by the pyjama collar.

'Oh thank goodness!' I said in relief as I knelt down in the hall and did that thing that mums do, as though checking for broken bones. I held Connor's arms out and scrutinized him and then looked up to our knight in shining armour. 'Thank you *so* much for bringing him back,' I said, as I relinquished my hold on Connor. 'Where did you find him?'

The man grinned and held his hand out to shake. 'You must be Casey, then. I'm Nev. Nev Thompson. From number 42.' He grinned again, and ruffled Connor's hair. In the short time of their acquaintance, our little escapologist had obviously managed to charm him. 'In my shed,' he finished. 'Hunkering down with all the mice and spiders.'

I decided I'd better attempt to give our neighbour some kind of explanation. 'My husband Mike and I are foster carers,' I said. 'He's out with my foster son looking for this young man as we speak. Connor here is staying for the weekend. There was a bit of an altercation between the boys, and ... well, as you can see ...'

Nev held his hand up. 'No worries. I know how it goes. I'll leave you all to it.' He then patted Connor's shoulder. 'And perhaps you can have a chat with Mum ... erm ... this lovely lady, and tell *her* what you know about the bones under the floorboards, lad, eh?' He then winked at me. 'Save calling the police out unnecessarily ...'

'Bones, Connor?' I said, confused. 'Bones under the floorboards?'

'Hundreds of them apparently,' Mr Thompson confirmed. He was clearly enjoying this. 'Of all the foster kids who've apparently been starved to death and then buried under the floor. And as I said to young Connor here, you might be keen to hear about them. Only you've not lived here that long, have you?'

'Erm, no we haven't,' I confirmed, looking pointedly at Connor, who, if it had been humanly possible, I think would have screwed his head right down into his pyjama top. As it wasn't, he had no choice but to face it out.

'Bodies?' I asked again.

But it seemed Connor had nothing to add at this point, so I thanked Mr Thompson. 'And we'll be sure to investigate the starving foster-child situation,' I added, trying not to grin.

But, of course, this was really no laughing matter, and any displays of mirth were as much about relief that he was back safely as about the ridiculous nonsense he'd concocted. Street-wise and old for his years he might be in some ways, but in others he was eight through and through.

'Where on earth did you think you were going, love?' I asked him once I'd herded him into the living room and texted Mike and Tyler that he'd been returned. 'What did you think you were going to do? Spend the night in a garden shed?'

'I've slept in worse,' he huffed sullenly, his shoulders now drooping. 'You don't know the half of what I've done. You really don't.'

Then he burst into tears.

I did as I'd always do at that point. I pulled him close to me and rocked him while he cried, and though he was stiff at first, he soon wilted and let it all go.

'I'm sorry, Casey,' he said eventually, still not raising his head from my chest. I stroked his hair, which still smelt of cold and fresh air, acutely aware of Mike and Tyler heading home, and wondering if they'd be quite as sympathetic. 'I just got a bit giddy an' all that. Like I do, sometimes. You know, lose it a bit. Go off on one.'

'Well, you certainly did that, love.'

'But I never mean to. Not really. You know, not to *really* run away. I was just messing about,' he finished – oddly, given what he'd only just told me. 'Am I in big trouble?'

I thought for a few moments before answering. It would have been so easy, given my relief, to tell him that no, that was an end to it. That we'd now finish our evening, and that everything would be fine. That way, we could trundle on with the business of containment till Monday, as per the plan. But I couldn't, because that suddenly felt all wrong. And particularly wrong, given that Tyler was involved. Conscious that I needed to be able to tell him I'd thrown at least half the rulebook at Connor, I knew I had to take a firmer line.

'No, not *big* trouble, Connor, but this isn't something we can just brush off. We had to report you missing to the police, love. It's the law and we were very worried about you. And we've potentially wasted lots of their valuable time.'

He was suddenly animated. 'The cops!' he spluttered. 'You phoned the cops! You grassed on me?' He looked dumbstruck. 'God, you'd get your fingers chopped off for that in London!'

It was so unexpected that, again, I had to suppress a smile. And another mental image; of the place in London where you might find acrobatic dwarfs who hung about with ladies of the night, while gangsters removed people's fingers.

Not to mention where foster kids were routinely murdered and buried beneath the carpets. What a curious collection of stuff Connor had in his head. 'Relax,' I said. 'We only reported you missing, love. That's all. But they won't be too pleased to know that you've been giving everyone the run around. Imagine if a really serious crime had been committed while you were hiding, and there were no police to go and solve it because they were all busy looking for you? A missing child as young as you means that everyone drops *everything* to go find them, Connor. And not just the police. Mike and Tyler have been out searching for you for an hour. What do you think *they* are going to have to say when they get back?'

He looked at me with a completely different expression then. 'Really?' he said, as if genuinely surprised. 'Blimey. I thought that Tyler kid hated me.'

The front door banged before I had the chance to reply and, half a minute later, in came Mike and 'that Tyler kid' himself.

'So the prodigal son returns,' Mike said as he took his coat off. 'Mate, you've caused quite a bit of trauma this evening. I hope you've got a good explanation, because we can't be having this. None of us can.'

Connor's face was a picture of contrition. 'I'm sorry, Mike; an' sorry, Tyler,' he said, looking from one to the other. 'Honest to God I am. I never even knew how long I was gone.' He gestured with a thumb. 'I was only hiding in a garden shed over the road. I thought you'd find me straight away, like. Honest I did.'

'Yeah, right,' Tyler said irritably. '*Course* you did.'

* * *

With Saturday evening fast disappearing beneath us, I decided that now wasn't the time for a post-mortem. With everybody tired I said the matter was closed – at least till both boys were up in their bedrooms, and I'd had a chance to debrief Mike first.

I made Connor a hot chocolate – Tyler hadn't wanted one – and filled Mike in properly while the marshmallows on the top began to melt. Despite the way our evening had been so comprehensively hijacked, I thought he'd at least find Connor's bit about the bodies under the floorboards amusing.

He didn't. 'Well, that's all very well coming from a neighbour down the street, because most of them know what we do. But imagine him telling that to a complete stranger? I mean, I know it's too ridiculous for anyone sensible to believe, but what with the things you hear on the news these days …' He shook his head thoughtfully.

'Love, I can't imagine anyone would give it so much as a moment's consideration,' I said. 'Honestly – can you?'

'Yes, but if a child makes an accusation, you know how it works, Case. It has to be *acted* upon, doesn't it? Has to be seen to be looked into.'

'Honest, love,' I said. 'I don't think we have to start worrying about the Keystone Cops flying round and pulling up the laminate!'

I was grinning, but he looked mildly exasperated. Which I suppose he had a perfect right to. 'I'm not saying they're going to,' he said. 'I'm just pointing out that he'll be leaving here on Monday and might tell all sorts of porkies about his time here. Things that people conceivably *might* believe.'

Mike was right, of course, but there was nothing to be done about that and, besides, I thought, as I trotted upstairs with the drink, Connor had a file thicker than Tyler's. So everyone would know what a troubled kid he was.

And certainly one with a vivid imagination. 'Bodies under the floorboards, indeed,' I gently chided him as I took in his hot chocolate.

Since he was already tucked up in bed, reading a comic and looking like butter wouldn't melt, I placed the mug down on his bedside table. I then sat down on the bed and drew a hand across his forehead to smooth his hair back. 'Next thing you'll be telling me we have fairies at the bottom of the garden.' I grinned. 'Or are fairies too wet for a hard man like you?'

He grinned sheepishly. 'I was only joking,' he insisted. 'Honest, Casey. Just pulling the man's leg.'

'Well, those aren't the kind of jokes that are funny,' I told him gently. 'If you tell fibs all the time and make stuff up, how will anyone ever know if you're telling the truth? And you never know, the day might come when it really matters that someone does. Have you ever read the story about the boy who cried wolf?'

He shook his head. 'Nah. I don't like proper reading much. I prefer me comics.'

'No need to read it,' I said, rising. 'I'll tell you it tomorrow.' Then I had a thought. 'Tell me, Connor,' I said,

'Sammy the Dwarf and Lydia the Porn Queen – are *they* real?'

He looked confused. 'Course they're real!'

My expression must have told him I thought otherwise because he wriggled into a more upright position. 'Honest they are, Casey. They're me dad's mates. They used to look after me.'

'*Really*, Connor?'

He nodded vigorously. 'Yeah, yeah. Real as I am. Used to be round ours all the time – well, when me dad was home, anyway. They used to sleep over sometimes too.' He grinned at a memory. 'It was Lyds who taught me how to play pontoon.'

Lyds. As presumably in Lydia, as in the Porn Queen.

'And seven-card brag,' he enthused. 'Least I think it was seven-card. Might have been five-card. Whatever. They were like me best mates, them two, they really were.'

He looked sad all of a sudden. Genuinely bereft. 'You must miss them, then,' I said.

He nodded. 'Like mad.'

He seemed to think a moment, as if unsure whether to open up to me more about them.

'So when did you last see them, then?' I asked.

'Oh, it was ages ago now. I shoulda been allowed to stay with them. That was what me dad wanted.'

'For them to take care of you?'

He nodded. 'While he was inside, yeah. And they could've done, too. I stayed with 'em a whole week once. Hid under the stairs when the cops came so they couldn't take me back into care while me dad was inside for the week for his fines an' that.'

We were returning to the realms of, if not the wholly unbelievable, certainly the 'somewhat muddled, perhaps, in the telling'. I couldn't imagine how the authorities would allow that to happen.

But it apparently had. 'Lydia never told the cops I was there. She gave them some cock and bull story about me having gone round a friend's and that. Then they stayed and looked after me when the cops went away. They kept saying if the cops came back they'd have to hand me over, but they never did.'

He looked thoughtful again, perhaps imagining a world in which he could stay with his 'best mates' for ever, rather than being shunted from care home to care home, already a loner and social outcast. Discarded by his mother, let down by his criminal father, with only a couple of what appeared to be also social misfits taking care of him – his only points of reference in a very cruel world.

'I'll bet they miss you, too,' I said. 'And who knows?' I added, aware that Connor was still in contact with his dad. 'Maybe you'll see them again at some point, eh?' I bent to kiss his forehead. 'And I'll bet they'd like that, too.'

Chapter 9

Having tucked Connor in I padded across the landing to check on Tyler, a thought already half forming in my head. Poor old Tyler, whose day had been derailed as well, and with whom I'd barely had a proper chance to chat – particularly given that come Monday he'd be off on his football-skills course.

He had his back to me, curled on his side, his headphones plugged in; obviously listening to music on his iPod. 'Hey,' I said, touching his shoulder, causing him to roll towards me sleepily. 'Maybe time you took those out and got some shut-eye, eh?'

I helped him remove the plugs from his ears and kissed him goodnight. 'Quite a day we've had today, eh?' I added as I switched his bedside light off. 'Like a whirlwind, that one, isn't he? Hope he didn't completely ruin your day.'

'Is that what I was like?' he said sleepily. 'Was I that bad when I first came?'

'Oh, you were *much* worse,' I ribbed him. 'Absolute *nightmare*, you were. They broke the mould when they made you, as you already know.' I jumped on him and gave him a bear hug through the covers. Tyler liked hearing about what a 'nightmare' he'd been in much the same way as some kids – kids with less complicated pasts – liked hearing about the antics they got up to as toddlers. Mad but true. Especially when I finished up, as I always did, by telling him how Mike and I fell so in love with every little part of him that we couldn't, shouldn't, *wouldn't* let him go. 'And you're alright, love?' I finished. 'You know. About Connor being here?'

He nodded through half-closed lids. 'I'm fine,' he said. 'Honest. You'd never manage him without me in any case, would you?'

I gave him a last kiss and conceded he was probably right.

It's amazing what a couple of glasses of wine and a DVD can do to restore your flagging spirits, because the next morning Mike and I were both feeling positive and energetic. 'We'll pack the car up, *whatever* the weather decides to chuck at us,' Mike had suggested. 'Just drive out to the country, have a picnic, play football, feed the ducks, or the swans, or whatever they have there. Make a day of it. Tire the little tyke right out.'

I'd agreed, so we were now doing exactly that; preparing and packing a huge picnic, hunting down old trainers and right-size wellies, and throwing bats, balls and buckets into bags. If containment it was to be then we'd do just that, via the perhaps unlikely but probably easier option of containing him in the great outdoors.

We'd not heard another peep from EDT and didn't expect to. As things stood the plan still was for them to have him collected on Monday morning, a plan I imagined they'd confirm at some point on Sunday night. 'But what if they don't?' I said to Mike while the boys were upstairs dressing. 'Or what if they tell us it might take another few days?'

In truth, the thought that had been forming in my own mind overnight was that if it did take a few more days, it wouldn't be a major problem. With Ty going off on his footie course on the Monday morning, I could devote all my energies to Connor, at least for a couple of days. Better that, I'd pretty much decided, than have him dragged off somewhere horrible – some grim secure unit in the middle of nowhere. And with the kind of fostering Mike and I usually did, I knew about such places, and with the kind of file Connor had, I knew it was highly likely – particularly given the violent incident – that a grim secure unit might be exactly where he would be headed. Unless they had the luxury of a few more precious days to track down a carer with a tad more positivity.

Mike turned towards me. 'You're not thinking what I *think* you're thinking, Case?' he asked, looking pointedly at me.

'Well, um, no, but, yes, but … oh, I don't know,' I confessed, feeling scrutinised. 'We'll cross that bridge when we come to it, love, shall we?'

'Blimey,' Tyler said, having bowled into the kitchen. 'We camping for a week or summat? How much food is *in* this bag?'

Saved by the proverbial bell.

Chapter 10

We drove out to a spot that we'd been coming to for decades. A big country park with a few acres of forest, a big river running through it and, beyond it, accessed via stepping stones, a swathe of open land that was perfect for picnics and ball games. And with the various travails of yesterday apparently forgotten, both boys seemed in good – and high – spirits.

Perhaps slightly too high spirits, as it turned out.

I've never been particularly sure-footed in such situations, so though the water couldn't have been more than two or three feet deep at that point, getting me across was something of a military manoeuvre. Rather like in the story, Mike had to plan it carefully, taking all the stuff that I'd been carrying across the river first, then, his hands now free, coming back over to collect me.

'You're not going to have him give you a piggy back, are you?' said Tyler, laughing. 'Because if you are, give me a mo so I can pull out my phone and film it.'

I gave him a pretend cuff around the ear for that – in fact, the idea *had* crossed my mind – but in the end I was able to cross to the other side without incident, all by myself, using Mike's hand to give me precious confidence.

And I was just congratulating myself on my achievement when I heard a splash. Groaning inwardly, I turned, expecting to see Connor, messing about. But it was Ty I saw, knee deep in the glittering water by the bank, his expression thunderous but his phone thankfully still in his hand.

'I was trying to effing help you!' he roared at Connor. 'What the hell did you do that for?'

'I di'n't do nothing!' Connor responded, hopping nimbly up onto the bank and rushing across to help Tyler out. 'I just tried to grab his hand, Casey, honest!' he said, turning to both of us. 'An' then I slipped! Here, let me help you, Tyler. Gimme your phone before you drop it!'

Tyler scowled at him. 'Yeah, right – and yanked me right into the water! Cheers for that, mate,' he said. 'Great job!'

Mike hurried across and held a hand out, pulling Tyler to the bank easily, while our furious teenager batted Connor's outstretched hand away.

'Oh, God, mate,' Connor said. 'I'm so *sorry*. I really am. Have we got any spare clothes, Casey? Tyler, d'you want to wear my trackies? They'll be a bit short on you, but –'

'No, I do *not* want to wear your trackies!' Tyler said, accepting a towel from me while Mike held his phone. 'I'll be fine,' he said, looking at me. 'I'll put my board shorts on instead.'

'Good idea,' I agreed, anxious to defuse the situation and hugely glad I'd packed some swimming shorts. 'They'll dry in the sun easy enough, won't they?'

But Tyler wasn't to be mollified. Having divested himself of the wet trousers and sodden trainers, he stomped off in shorts and flip-flops to the picnic area.

'Thank heavens for Mary Poppins, eh?' Mike joked, obviously also trying to make light of it as we followed Tyler up the path to where the picnic benches were. 'We may all scoff, but where would we all be without her? Up blankety-blank creek without a paddle, I reckon, Connor, don't you?'

But Connor, whose hand I was holding, was on his own track. 'He's going to really hate me now, isn't he?' he whispered, tugging on it lightly.

'Oh, he'll come round,' I reassured him. 'After all, accidents happen, don't they? And you'd be amazed what a difference a jumbo sausage roll makes. And an apology from you, okay? Even if it *was* an accident. A proper apology makes all the difference in the world.'

He nodded. 'I'll tell him I'm sorry. I *am* sorry, Casey. I was just thinking this morning how he seemed to be getting okay with me now.' He sighed. 'And now I go and do that. D'you think his trainers are gonna be okay?'

'They'll be just fine,' I promised him. 'And they're only his old knocking-around ones, don't worry. Quick spin in the tumble dryer and, spit-spot, they'll be good as new.'

'Like in *Mary Poppins*?'

'*Just* like in *Mary Poppins*,' I reassured him.

Chapter 11

Connor did apologise and, as predicted, Tyler did come round. So much so that by the end of the day I was feeling quite relaxed. Kids had spats, kids had fall-outs. All these things were normal. Heaven knew, I'd seen it enough with my own two. And it was lovely to watch the three of them – Mike being one of the boys as well, of course – kicking a ball around and laughing and joshing with one another, just like every other family at the country park that day. But I was still knocked for six when, just before we were leaving, Connor came over – Mike and Tyler were playing competitive keepy-uppy by this time – and flung his arms around my neck.

I was on my knees at the time, packing up the picnic things, which made it easier, given his diminutive size. He also almost knocked me for six, literally.

'Well, well,' I said, when he released me and looked self-consciously at me through his fringe. 'To what do I owe this unexpected pleasure?'

He knelt down and started helping me. 'Nuffing,' he said. 'Well, nuffing in particular.' He sat back on his heels and shrugged. 'I dunno. I just love being with you lot,' he said. 'I never get to do stuff like this. Well, 'cept with school and then it's *mega*-boring.' He did one of his heavy sighs. 'I wish I didn't have to go tomorrow. I wish I could stay.'

I grinned at him, my heart melting, quite without my telling it to. 'Well, there's a turn-up,' I said. 'I thought we were losers. And what about all those bodies under the floorboards, eh?'

'*Even* with the bodies under the floorboards,' he said, leaping up again, seemingly embarrassed by what he'd said now. Which kind of let me off the hook, because I really didn't know what to say.

We were all exhausted by the time we got home, not least because of the many miles we'd covered, quite apart from anything else and, given that it was Sunday night and Tyler had an early start the following morning, I sent the boys up to get themselves organised while I put Tyler's trainers in the dryer and Mike emptied out the picnic bag.

'And, seeing as we've been so good, Casey,' Connor chipped in, 'and seeing as how this will prob'ly be my last night, can I please, please be allowed half an hour to play Xbox with Tyler before bed?' He looked across at Tyler hopefully. 'Just for a little while? Nothing naughty or anything. Just the footie game? *Please*?'

Tyler didn't seem that fussed – he was probably more interested in getting packed and chatting to his mate Denver, I reckoned – but he nodded. And with Connor's small hands pressed together as if in prayer, how could I say no?

'Go on, then,' I said, turning back to the sodden trainers, 'but I warn you, bath first and then I'll be up to turn everything off in half an hour, so chop chop! You best be quick, hadn't you?'

They both scooted off and, once we'd finished off the chores, Mike and I went for a brief but welcome sit-down. We'd not yet heard from EDT about what was going to happen in the morning, but I was feeling pretty relaxed about that now and I wondered if Mike was, too. I told him what Connor had said about wishing he could stay with us.

Mike lowered the volume on the TV he'd only just switched on. 'Casey, are you saying what I think you're saying?' he asked me.

'I'm not saying anything,' I replied. 'I'm simply telling you what he said. Though I have to say, now that he's settling down a bit, it does seem a bit unfair to shoo him out the door after just one weekend. Not if he's only going to be shipped off to some God-forsaken unit somewhere. How's that going to help him?'

'Love, have you forgotten that this kid attacked his social worker with an iron bar?'

He was astute, Mike, I had to give him that. Because I hadn't forgotten – of course I hadn't – but, on the other hand, I sort of had. It was just becoming so difficult to reconcile the story we'd been told early the previous morning with the slip of a little lad who was currently in the bath upstairs and about whom I was in the middle of a big reassessment. Perhaps the outlook didn't need to be so bleak for him after all.

Mike sighed, obviously reading my mind. 'Love, it's out of our hands anyway. And it's alright having one good day, but we have to think about Tyler, too. Besides that, my guess is that they already have somewhere for him. If they hadn't, I'm pretty sure they would have been on the phone by now, buttering us up.'

'I know,' I said, 'but you know what's likely to happen. They'll just take him off us and bung him anywhere they can find a space. I just think that what with Tyler heading off to footie tomorrow, it's not like it would be a problem for us to hang on to him for a couple more days. You'll be at work anyway and I'm just thinking –'

'That you can burrow beneath the surface, find out what makes him tick, see something in him that no one else has, do him some good, and –'

'And what's wrong with that? Isn't that what we're supposed to try to do?' I wanted to know, feeling myself getting chippy.

'Love, there's *nothing* wrong with that. I just think it would be madness to go off half-cocked about a child you know so little about. Committing to stuff. Getting his hopes up. You haven't said anything to him, have you?' he asked, suddenly looking alarmed.

I shook my head. 'No, of course not!' I said. 'And before

you ask, I haven't said anything to Tyler either.'

'Good,' Mike said. 'Because you can't think about doing anything till you've spoken to him anyway. See how *he* feels about it. It's not just what *we* want. We have to take *his* feelings into account.'

I promised I wouldn't do anything before speaking to him, and once Connor was tucked up in bed I went into Tyler's room to help him finish off his packing. But before I could bring the subject up, Tyler did himself, and I wondered if Mike wasn't the only one able to read my mind.

'So he's going tomorrow then, Connor, is he?' he asked, as I redistributed his shin pads.

I nodded. 'In theory. I've not spoken to EDT yet, but yes, love, that's the plan.'

'They haven't called you, then? To ask if he could stay with us a bit longer?'

'No, they haven't,' I said. 'I imagine they'll pick him up mid-morning. Why d'you ask?'

Tyler glanced at me. 'I was just wondering,' he said. 'You know. He really likes it here now. *Really* likes it. Did he tell you?'

'Yes, he did,' I said. 'We seem to be flavour of the month now, don't we? Bless him. Not that it's hard. He's barely ever known a real home up to now, has he?' I let the thought lie. We both knew that Tyler knew *all* about how that felt. 'What a difference a day makes, eh?' I said eventually. 'Anyway, we'll see. But would you like it if he did, then? You know, just for a bit? Till they can find him somewhere long-term? I rather got the impression earlier that you could have cheerfully throttled him.'

'We-*ell*,' he admitted. 'That's true. I did. But, you know. Whatever,' he finished, turning back to his case. 'If you think you should – that you can help him – that's fine.'

'"Fine"?' I pressed. '*Really*? Not "if you must"?'

'No, really,' he said. 'Honest. It's *fine*.'

Chapter 12

Having told him how much we loved him, I left Tyler to it, and when I went downstairs again Mike and I talked at length. No, we wouldn't commit to anything long term – if he was lucky enough to be found a home rather than a children's home, which was a long shot, Connor really seemed to me to be a boy who needed to be an only child. I might have got a bit misty-eyed about the hand life had dealt him, but I wasn't stupid. His notes were detailed enough for me to know that just as one swallow doesn't make a summer, one agreeable day doesn't the perfect child make. As Mike had pointed out, this was a boy with a very violent episode under his belt less than 48 hours earlier.

But a few more days with us might make the difference between him being carted off to a secure unit and being found a placement that might be altogether more positive for him in the long term. I never forgot that the first child Mike and I ever fostered had come with an equally long list of 'crimes' and it was either us or be banged up in such a place.

Our position decided, I wrote up my log and emailed EDT with my thoughts. It was probably too late to phone them – well, to discuss something like this, anyway – but whoever dealt with it first thing could act on it then. I also copied John Fulshaw in, mostly as a box-ticking exercise. He was only due back home from holiday that morning, and I doubted he'd look at it till he returned to work. Which was fine. He really didn't need to be bothered on this one. My main plan was to see Tyler off first thing in the morning, then, when EDT called me, to just clarify that we'd discussed it and that if the plan was to take Connor temporarily to a secure unit, that there was an alternative that would give them the luxury of a few extra days.

I then went to bed and slept the sleep of the righteous – well, till, about 3 a.m., when something must have woken me.

I lay in the dark for a few minutes, trying to work out what it was that had pinged me into wakefulness so suddenly. It clearly wasn't Mike. Curled up on his side, he wasn't snoring, so it hadn't been that. Then I heard it again. Indistinct, but definitely there.

My first thought being Connor, I slipped from under the covers with the intention of going to check on him, but as soon as I opened my bedroom door I could tell that the sound was coming not from Connor's room but from Tyler's.

And it was the sound, to my surprise, of Tyler crying.

I hurried across, opened the door and then shut it silently behind me.

'Oh, sweetheart!' I said as I saw him sitting up, clasping his knees, in his bed, 'What is it, love? What's the matter?' I asked him, hurrying to his side.

He sniffed and shook his head, 'I'll be okay, Casey. It's nothing. Just a … a nightmare, or something.'

'Or something?' I put my arm around him. 'Tyler, you know me, love. I'm not going anywhere until you tell me what's wrong. What kind of nightmare? What happened? Bogeymen? Monsters? Dropping your mobile down the toilet? Or something *else*?' I clasped him tighter. 'Come on. Spill.'

It took Tyler a moment to compose himself. Then he did spill. 'Do I have to go to the football course tomorrow?' he asked me tearfully.

'Why ever wouldn't you want to?' I asked him gently. 'You've been looking forward to it for weeks.' Then I had a thought. 'Have you and Denver had a falling out?' I asked him.

He shook his head. 'No, it's not that. I just … I just …'

'What, sweetheart? What is it? Come on. You know you can tell me.'

He sniffed some more. I could tell he'd been crying for quite a while. 'I can't …'

'Yes you can. Anything. Come on. Spit it out.'

'It's just … it's just I don't want to go. I just want to stay here and …'

Another long pause. 'And?'

'And make sure *he* doesn't ...'

'Who doesn't?' And then it hit me. 'Connor?'

I felt Tyler stiffen then. Felt the burgeoning adolescent muscles tense under his pyjama top. 'He's a *liar*, Casey. You don't realise!' Tyler almost spat the words out. And then, bit by bit, out it all came at last. It seemed their little Xbox session hadn't been that at all. It had been a 'chat'. About how Connor was going to be moving in with us while he was out of the way. How he knew how to 'play' us. How he knew a good thing when he saw one. How he'd soon have us 'on side' and be the one we 'loved best'.

'And he means it, too,' Tyler finished. 'You don't realise, Casey. Me going in that river? That wasn't an accident. He yanked me in on purpose! Honest, I wouldn't lie to you –'

'Tyler, I'd never doubt you for a moment. You know that.'

He sighed miserably. 'An' I can't *bear* it. To be going off and him standing there all smug, like, waving me off. And still being here when I get back. He'll ruin everything. He will, Casey. I know you've got to do what you're doing, an' I know you feel sad for him – an' I know Mike does as well – but, honest, he'll ruin everything. I *know* he will!'

I held him tight and soothed him, feeling in five kinds of shock, which was ridiculous. That an eight-year-old child could pull the wool over my eyes so completely. That I could be so blind as to not notice how stressed Tyler had been. That I'd the confidence – no, the *arrogance* – to forget all my training, and think I could swoop in and be bloody superwoman where others had failed.

I comforted him and reassured him and promised him things would be fine. That he could go off with Denver secure in the knowledge that when he returned things *would* be back to normal.

I thought about my log and the email I'd already sent, and it took a while for me to settle down again. All I had to do now was expedite it, knowing even as I thought it that EDT might well have already acted upon my message, i.e. *not* acted, no longer being in any sort of rush.

I also had a lot of thinking to do. Not least analysing what an idiot I had been. Thank goodness I'd heeded Mike and not given Connor so much as an inkling that he could stay with us. Only thing was that I now had a potential situation in which we had no choice *but* to keep him, at least for those few days I'd breezily promised and which I could now repent at my leisure.

And even the hardening in my heart was a tricky one. Much as I'd felt angry that Connor had duped me so effectively, there was a part of me that felt the extent of his pain even more. To be just eight years old and to see the world as a place where your fellow human was reduced to being a 'player' or being 'played'. And why wouldn't he try to play us? He'd glimpsed a different sort of life with us. One where the transient carers that he was used to in the various children's homes were replaced by a home and a loving, caring family. Did it matter that he felt not a flicker of emotion for us? No, it didn't. It was a far superior billet than his previous one and, being so 'streetwise', I didn't doubt he knew would be superior to his next.

The behaviour, not the child. That was the mantra I tried to stick to. And, who knew? As his unguarded words about Sammy and the Porn Queen had already hinted at, there always remained the hope that Connor *could* be redeemed in some way. So, yes, a part of me, though my head said *we* couldn't be his redeemers, still felt bad that the alternative was looking so bleak.

It took me a long time to fall back to sleep.

Chapter 13

My alarm went off at 7.00 a.m. on Monday morning and for a while I just lay there, trying to work out just how little sleep I'd had. I could hear Mike in the shower, so, while I waited for it, I crept out onto the landing, then crossed it and quietly opened Tyler's door. He, too, was already up, thankfully, though still in his pyjamas, and on his knees rummaging through his little wheelie suitcase.

'Are my black footy socks in here?' he asked. 'As well as my red ones? 'Cos I just checked the list and it says we need both. And now I can't find them. D'you remember me putting them in?'

'Stop flapping, worrywart,' I said, pleased to see him focused on his course again. 'Everything you need is in there, *including* a new toothbrush. Speaking of which, have you washed yet? Because time's getting on.'

'Just about to,' he said, jumping up and rushing past me through the door.

* * *

Changing my mind – I could shower later – I left Tyler to it and having been back to the bedroom to grab my dressing gown, then went down to the kitchen to boil some eggs for breakfast. I was immediately accosted by Connor, who appeared from behind the kitchen door, going 'Boo!'

'Morning, Casey!' he added, beaming. 'Did I make you jump? Sorry.'

'You did indeed, love,' I confirmed. 'What you doing up so early?'

His expression changed and he sighed as he pulled out a chair at the table. 'I couldn't sleep,' he said. 'I was worrying. Wondering where they were going to take me. Has anyone told you yet? Are those men in the van coming again?'

Amazing how you see things differently when someone has turned the lights on for you. And I was glad to be able to answer him truthfully.

'I don't know yet, love,' I said, 'it's a bit of a case of we'll know when we know. But perhaps getting some breakfast inside you will cheer you up a bit, eh?' I went over to the fridge. 'Ah, and here's Mike,' I added. 'Hello, love. One egg or two?'

But there was scant time for Mike to tell me because just at that point there was a sharp rapping on the front door.

Tyler had walked in just behind Mike and now looked up at the kitchen clock.

'That can't be Denver and his mum, can it?' he said. 'God, they're early.'

They would indeed have been. They were due at 8 and it still wasn't quite 7.30. 'Grab yourself some breakfast, love,' I told him. 'I'm sure it's not them. Probably just the postman with a parcel or something.'

I hoped it would be, too, since I wasn't averse to a bit of online shopping. So I was open-mouthed to see John Fulshaw standing on the doorstep.

'And a very good morning to you, too,' he said, as I hauled my jaw up and ushered him into the kitchen. 'Morning, Mike; morning, lads,' he said. Then he sniffed. 'Can I smell coffee? All over the place I am, with this flipping jet-lag nonsense. So I could definitely do with one, if you don't mind.'

I went to pour him one, making a 'no, I don't know either' face at Mike as I did so.

Who then spoke for me. 'Good holiday?' he asked John.

'Best one in years,' he said. 'Brilliant.' He'd taken his family to Disney World in Florida, so I didn't doubt it for a moment. But why was he *here*?

'So to what do we owe the pleasure?' Mike added, still as confused as I was.

'I'm here to pick up this young man,' he said, turning towards Connor and smiling down at him. 'Got some transport laid on – picking up from the office,' he clarified. 'And in less than an hour from now, so I thought we'd better crack on.'

Connor's expression was hard to watch as John placed a friendly hand on his shoulder and told him not to bolt his food, but that when he was finished he needed to trot upstairs and get his belongings together. 'Time and tide wait for no man, I'm afraid, mate,' he added cheerfully.

Cheerfully, and oddly. 'What, *now*?' Connor said, looking at Mike and me in turn. 'Now this minute? Like, for deffo? Where are you taking me?'

'To the seaside,' John said equably. 'Well, not me personally, obviously. But that's where you're headed. I'll be able to tell you all about it on the way.'

'What, *now*?' Connor asked again, as though he'd not heard him the first time. 'But what's the rush? Why does it have to be today?'

Once again, he looked at me and I struggled to look back at him. He looked as young and vulnerable as a five-year-old, and also close to tears. I felt my resolve slipping down into my boots. Well, my slippers.

'I'm sorry, son, but yes, it does have to be today,' John said gently. 'I can see you've enjoyed your time here, but everything's arranged now, I'm afraid.'

Mike moved towards him. 'Come on, lad,' he said. 'How about I come up and help you get your bits together, eh? And a couple of toys to take with you,' he added, glancing at me. 'How about that?'

Connor went with him, exiting the kitchen on very obviously reluctant legs, and no sooner was he headed upstairs, with Mike right behind him, than the door went again. This time is *was* Denver.

'I'll just get off, then,' Tyler said, the lightness in his legs as he went to grab his case reflected in his voice as well. 'No need to come to the car, Casey,' he said. 'I'll just leave you to sort everything out.'

'Not so fast,' I said, rushing after him and catching up

with him on the path. 'You *really* think you're getting out of here without a hug?' I duly gave him one, while simultaneously waving to Denver's mum, who was sitting in her car. I then inspected him carefully. 'Are you okay?'

Tyler grinned. 'More than okay. *Definitely* more than okay. Now – *please* – let me go, woman!'

'Not so fast,' I said. 'You've not put in your tea order for Wednesday.'

'Meatballs and spaghetti, please!' he yelled back, before jumping in the car. 'Just like normal!' he added through the open window.

Having waved the car round the corner I hurried back inside, my mind at sixes and sevens. 'So where exactly are you taking him?' I asked John, who had been watching me from the kitchen window.

'A place in Kent,' he said. 'Another semi-secure unit.' He must have seen my face fall. 'Casey,' he said, 'you have actually *read* the information you were given, haven't you?'

I nodded. 'Read it and digested it but, oh, John, he's only *eight*.'

'I know,' he said. 'But it's not like the picture I know is in your head. Only three other children ever in place there at one time – so we were lucky. Two staff to each child, and a *very* strict regime. One designed to set firm boundaries and try to prepare children like Connor for living within the confines of a family. A task and a half, but one that's proved to be just the ticket in the past. He'll soon get used to it.' He smiled. 'He'll have to, won't he? Casey, I don't even know why I'm telling you all this.' Then he narrowed his eyes. 'Or – hmm – do I need to tell you it all again?'

But there was no time. Connor was back down and clutching a box Mike had found for him. It was full of toys and games but, from his expression, you'd have thought they were snakes.

'Tell her what?' Connor asked, his cherubic face now set and angry.

'All about your new home, mate,' John said brightly. 'As I was just telling Casey, it sounds lovely. Just the ticket. Anyway, we'd better press on. I think you know the fellas who are going to be driving you down there.'

Connor looked appalled. 'Not them gayers!' he exclaimed, huffing. 'I've already put the hard word out round about them three. An' that dark one better watch out 'cos I've got a flick knife in me bag.'

John smiled as he put down his coffee mug. 'Okay, mate. Whatever you say. Say goodbye, then. It's time we hit the road.'

Connor duly turned to Mike and me. 'Laters, you two,' he said. 'Never wanted to be here anyways with you pair of old farts!'

On which note, he was escorted out of the front door by John, marched down to his car, helped inside and belted up. We followed them down the path, Mike trying hard not to laugh, while all I could think of was that, sometimes, you did have to laugh about stuff like this happening. Or you'd cry.

John walked around the back of the car and opened the driver's door, smiling at us both over the roof.

'Sorry about that,' he said. 'You know, turning up unan-nounced so early.'

'It was certainly a shock,' Mike said, glancing at me. 'We were expecting a call from EDT first.'

John met my eye. 'Jet lag, like I said,' he explained. Or rather didn't explain, because actually, he didn't really need to. 'Let's just call it – let me see, now – an "executive deci-sion",' he said, dipping down and climbing into the car. He then started the engine and buzzed down the passenger-door window. 'As me laddo in the back here says, laters!'

'Are you going to tell me what all that was about?' Mike asked as we headed back up the path.

'I think so,' I said. 'Well, once I've figured it out myself. Which might take some time.'

'You're telling me,' Mike agreed. 'Still, as they say in Memphis, it would appear that Elvis has left the building.'

As had superwoman. That much I *did* know.

Epilogue

A few days after Connor had left us, John Fulshaw popped round, as he does, for a coffee, and explained that, as I'd presumed, he had indeed opened and read my late-night email, and, to use his words, 'could read between the lines and see a disaster in the making, clear as day'.

And, of course, he'd been right. There was no way we could hang on to Connor, because we had to make a choice and our choice had to be Tyler. Sometimes you have to accept that you really can't be all things to all people – all *children*. So I was very grateful for John sweeping in like a one-man SWAT team that Monday morning and taking that difficult decision out of my hands. As I've always said, sometimes my agency link worker knows me better than I know myself.

* * *

When I think about Connor – when I think about fostering generally – I am oddly reminded about a really sad poem I learned as a child. It's by Edgar Guest and called 'A Child of Mine (to All Parents)', and it spoke about the fact that children are only on loan to us for a while. Although this poem has been used over the decades in the most unfortunate of circumstances – often at funerals and memorial services – when children come and go in and out of our doors and our family, the sentiments in it always come back to me.

Mike and I both realise that the children who come and live with us are 'borrowed' children. Their stay may only be brief, but however fleeting it turns out to be, we have a duty to try to have some positive impact on their young lives. I can't lie to you and say that this is always easy, and I can't swear that we can instantly fall in love with every child. We can't. What I can tell you honestly is that we try our best, in whatever time we have, to make their life a little more bearable, and to ensure that they have somewhere warm, safe and loving to hole up until it's time for them to move on.

That's why it hurts if a child – in this case, a child called Connor – has to leave us and we feel we haven't done quite enough. Even when we know we've tried, if we have to hold our hands up and admit that we are stumped and can do no more, we feel inadequate. I suspect that's human nature. It's also difficult because it's like someone has torn the final chapter from a favourite book before we've finished it, before we've had a chance to find out how the story ends.

Happily, for Mike and me, these occasions have been rare, and even on the odd time it *has* happened, we've been lucky enough to have John on the case and to eventually find out what happened next. Connor's story is still being written, of course, and with it out of our hands all we can hope for is that the next place he stayed managed to do good things with him and that one day soon he *will* be placed in a family unit. Who knows? It might be happening as I speak.

As for us, well, I'm still beating myself up about Connor. Irrational, I know – that's what Mike tells me, anyway. Because I'm not superwoman. Never was. But writing about Connor has been cathartic and helpful. And if it helps anyone understand the complex world of what we do even a little better, then it's been worth it.

Here's to a much brighter future in prospect for that little boy with such a terrible past.

Casey Watson
May 2015

Scarlett's Secret

Scarlett's Secret

I've never been much of a one for long, boring meetings. Much less lectures – all that sitting still for ages, having to concentrate. I always get ants in my pants. But there was a talk I remember going to during my fostering training, which taught me something that's always stayed with me. It was when the speaker, who was talking about what we could learn from kids' behaviour, asked us to imagine communication like an iceberg. At the top – the part above the waterline – was the behaviour we could see, and beneath it – by far the greater part of any iceberg – were all the reasons why the child might be displaying that behaviour, but which we couldn't see, and so could only guess at.

It seems self-evident, but it's easy to forget, too. And it reminded me of one of the most valuable lessons I learned about communication: that when a child's acting up there is always a deeper reason, and if we can find out what that reason is, rather than just labelling the child as 'naughty', then we have a much greater chance of dealing with the underlying problems. Take the other approach, and the child will just get naughtier.

None of which crossed my mind on the bright August morning when I met Scarlett and Jade – that only happened afterwards. I was busy reporting for duty as Team Leader for a youth-centred project, and was much too busy feeling excited about my new job. This was back before I'd ever thought of becoming a foster carer, even before I ran 'The Unit' in the local comprehensive school. This was back when my own kids were still in their mid-teens and I was a youth worker employed by the council.

Our work on these projects – each was about four months in duration – centred around recruiting and supporting NEETS. Lots of people know the term now because it's in pretty common usage, but back then it was one of the trendy new buzzwords. It means Not in Employment, Education or Training Scheme and in this case that might mean kids with drug or alcohol issues, kids in care, kids who might have been in trouble with the law, as well as some who, for whatever reason, simply couldn't find a job. Those were the kinds of kids we wanted to sign up for the course: kids who had slipped through the net and needed help. ones who lacked many of the skills they'd need to be a useful member of society and who, as a consequence, felt lost.

Far from being lost, my assistant, Katie, was all about this morning. And with her mane of hair and bouncy manner, I had privately nicknamed her Tigger; fresh out of uni, she was a blur of smiles and ambition and optimism, and had been a breath of fresh air on our two-week training course. I knew I was going to really enjoy working with her.

'So,' she said, jogging into the office, grinning widely, 'ready for day three? Do we have a smiley-facey Casey, all ready to wow the troops?'

I laughed. That had been one of the edicts during training; the importance of us wearing our smiley faces at all times. (Except when we had to wear our stern ones, obviously.) But Katie didn't need to put it on; her enthusiasm was infectious and it was clear the kids loved her. I was so pleased I had been part of the selection process when the bosses had been interviewing prospective candidates for the job. Yes, she was less experienced than the other candidates, but with her not being much older than the kids herself, she had an extra something that I didn't. They seemed to know that she really understood where they were coming from.

'We do indeed have a smiley Casey this morning,' I said. 'And we have lots to do before they arrive.' I passed Katie a pile of papers and a stapler. 'Here you go,' I said. 'You can put these into batches of three for me while I arrange the tables.'

The kids had an English test that morning, so we had to have a bit of a reshuffle of the arrangement we'd had the furniture in for the previous couple of days. The room that the council had allocated for us was in one of their large training centres, based on a small business estate, and was rather like a large classroom, which I hated. These students would not have long left at school and the last thing they would have wanted was yet another gloomy class to sit in. With that in mind, I had immediately Casey'd it up with bright pictures, comfortable scatter cushions, and colourful cups and saucers, etc. Part of the programme we offered included an adult qualification in Maths and English – it was about the only 'schooly' thing they did, and I wanted them to feel at ease when they did it.

I wanted them to feel at ease, period. That was what we were all about. As they'd said in training, getting these kids comfortable was key to helping support them, because though we might know where we wanted them going – out into the world, with greater confidence – what we didn't know was where they had been.

We'd got off to a good start, Katie and I. An incredible start, actually, because after a week or so going round all the places that might refer kids to us – job centres, schools, the local Young People's Service – we already had fifteen young people enrolled and had even had to set up a waiting list for the next course.

Right now, however, we had a lot to get through with our first batch, who'd spent their first couple of days with us shyly – and in a couple of cases, slightly reluctantly – getting to know both us and one another. In just a couple of days we'd be taking all fifteen away, and that's when we'd really start bonding. We'd be pushing them hard – taking them rock climbing, abseiling, raft building and so on – and in a team-building environment, away from usual routines, hopefully out of their comfort zones, too. That was the plan – that the intensity of the experience would get to them and that barriers might start coming down. In training we'd been told to expect some highs and lows; with so much opportunity for one-to-one time, kids would open up to us: things were got off chests, and feelings were aired.

I was looking forward to it, too. There was only one thing niggling me: that I'd be leaving the family again (I'd had to, briefly, as part of my training), which I knew wouldn't go down well with my son Kieron. He was fifteen, but with his Asperger's, he still found changes like that challenging. Still, I reasoned, my husband Mike coped last time, and would do so again, and while I was doing rewarding work with my bunch of disaffected teenagers, I knew my own younger teenager would be learning valuable coping skills of his own.

I pushed that small anxiety to one side and concentrated on the task at hand, and on one other potential problem that had already raised its head and would definitely need addressing before we left. We had seventeen-year-old non-identical twins with us, Jade and Scarlett, a pair of petite, auburn-haired girls, with the same pretty green eyes. On the face of it, they seemed well adjusted – they certainly talked a lot. Though, as Katie and I both noticed, it was mostly to one another, though there was a tension beween them that I couldn't quite put my finger on. It was something we were gently trying to address by splitting them up for activities – something we were keen to encourage when we went away.

Jade was clearly the brighter of the two – she seemed to 'get' things really readily – but there was one problem; she had this really, really unpleasant smell about her. It was strong, too; the day before, we'd had to throw all the windows open, just to stop from gagging – you could actually smell her coming in before you saw her. It was so bad, in fact, that the smell was still lingering when I'd arrived at work this morning, and as a consequence I'd hastily re-jigged the schedule to fit some more outdoorsy tasks in as soon as the English test was over

'Did you notice?' Katie said now, as I set about handing out the now stapled examination booklets. 'How Scarlett got that body spray out yesterday afternoon and started spraying it on herself so pointedly?'

I had. I'd seen it more than once. She'd get it out and make a big show of freshening herself up, then quietly urge her sister to do the same. Which Jade would do, albeit snatching it from her with an angry scowl on her face.

'I know,' I said, 'and I'm still mulling over how best to approach it. Scarlett clearly knows how bad it is – you can see how she's embarrassed …'

'And it's probably why they're both so keen on sticking together, don't you think?' Katie said. 'Scarlett particularly – it's like she's protecting her, isn't it?'

'Or trying to protect the rest of the group from having to get too close to Jade,' I said. 'I get the impression she's more anxious that something might kick off. With Jade, I mean – if someone says something. Don't you?'

I'd been studying the girls closely, in fact, wondering how best to approach things, because it was clear something would need to be done before we set off for the residential centre – all those hours in a mini-bus followed by a week in a remote hostel, sleeping and living in such close quarters: it would be a challenge for anyone not blessed with a particularly heavy cold. I'd be tolerant of it, of course, but it made my nose wrinkle even thinking about it – and I knew her fellow course mates would be less forgiving. So speak to Jade or speak to Scarlett? I was still undecided. Something told me, however, looking at the way the girls interacted, that there was more to Jade's astonishing lack of personal hygiene than met the eye.

Katie agreed – and she was obviously on the same track as I was. 'Sun,' she commanded, looking out of the window and pointing a finger skywards, 'we're relying on you to be here next week, okay?'

But with the British weather being unpredictable at the best of times – particularly in August – wishful thinking wouldn't be enough. I would have to speak to one or both of them. You couldn't stay outside the *whole* time, after all.

But as often happens when you spend time dithering over a plan of action, I was beaten to it. I had decided to look a little deeper into the twins' background before saying anything, and while there was nothing on their application that hinted at an obvious issue with Jade compared to Scarlett, there was a contact name given – for a lady called Jan. She was the Pastoral Care Manager at the school the twins had attended and, by happy coincidence, I knew her slightly. So I called her to see if she could tell me more.

'Well,' she said, 'the one thing I can tell you about them you probably already know. That they were removed from home by social services just before the spring term in year eleven and were both put into care. They never returned – and as far as I know – missed taking their GCSEs as a consequence.' She paused. 'I'm told it was a serious child-protection issue, Casey, but, as I say, you probably already know this, don't you?'

I told her I didn't.

'Well, in that case,' Jan said, 'there's something else you might not know, either. I heard afterwards that Jade was pregnant – though I don't know the exact circumstances. I'm assuming she had a termination, but that's all I know. I was wondering if it might be related to the reason the girls were removed from their home …'

She didn't need to say any more. A family member perhaps? It happened. I was shocked, though. There was nothing in either of the girls' applications or interviews that would hint at such traumas having happened in their young lives, nothing about Jade that suggested something so sad had happened to this young girl. Apart from being a bit nervous and, in Jade's case, having the body odour issue, they'd come across as quite grounded young girls.

Jan's comment about the reasons for the girls being taken into care lingered with me. What could have happened? What had they been subjected to? And by whom? Well, I thought, at least they were part of something now that might help them to open up and start to deal with it. After speaking to my manager, just to keep him in the loop, I resolved to make a particular effort to spend time alone with the girls while we were away, just in case it was an opportunity they wanted to take advantage of. That's what the courses were for, after all – to give troubled kids a chance to put their troubles behind them and start to take their place in the adult world.

But, like I say, the opportunity came about before we even left, and not in the most harmonious circumstances.

It was the Friday; the final session before setting off on the Saturday, and we were completing our last preparatory session – an exercise in risk assessment. I'd just given a presentation on risk and danger and we were now talking about the business of why it was a good thing to push yourself to your own personal limit. Katie and I stood up to demonstrate an exercise about trust. It was one in which you got into pairs: one would stand with feet and arms outstretched, legs and feet steadied, while the other stood in front, just a couple of feet ahead, with their back to the other. The person in front then closed their eyes and fell backwards, trusting that their partner would catch them.

Having demonstrated it (to some amusement, given that I'm five foot nothing and Katie is five six, and it was me doing the catching on this occasion), I told the group that we'd split into pairs and head to the park so we could practise some more variations out in the sunshine. I then left

Katie to split the groups into pairs while I went off to the kitchen and filled bottles with squash.

I heard the rumpus as soon as I turned back into the corridor, and ran into the room to find all hell had broken loose. Everyone seemed to be involved in a huge, noisy argument, in the middle of which was Katie, clutching her nose.

'Right!' I shouted over the din, as I hurriedly put the bottles down. 'Can someone please tell me what the heck is going on in here?'

The crowd parted slightly, enough for me to take in the scene. Katie's nose was obviously bleeding – I noticed that one of the girls, Dawn, was over at the sink grabbing paper towels to staunch it, and there was a boy seated – a tall, stocky lad of nineteen, called Carl. Scarlett's face was a match for her name – actually, no, it was closer to beetroot – and Jade was standing next to her, sobbing.

With Katie unable to speak – she had her head tipped back, pinching her nose, and could only gesture towards the twins mutely – it was Scarlett who was keenest to provide an answer.

'Ask these bastards!' she screamed at me. 'Me an' Jade are going now! You can stick this up your arses!'

I was gobsmacked at her hysterical tone, as she was usually so measured. She seemed livid. I could see she was close to tears as well.

Dawn brought the paper towels and Katie set about staunching the flow of blood. Who'd hit her? I didn't know where to start, so I took the executive decision to get everyone – as far as possible – down to one level.

'Right,' I said again, keen to appeal to everyone's higher sensibilities, 'I want everyone – you included, Scarlett – to calm down and *sit* down. We need to see to Katie and, Carl – are you hurt as well?'

He seemed to be. He had one hand clamped to his reddening cheek, the other round the same upper arm. He looked distinctly sorry for himself as he nodded.

'Is it your face?' I asked, gesturing for him to lower his hand. And it obviously was. His left cheek was even redder than Scarlett's face.

'And what happened to your arm?' I asked him, as everyone – to my relief – did as I asked them. Bar Scarlett and Jade, anyway.

'She did it!' he said, glaring at Scarlett. 'Fucking slapped me *an'* fucking punched me! Fucking lunatic!'

'Enough of that language,' I said firmly. And was about to ask for more details when Scarlett shouted over me.

'And you're a fucking twat!' she rounded on him. 'And you deserved it!'

'Scarlett!' I said to her. 'Shouting won't help anything, will it? Will you please sit down? Come on – you and Jade. Come and sit by me, both of you –' I pulled a couple of chairs out. 'And let's hear – calmly, please – what's brought all this about, eh?'

The girls seemed undecided – they looked like they might bolt and never come back, in fact, which was the last thing I wanted – but another boy, Mattie, who'd been quiet from the outset but seemed quite together and sensible, touched Scarlett's arm encouragingly, and this seemed to do the trick. The three of them sat down together in front of me and while the others sat around looking sheepish and, in some cases, guilty, Mattie and the girls explained what had happened.

'It was the pairings,' Mattie explained, looking slightly embarrassed. 'Katie told us we must pair up with someone we felt we didn't really know yet, and, well ...' he hesitated. 'No one wanted to pair up with Jade.' There was a short silence. 'It's because of the smell,' he said quietly.

'See!' Scarlett burst out. Mattie visibly cringed. 'See how fucking horrible they all are?' She put her arm round her sister and crushed her towards her.

'But it's the truth,' Dawn said. 'No one wants to be mean, honest. It's just that, well ...' she paused, too. 'It needs to be said.'

Katie's nose, by now, seemed to be recovering from its flood. She nodded her approval of Dawn's honesty.

'No, it doesn't,' Jade said miserably. It was the first time she'd spoken and all heads swivelled towards her. 'You think I don't *know* I smell? Then you're idiots. And you know *nothing* about how shit my life is. Nothing.' She turned to Carl then. 'And you're just a *dick*,' she finished, wiping her eyes and looking like she'd quite like to slap his face, too.

I looked to Katie for more information. She obliged.

'Caught in the crossfire,' she told me. 'This wasn't intentional, was it, Scarlett?'

Scarlett shook her head. 'No, it wasn't – an' I'm sorry, Katie, honest I am – it was intended for *him*!'

All eyes now turned to Carl, of course, who had so far seemed quite a nice boy. A little bit of attitude perhaps – he struck me as a teenager who had suffered from a slight lack of boundaries – borne out by the evidence on his application: he'd been in trouble with the law for petty crime and general disturbances on his estate, but so far on the course he'd done nothing to alarm us.

But now he had, and had clearly got some grief for it, too. I tried to picture Scarlett flying at him – all five foot two of her – and imagined he must have been as surprised as I was by the idea.

But she clearly had. 'Go on,' she prompted now. 'Tell Casey what you said to Jade.'

Carl rubbed his arm again, is if to emphasise that he'd suffered enough. 'I just said …' he began haltingly.

'He just *said*,' Scarlett snapped, 'that he'd rather plant his face in a pile of dog shit than pair up with Jade, because at least dog shit wouldn't stink so bad. *That's* what he said to her!'

There was another heavy silence. 'Didn't he, Mattie?' Scarlett demanded. 'Thought he was *so* fucking funny. He just didn't realise that *I* heard it, too!'

She stood up then, and yanked her sister up onto her feet with her. 'C'mon, Jade,' she said. 'We're going. And we don't have to come back, either. We don't need any of this shit.' They started heading for the door.

I was just rising from my own seat to try to diffuse this unfortunate situation when Jade pulled away from Scarlett slightly and turned around. 'Oh, I'm coming back,' she said, surprising her sister, I think, as much as the rest of us. 'Take a lot more than that *dickhead* to scare me off!'

At which point they did leave, and the rest of us breathed out. Not that the day was quite done. Apart from the incident reports we'd have to file and the words we'd need to have with Carl privately, it was an important function of the course to deal with issues, rather than bury them, so I took the opportunity, once Katie had reassured me she wasn't actually wounded, to discuss with the team how – *as a team* – we could best make the situation right.

Dawn was positive, thinking that now the problem was out in the open Jade's personal hygiene might improve. And a couple of the others admitted that they felt really bad, and would make a special effort to include, rather than avoid, her. In the end, given that Carl had already received such an embarrassing physical pasting from Scarlett, I decided to leave him till an opportune moment once the residential trip was under way. But, though I was pleased overall that we'd straightened things out as best we could for the moment, it still felt like the tip of that proverbial iceberg.

And it was. The next morning, I was at the centre at 8 a.m., bright and early, to prepare for the team's arrival at nine. And as I rounded the corner I was surprised to see Scarlett sitting on the wall outside.

'Hi, Scarlett,' I said. There was no sign of Jade. 'What brings you here so early?'

She stood up and brushed the seat of her jeans off. 'I needed to speak to you,' she said, as I unlocked the door, 'before Jade gets here.'

'That's fine,' I said, ushering her over the threshold. I remembered they lived separately, so perhaps they weren't inseparable, after all. 'What about?' I said, hoping it might be Jade's problems. That would definitely be progress. I headed straight for the kitchen and she followed.

'Casey,' she said, 'can I tell you a secret?'

I turned to face her as I turned on the tap to fill the kettle. ''Course you can,' I said, keeping my voice casual.

She chewed on her lip. 'I can't really talk about it – not just yet, but, well, me an' Jade have had some bad stuff happen to us – you know we had to go into care, don't you?' I nodded. 'Well, it involves my dad and mum –' she paused. 'And, like I say, I can't really talk about it, but, well, I'm *fine*. I'm over it. But ...' she hesitated, as if unsure whether to continue. 'Well, it's just that it's different with Jade,' she continued finally. 'She deals with it differently, you know? That's the thing.'

Not knowing what the 'it' was that Scarlett felt she couldn't tell me made it difficult to know what to say. So I said nothing. Just nodded, and let her carry on. Which she did.

'She got involved with a druggie, that's what happened. An' he was on the sex offenders' register and she had her kids took off her.'

'Her kids?' I was trying to catch up, but there were too many questions blocking the route. 'Kids plural?'

Scarlett nodded. Yeah, she had two with him. I *told* her, I *did* …'

She tailed off. I could see she was worried that she'd said too much already. I put a hand out and squeezed her arm. 'You want a coffee?' I said. 'I'm having one. Can't function without my coffee. And, look, you don't have to tell me any more if you don't want to. Not if it's upsetting you.'

Scarlett opened the cupboard and got down two mugs. 'No, I need to. I mean, I just need you to know. That's what it's about. I mean, she hasn't said so, but, well, I think she makes herself smell on purpose. I've been thinking about it lots. She hardly ever has a wash or changes her clothes – and she doesn't wash them either – and her flat's just as bad. It's covered in dog shit, and hairs, and she never cleans up, and she says it's just since the babies went and that, but it isn't. It's always been that way, ever since she moved in.'

'You didn't move in together, then? You know – when you had to leave home?'

She shook her head. 'No, that was never happening – she was already seeing that knobhead.'

'So it might have been partly down to him, then?'

'She shrugged. 'I guess. But I don't know … It's just that I wanted you to know. It's not that she means to make everyone hate her. It's just like, well, I think she does do it on purpose – you know, wearing her stinking old clothes and everything – so that everyone will hate her. Well, not hate her exactly, but, you know, back off. Leave her alone.'

I considered her words. And given the background – I was still in a state of shock about those two babies – it made sense, and I was impressed that Scarlett had thought it through and been so perceptive. What to do about it, however, was another matter entirely.

'I think you might be right,' I said, 'given what you've told me, Scarlett. And thank you for doing so. Yesterday must have been an unpleasant experience for both of you, and your coming here helps me understand better why things kicked off the way they did.'

'And I'm going to say sorry properly to Katie,' she said. 'I *am* sorry, really. It's just when people like him ... well, like I say, I'm really sorry.'

'I know you are,' I said. 'I can see that. The question now, however, is how best we can help you both. Is there anything I can do?'

'Well, I suppose you could try,' she said, looking hopefully at me. 'It's just that she's gotta keep herself clean and fresh and stuff or it's just going to be awful when we go away, but if I say anything she'll kick off again. I know she will. I daren't even say *anything* to her. It just makes her worse.'

'Don't you worry,' I said, 'you can leave it with me.' Because, actually, in comparison to what I'd just heard, that part was easily addressed.

'So,' I announced, 'on this eve of our adventure, I can reveal that I have gifts for you all!'

There was a small cheer as I delved into my bag. It was the end of the day, and we were just finishing off our last-minute tick lists. We'd sorted shopping lists and menus and rotas and teams and I was tickled to see how much these kids seemed to be looking forward to what a lot of people my age would consider a chore – cooking meals for each other all week. But then, for some, these simple things were new experiences. Tomorrow morning would see us heading off to the wilds of the countryside and we were, by now, as ready as we'd ever be. The teenagers were palpably excited. There'd been no recurrence of the unpleasantness of before, and though Jade was still wary, she'd been true to her word about not leaving; she seemed determined to see things through and that in itself gave me hope that whatever the appalling circumstances of her recent past, she could find a way out and go on to something better.

My gifts, which had been bought out of the residential budget, were a toilet bag for each of them, complete with all the usual toiletries: soap and shower gel, shampoo and conditioner, toothbrush and toothpaste, deodorant, and as I handed them out I made a reference to being a mother with a teenage son, and how I knew all about boys and their smelly habits if left unchecked.

Everyone knew the truth, of course – after the incident earlier in the week, how could they not? – but it was at least a way to emphasise hygiene without singling Jade out, and I could see Scarlett was grateful.

And happily, for the most part it worked. For all my worries about how things would pan out in the close-knit environment of a full-on residential week of new experiences and challenging activities, Jade's personal hygiene seemed no longer to be a problem. No, she wouldn't be winning awards for Miss Squeaky Clean any time soon, but she definitely smelt less offensive than previously and she did, if not that willingly, shower.

'Group dynamics,' Katie observed sagely, as we beavered away together trying to load the minibus so that we'd get everything in – no mean feat – on the final morning. 'I remember learning all about it in college. It's all down to peer pressure, what we've witnessed this week, wouldn't you say? It's one thing turning up at the centre every day, in clothes *you* chose, washed or unwashed – unwashed, in this case – ready to take on anyone who crosses you, but quite another when you're living cheek by jowl with other people, isn't it? Makes it so much harder not to conform. Everyone else goes to the shower block, then you go to the shower block. Not showering, instead of being something you just didn't get round to, becomes an act of defiance. Different thing.'

'Different thing entirely,' I said, grunting as I tried to shoehorn in a plastic box of bats and balls. And she was also spot on, I decided.

But my pleasure in seeing how well the week had gone – and it had; it had been a blur of activity from the moment we set off – was still tempered by the knowledge I now had of these poor girls. I didn't know what had happened to them to make social services take such drastic action (unusual in girls of their age), but what had happened with Jade subsequently made me think the worst. She must have been in a very unhappy place, whatever happened – which would have made her vulnerable to a predatory male.

I also knew now that it weighed heavily on her sister, and though Scarlett hadn't sought me out to talk further while we'd been away, I had a feeling she might once we returned.

I was right. We were back mid-afternoon – a little later than scheduled – and as the kids were in high spirits, Katie and I made the decision that rather than have them start on their folders, we'd let them go for the day. It felt too mean to drag them indoors after their exciting week – time enough to do that on the Monday.

One by one they dispersed, including Jade, and also Katie, and eventually it was only me left. Me and Scarlett, who seemed curiously reluctant to leave.

'Is there anything I can do, Casey' she asked me, 'before I go? To help, like?'

'Well,' I said, 'I have to clean out the minibus before it goes back. You could help me do that if you like.'

She nodded, so I threw a roll of bin liners at her, and she immediately tore one off and jumped into the bus to gather up the stray crisp packets and bits of rubbish that still lurked here. I soon joined her, now armed with a bucket of soapy water and a couple of cloths, and we both set about the task in hand.

We'd been at it about ten minutes, one at either end, idly chatting, when she suddenly said, 'Casey, you know our dad is in prison, don't you?'

I shook my head. Then mentally recalibrated. She probably just assumed that I'd know that. Social services were part of the council; *I* worked for the council … 'I didn't,' I told her. 'What for?'

'For what he did,' she said. 'For raping and abusing me and Jade.' I stopped what I was doing so I could look at her. She was wiping a window furiously. 'He abused us right from us being little girls to just a few years ago. My mum used to go out for a couple of hours an' he'd make us watch dirty videos with him, then he'd mess with us.'

She stopped wiping then, and stared out of the minibus window for a few seconds. 'Both of us, together. In the same room. It was *disgusting*,' she finished quietly.

I didn't know what to say to her, so I just did what felt right. I stopped what I was doing and went down to the back of the bus, where she was, urged her to sit down and put my arm around her. She began to cry then, and I realised this thing she'd just told me must have been a *huge* weight she had to carry around.

'It's okay, love,' I soothed. 'It's okay. I'm here for you to talk to. I can't imagine how horrible that must have been.'

'I don't think you could imagine,' she said. 'How could you? And you know what's worse?' I shook my head. 'What's worse is that we think our mum knew. We think she must have, because she used to put us in our pyjamas – stupidly early – and then she'd be, like, asking our dad what time she should come back.' The tears were streaming down her face now, so much so that I wondered just who she had shared this with before. My hunch was hardly anybody. Her voice was just too full of horror – as if she was revisiting a place she hardly dared to go.

'So how did it end?' I asked. She gave a little shudder, almost a physical embodiment of what she'd been through.

'It was me,' she whispered. '*I* stopped it. In the end, I just *had* to.'

'Of course you did …' I began.

'Yes, in the end,' she said, 'but you don't realise. For a long time we thought it was normal. He was our dad, and he'd do stuff, and we didn't like it – *'course* we didn't – but we didn't know any different, did we? And then, when we got a bit older – old enough to know we didn't like it, and didn't want it happening – we'd ask Mum not to leave us with him and sometimes, if we cried enough, she'd stay at home. But this would just get him mad and he'd be really horrible and pull her hair and punch her about and really frighten us …' she sighed. 'We tried *everything*. We tried saying we were ill, we'd pretend to be asleep. But he'd just do it anyway. And then one day, I don't know why, but something just seemed to snap in me. And there was this lady who lived next door and she would always be asking if everything was okay all the time, you know? I think she was worried about all the beatings my mum got – maybe she could hear it. Anyway, one day I was at home alone, just sat in the garden. I think Mum was out somewhere with Jade and Dad had gone into town, and I was just sitting in the garden and I must have been crying or something, because suddenly she came out and asked me what was wrong and I just told her.'

Scarlett looked at me as if she still couldn't quite believe she'd taken such action. 'I just told her everything. Just like that. And it all went from there, really. She took me into her house, and she called the police, and then the next thing you know, there was our dad going off to be locked up and me and Jade were put in care.'

I noticed Scarlett had stopped crying now and that her voice had grown hard and bitter. I put both arms around her and just held her for a bit. The silence lengthened. Which was fine, because I didn't trust myself to speak. Not for a while anyway. Some things are just beyond words.

'Are you seeing anyone, Scarlett?' I asked her eventually. 'Having any counselling or anything?'

I felt her nod. 'Yeah, I have been. But not Jade. She won't talk to anyone. She just refuses. She blames me, I know she does. For splitting up the family. Which is true, and it was horrible – specially having to move out of home. So Jade wouldn't tell, wouldn't admit to the police what had happened. She told them it was all me – that it might have happened to me, but it didn't happen to her. She said if she didn't then Mum would end up in the nut house 'cos of what I'd told them, and that she couldn't cope without Dad and that I had ruined everything. She did tell in the end, like, a good bit later, so he was charged with what he did to her, too, and they increased his sentence. But it's like it never happened now – not for Jade. She just wants to forget it – completely block it out. But I know she still blames me, and I just don't know what to do.'

'Scarlett,' I told her, 'you know you have done nothing wrong, don't you? You are not responsible for *any* of this and you don't have to feel guilty that your sister can't face up to her past. It's not your fault, okay? None of it. Yes, Jade probably does need help to come to terms with it, I'm sure she does, and when she's ready to accept that, it will be there for her, but in the meantime all you can do is support her however you can.'

'That's just it,' Scarlett said. 'I don't know how to. I know – I just *know*,' she said, her voice gaining strength, 'that if she could just deal with it – talk about it with me – it would help her to get better. But you've seen what she's like. Yeah, I can nag her about her clothes and stuff, but if I so much as mention Dad's name, it's like – whoosh! She's off like a rocket. Like she's got this switch. Trust me, I have tried and tried and tried.'

'So are you saying you'd like me to try to speak to her for you?' I asked gently.

'Could you?' she said. 'Oh, God, Casey, *could* you? I don't know where she's going to end up otherwise, I really don't.'

I had never been so grateful to return to the bosom of my family than I was that afternoon. After the high of the week's adventures, the thrill of doing a job I so enjoyed doing, the pleasure in seeing this raggle-taggle bunch of largely disaffected kids blossoming, what Scarlett had told me had made it feel like someone had stomped up and ripped the sun out of the sky. I wasn't naïve; I knew such families, such horrors, such evil characters existed, but at the same time the thought of walking a mile in Scarlett or Jade's shoes filled me with so many emotions – anger, disgust, compassion, hopelessness, and more anger. Too much emotion to take home to my none-the-wiser husband

and children, who were looking forward to their usual smiley wife and mum. So I sat for a good while before heading home to them, just so I could regain some of my earlier *joie de vivre*.

And I was glad I did, because a bit of *joie de vivre* was clearly needed. 'It's been the week from hell,' Mike announced dramatically, once Kieron was out of earshot. He was so pleased to have me home that he talked with his feet – trotted immediately back to his bedroom, the world now being back on its proper axis.

I resisted the urge to make comparisons; after all, Kieron's immediate disappearance was evidence of his relief. I was back, so now life could go on as it was supposed to. Mum downstairs doing Mum things, Dad at work as per usual, big sister Riley, being big sisterish (i.e. mostly annoying him), leaving him to do what he liked to. Alone. Back on track.

'It really has,' said Mike. 'The food issue, the "staying in" issue, the "Where are you going, Dad?" issue. Let me tell you, if I have to so much as glance at the trailer for any movie with the words "fantasy" or "dragons" or "Superman" in it, I think my head might explode.'

'How *did* the food thing go?' I ventured, remembering how alarmingly quickly Kieron went off eating the last time I'd been away. 'And what do you mean, "staying in" issue? You didn't make him stay in all week, did you?'

Mike pulled a face. 'I meant as in I couldn't get him to go out! Here was me, thinking he'd be off with his friends playing football after school every night, but no chance.

No, love, I think we have to accept that if you're not around, everything is definitely not right in Kieron's world.'

'Oh, bless him,' I said. I suddenly felt tearful. So much so that it must have shown on my face, because Mike put his arms around me and gave me a reassuring squeeze.

'We all feel a bit like that when you're not here, love,' he said, chuckling. 'I say it's Kieron, but it's mostly just a ruse to keep you here ...'

'What, even Riley?' I joked. Mike could always make me feel better.

'Riley? Oh, you mean that pretty, black-haired seven-teen-year-old who I'm told possibly lives here? That the one?'

'That's the one,' I agreed.

Mike grinned. 'I wouldn't know. Made a couple of pithy announcements about not hanging around with her "freaky" brother, then spent most of the rest of the week in David-land. Far as I know.'

I wasn't surprised to hear this. Riley had only recently started seeing this lovely boy called David, but had already dubbed him as being 'the one'. We thought we'd wait and see, but, well, I also knew my daughter ...

Which made me think of Jade and Scarlett, two seven-teen-year-olds with very different life experiences. Not to mention very different concepts of 'home'. I hugged Mike even tighter and counted my blessings. And I resolved that I would try to get those girls help.

* * *

After reassuring Kieron that I would be home at teatime, as per usual, I returned to work on Monday with renewed energy and enthusiasm for the rest of the course. Everyone was busy with their folder work, writing up their experiences, Jade and Scarlett included, so I had ample time to ponder what best to do. The last thing I'd asked Scarlett before the weekend was the name of her counsellor, which was Karen, and whether it would be okay if the two of us had a chat. And as Scarlett had agreed, I decided I'd call her, so, leaving Katie to keep everyone on task in our group room, I went along to the office to find myself a phone.

And I was in for my next surprise. It was easy enough to track down her number, because Scarlett had added her as a referee on her application to join the course, but when I did, it was to find that she wasn't actually a counsellor at all – just a lady who worked for an agency which found employment for teenagers. 'Though we do try to forge close relationships with clients,' she explained, 'and get involved in other services where possible, too, such as helping them to find accommodation and filling out benefit claims, that sort of thing.'

'But you know Scarlett's background?' I asked.

'Oh, yes, certainly.' She went on to explain that Scarlett had told her everything – had blurted it out, much as she had to me. This had been two years back, not long after their father had first gone to prison, and she told me that as far as she was aware anyway, there was no one else now involved in the girls' care.

A sad but all too believable picture was emerging. It looked like, once the case was closed, they had pretty much dropped off the radar, Jade's first pregnancy notwithstanding. By then she was living with the guy who'd made her pregnant, and was already on the depressing trajectory that would end in her having the baby removed from her care. And relations with the girls' mum – what should have been a source of comfort and support – had continued to be difficult, too. Once the girls had been placed in care, Karen told me, she'd moved to a bedsit, taken up drinking as a hobby, and spent most of her time – according to Scarlett, anyway – out in bars, picking up random men. As far as Karen knew, Jade continued to visit her mum sporadically, but Scarlett had been adamant that she'd have nothing to do with her till she admitted that she had known what had been going on all along.

'But, of course, she was never going to do that, was she? Or she'd possibly face charges, too. No, I think, sad to say, that the situation reached an impasse, of the not-terrifically-helpful-"least-said-soonest-mended" kind.'

Which had mended nothing, by the looks of things. Both girls clearly had issues – *big* issues: half-a-lifetime-of-sexual-abuse-type issues – but the resources of social services hadn't managed to stretch to getting either of them professional help.

But perhaps I could try to help them exorcise their demons. I could certainly do as Scarlett asked and try to get Jade to open up to me, and I could suggest – to Scarlett at least, because Jade might be more wary – that proper professional counselling might be the next step for both of them, if they were going to move on from the horrific abuse they'd endured. I felt sure that support was out there – in fact, I knew it was. We just needed to go out and find it.

Pinning Jade down wasn't going to be the easiest thing, I knew. I needed to speak to her without the rest of the group being around, but something told me that if I tried to get her to come and chat to me in my office, she might shy away. Even leave, given what Scarlett had told me. I was still mulling it over a couple of days later, in fact, when an opportunity seemed to present itself.

One of the team projects that had been decided upon as part of their four-month engagement was to repaint a local council community centre. Alongside this there was a plan to provide some new furniture, and to this end some serious fundraising needed to be done, such as packing bags in supermarkets, a couple of cake stalls and so on. One of the schemes – dreamt up by the kids themselves, which really impressed me and Katie – was to provide a car and van washing service for the local businesses. It was ideal for all, as with so many businesses packed into the estate, they had a ready and willing clientele on site.

On this day, as I was in my office, going through some paperwork, I realised that Jade and Scarlett, who, despite their differences, still stuck together like glue, were both washing cars outside the offices opposite. Best of all, they were alone, the team being scattered over the locality on their various fundraising tasks.

'You know what?' I said to Katie, whom I'd brought up to speed with the girls' situation, 'I think I'm going to chance my arm and go and speak to them together.'

She looked up and grinned. 'You want me to go and grab you a hard hat first?'

Bless her, I thought. She was such a lovely girl, she really was. And if she stayed in this line of work, she'd go far. In theory, she could have pressed charges for assault after what had happened on day three, or, at the least, made an official report implicating Scarlett, but she hadn't. 'It was an accident,' she'd said, 'and accidents happen. Part of life. And off the back of a difficult, inflammatory situation. And Scarlett's already apologised. Subject closed.' And that had been that.

I declined the hard hat, and instead donned some Marigolds, then went to join the twins in the adjacent car park.

'Lovely day for car washing,' I said, squinting up into the sunshine. 'You girls need a hand?'

'You could get us some clean rinsing water,' Scarlett said. 'That would be helpful.' She reached down to pick up the bucket beside her and held it out to me.

I took it from her. 'By the way,' I said, 'I meant to tell you, I've been speaking to Karen from the agency. And also to my manager. And they reckon that if you want to, they can sort something out for you – some sessions with a professional counsellor – you know, like we were talking about? Only if you want to, of course, but you know, I think you should really consider it, because they've dealt with many, many girls in your sort of situation' – I glanced across at Jade who was watching us both intently – 'and, as I say, love, I really think they could help.'

Scarlett's expression turned from one of interest to one of sudden comprehension, as it dawned on her that I was telling her this right now precisely because Jade would be able to hear it. She glanced across at her sister, who was staring back at her, looking daggers. Jade then threw down her sponge and marched around the car she'd been lathering, squaring up to her sister, hands on hips.

'What the fuck have you been saying, you stupid cow?'

Scarlett took a step back. She was clearly intimidated by her sister – perhaps one of the biggest obstacles to her being able to support her.

'It was only to Casey,' she said. 'Honest. I just – Jade, I just needed to *tell* her. I needed to talk to someone! You might not, but I *do*! I can't live like this, watching you – you – God, Jade, *look* at you! You just keep bottling it up and bottling it up, and –'

'I'm bottling it up because I want to forget about it – can't you get that? If I wanted to broadcast it, I would! Why can't you do that? Why the hell can't you just fucking do that?'

Scarlett stiffened then. 'And end up like *you*? Shacked up with that knobhead, losing your kids, living in that shithole, letting yourself get into that state … That's what I should be like, is it? *Is* it?'

She was shouting at her sister now and, in contrast, Jade deflated. And in that instant I could see that perhaps that was where the problem lay – that Scarlett couldn't help her sister because the first thing it involved doing was spelling out exactly how low she'd sunk.

And perhaps that didn't escape Jade's notice either. 'You think I don't *know* that?' she whispered, her chin beginning to wobble. 'You think I don't think about those babies every single minute of every day? You think I don't *care*? Scarlett, you have no idea how much I hate myself, trust me. So you hating me, too – you know? Whatever.'

She took a breath then, a huge gulping breath. Then sank to her knees, put her head in her hands and starting moaning – a horrible keening sound – and tugging violently at her hair.

I put the bucket down and rushed to her side, kneeling down in front of her, and trying to get my arms around her shuddering torso. Scarlett looked stunned, so I gestured for her to come over and support her weeping sister, but as she approached, Jade looked up. 'Just fuck off, Scarlett!' she sobbed.

'Jade, love,' I said softly. 'Please try to understand how your sister feels. She's hurting, too – she hurts every bit as much as you do, believe me. She just deals with it differently – *has* dealt with it differently. But you know, all she wants is to be there for you – and for you to be there for her. You *need* each other. And you need help, and all she wants if for you to get it. As do I. It's not right that you should just be expected to get on with it. You can't just "get on" after such terrible things have happened to you. You deserve better. You both do.'

Scarlett knelt down, too, then and Jade didn't stop her putting her arms around her, and as we knelt there, on the wet tarmac, the soapy water seeping into the knees of our jeans, I looked up to see a lot of curious faces looking out of the centre windows. Including Katie, who did a thumbs up. I did one back.

An hour later, we were back inside, clutching mugs of coffee, taking stock. Once the floodgates had opened it seemed there was no holding Jade back. And it began to emerge that by far the greatest problem in the girls being able to communicate was the spectre of something even more distressing than what their father had done to them. It was what he'd made them do to each other. From a young age he'd made them not only watch each other while he performed sexual acts on them, but also made them touch each other sexually.

It was this, above all things, that had created the barrier between them. That and the memories that swirled around Jade's head and gave her nightmares, compounded by the terrible, terrible guilt she felt about everything that happened subsequently. The terrible choice she had made, the loss of her babies, while her sister – at least outwardly – appeared to be so sorted. 'I can't even bear to think about it,' Jade said, weeping. 'Any of it. I had those kids and I lost them. I did wrong by them and I hate that. I just feel so guilty. And so dirty. I can't *bear* that you know all that.' She looked at her sister reproachfully. 'I feel it now. I feel sick. I just want to be able to rub it all away.'

'I can help you with that, Jade,' I told her. 'I promise. No, we can't change your past, but we can change your future, but first you need to accept that you need help. Because we can get you help – help to rub all those horrible thoughts away. What you're doing now is, well, just covering them up, running away from them. And it's not helping, is it?' I asked her gently.

Jade shook her head. 'Sis, she's right,' Scarlett said. 'It's not helping, not at all. I want to make it go away as well – just as much as you do. But if no one knows how bad it's been for us, how can they help us? They need to *see* what's been done to us, don't they?'

Scarlett leaned across and squeezed her sister's hand. 'It'll be all right,' she said quietly. 'Honest it will, Jade. It'll be *better*.'

I could hear movement outside. Chairs being scraped back, people reconvening before the lunch break. Katie's voice above the chatter, reassuringly bright. Somehow an hour had come and gone.

'Look girls,' I said, 'you've had a bit of an emotional morning, the pair of you. How about you head home and come back in the morning? In the meantime I can speak to whoever I need to speak to in social services to get that help for you. No need for you to stay now – you can catch up tomorrow. We're only doing some folder work this afternoon.'

The girls looked at each other and this time it was Jade who took her sister's hand. 'Nah,' she said, smiling at Scarlett. 'You're all right. We won't go home. We've got cars over there to finish washing, haven't we?'

I watched the pair of them go and, though the change in their demeanour was all but imperceptible, I could see it. I smiled. It was already better.

To my delight – not to mention shock – things moved impressively quickly after the girls made the decision to seek help. With Karen's assistance – she had a friend in the right department, as it happened – we were able to arrange counselling for both girls almost immediately; they began going twice a week, separately, for the remainder of the project. It proved to be the turning point they needed. And not only did they feel better, they positively blossomed as a result of it; along with more than half of their cohort, they both secured jobs at the end of the course. Katie and I couldn't have felt prouder.

I've seen both girls a couple of times since and things are so much better in every way now. Both have boyfriends as well as jobs and are putting their pasts behind them – no small feat, given the magnitude of the wrongs that had been done to them, and testament to both the efficacy of counselling and the simple fact of family – they have each other and though they have taken different paths, that bond has been key to their recovery.

Two years ago, Scarlett even made a compensation claim against her father and, after her home was ripped from under her, she received enough money to enable her to buy a small flat. Jade was more reticent, deciding that she didn't want to take action, but made the decision to do something equally life-changing – she changed her name by deed poll, so she no longer shared her father's surname.

Counselling had another beneficial effect, too – both the girls finally made peace with their mother. While, as an outsider, and a mum, I still couldn't quite get my head around what she'd let happen to her daughters, both Scarlett and Jade did, and as a consequence forgave her – realising that she had been a victim as well.

So, all in all, my first foray into team leading was a memorable one. And much more of the proverbial 'emotional roller coaster' than I could ever have expected. My memories aren't just about those two unfortunate girls, though, they are also about poor, unfortunate Carl.

It was a good three weeks later when a man came a-calling – a middle-aged, fit-looking, cross-looking man, with close-cropped hair and an air of displeasure. He was Carl's dad, apparently, home on leave from the Army, and he wanted to make an official complaint about a bullying incident he'd been told about, from earlier in the course, involving his son and 'some moronic thug' who'd thumped him.

'Erm, what incident would that be?' Katie asked him, confused. 'It's news to me – I think you must be mistaken.' He then explained that his wife had put him fully in the picture – that while he'd been away, this hulking lad had tried to beat up his son, and that, also according to his wife, who had 'seen the bruises for herself', nothing whatsoever had been done to bring the lout to book. It didn't matter, he finished, that his boy hadn't wanted to take it further. It simply wasn't good enough, and the bully should be punished.

It was something of a moment, that one, for sure. I remember Katie and I picturing all five foot two of Scarlett and trying not to giggle as the penny finally dropped. You could have fried an egg on poor Carl's cheek that afternoon …

CASEY WATSON

One woman determined to
make a difference.

Read Casey's poignant
memoirs and be inspired.

Five-year-old Justin was desperate and helpless

Six years after being taken into care, Justin has had 20 failed placements. Casey and her family are his last hope.

THE BOY NO ONE LOVED

A damaged girl haunted by her past

Sophia pushes Casey to the limits, threatening the safety of the whole family. Can Casey make a difference in time?

CRYING FOR HELP

Abused siblings who do not know what it means to be loved

With new-found security and trust, Casey helps Ashton and Olivia to rebuild their lives.

LITTLE PRISONERS

Branded 'vicious and evil', eight-year-old Spencer asks to be taken into care

Casey and her family are disgusted: kids aren't born evil. Despite the challenges Spencer brings, they are determined to help him find a loving home.

TOO HURT TO STAY

A young girl secretly caring for her mother

Abigail has been dealing with pressures no child should face. Casey has the difficult challenge of helping her to learn to let go.

MOMMY'S LITTLE HELPER

Two boys with an unlikely bond

With Georgie and Jenson, Casey is facing her toughest test yet.

BREAKING THE SILENCE

A teenage mother and baby in need of a loving home

At fourteen, Emma is just a child herself – and one who's never been properly mothered.

Eleven-year-old Tyler has stabbed his stepmother and has nowhere to go

With his birth mother dead and a father who doesn't want him, what can be done to stop his young life spiralling out of control?

What is the secret
behind Imogen's
silence?

Discover the shocking and
devastating past of a child
with severe behavioural
problems.

THE GIRL WITHOUT A VOICE

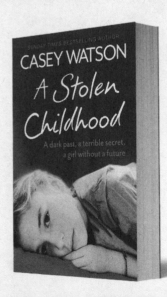

Kiara appears tired
and distressed, and the
school wants Casey to
take her under her wing
for a while

On the surface, everything
points to a child who is
upset that her parents have
separated. The horrific
truth, however, shocks
Casey to the core.

A STOLEN CHILDHOOD

Flip is being raised by her alcoholic mother, and comes to Casey after a fire at their home

Flip has Foetal Alcohol Syndrome (FAS), but it soon turns out that this is just the tip of the iceberg . . .

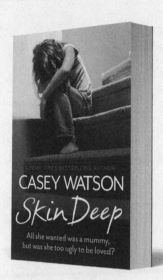

SKIN DEEP

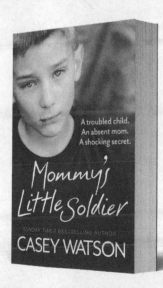

Leo isn't a bad lad, but his frequent absences from school mean he's on the brink of permanent exclusion

Leo is clearly hiding something, and Casey knows that if he is to have any kind of future, it's up to her to find out the truth.

MOMMY'S LITTLE SOLDIER

Adrianna arrives on Casey's doorstep with no possessions, no English and no explanation

It will be a few weeks before Casey starts getting the shocking answers to her questions . . .

RUNAWAY GIRL

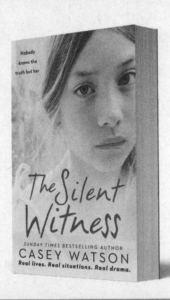

Bella's father is on a ventilator, fighting for his life, while her mother is currently on remand in prison, charged with his attempted murder

Bella is the only witness.

THE SILENT WITNESS

E-BOOK SHORT STORIES

Six-year-old Darby is naturally distressed at being removed from her parents just before Christmas

And when the shocking and sickening reason is revealed, a Happy New Year seems an impossible dream as well . . .

THE LITTLE PRINCESS

Jade and Scarlett, seventeen-year-old twins, share a terrible secret

Can Casey help them come to terms with the truth and rediscover their sibling connection?

SCARLETT'S SECRET

E-BOOK SHORT STORIES

Nathan has a sometime
alter ego called Jenny
who is the only one who
knows the secrets of his
disturbed past

But where is Jenny when
she is most needed?

NO PLACE FOR NATHAN

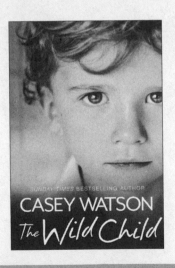

Angry and hurting,
eight-year-old Connor is
from a broken home

As streetwise as they
come, he's determined to
cause trouble. But Casey
is convinced there is a
frightened child beneath
the swagger.

THE WILD CHILD

Five-year-old Paulie has killed the family's pet rabbit, and been given up by his mother and stepdad

But Casey soon discovers that returning Paulie to his family might not be the best idea.

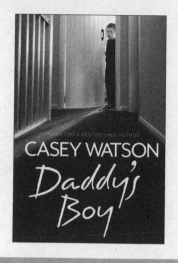

DADDY'S BOY

AVAILABLE AS E-BOOK ONLY

Cameron is a sweet boy who seems happy in his skin – making him rather different from most of the other children Casey has cared for

But what happens when Cameron disappears? Will Casey's worst fears be realised?

JUST A BOY

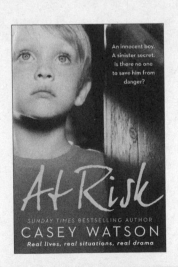

Adam is brought to Casey while his mum recovers in hospital – just for a few days

But a chance discovery reveals that Casey has stumbled upon something altogether more sinister . . .

AT RISK

FEEL HEART.
FEEL HOPE.
READ CASEY.

Discover more about Casey Watson.
Visit www.caseywatson.co.uk

Find Casey Watson on &

Moving Memoirs

Stories of hope, courage and the power of love…

If you loved this book, then you will love our
Moving Memoirs eNewsletter

Sign up to…

- Be the first to hear about new books

- Get sneak previews from your favourite authors

- Read exclusive interviews

- Be entered into our monthly prize draw to win one
  of our latest releases before it's even hit the shops!

Sign up at

www.moving-memoirs.com